Jay Gree

America's Unidentified
Serial Killers

Green Witch Publications

Published by Green Witch Publications

Cover image by Jill J Jenkins and back image by Designecologist are used with thanks.

Also by Jay Greenwich

Skinless Meat
Spinster Killer
Crack Whore
Fables for the 21st Century Vol. 1
Fables for the 21st Century Vol. 2
Men Who Kill Men

Dedicated to Megan

Contents

Foreword

ATTACHED TO SOME NAMES is a notoriety so terrible that they are instantaneously recognised virtually the world over. Ted Bundy. John Wayne Gacy. Jeffrey Dahmer. Richard Ramirez. These are some of America's most monstrous serial killers. Their crimes are well documented, their faces easily recognised and their names widely known. They are names that still strike fear and revulsion into the general public, many of whom may still remember following the trials in the media with escalating horror as the appalling and gruesome details unfolded in awful detail.

But at least these killers were caught.

Sometimes, despite law enforcement's best efforts, heinous killers *do* escape justice. Townspeople notice an unusual pattern of inexplicable disappearances. Police become alerted to a mass grave that should not be where it is. Investigators unearth a succession of bodies, all having similar characteristics, all killed in the same way. But when there is no face to attach to the perpetrator of these acts, when there is no name for the phantom walking amongst them – how much more unnerving the horror! Suddenly everyone becomes a suspect. People begin to mistrust their neighbours' motives and intentions. They fortify their homes and become wary of going out at night. And their suspicions grow and grow …

Mostly, law enforcers are able to use their investigative acumen to apprehend the killer in their midst. They gather evidence, build their case, level a charge, bring a prosecution and, if everything comes together, sentence and convict their suspect. But sometimes the killers are never caught. Sometimes no motive can be found other than the senseless slaughter of others for enjoyment, power or a raging lust. No connections can be found between the victims other than a certain "type". The killers, very clever or careful or lucky individuals, leave no evidence behind. They make sure there are no witnesses; they cover their tracks. All they leave in their wake are the victims and the devastating consequences of their evil acts.

These are the ones who have never been caught.

America has its fair share of such murders. Based upon FBI statistics, there are around 15,000 homicides annually. Experts estimate that serial killings account for no more than one percent of these murders. That suggests that around 150 people are the victims of serial murder every year in the US. The FBI goes on to estimate that at any one time there are between 25 and 50 serial killers operating within the US. This is not a reassuring statistic.

The image of the highly intelligent serial killer pitching his wits against investigators is a Hollywood invention, one that audiences actively seek to be thrilled by. Newspapers and the TV news love to suggest that serial killers have a debilitating mental illness that compels them to commit murder. The media depicts them as sad and lonely social misfits who come out of their lairs to kill by night, only to retreat again until the next time. The public thinks of them as white, middle-aged men with a nervous tic or strange stare.

The fact of the matter is none of these stereotypes is accurate. The characteristics of serial killers span the full range of the demographic spectra; overall their characteristics roughly correspond with those of society. Whilst it is a general rule of thumb that serial killers largely kill within their own racial type, all ethnicities are represented proportionally within the numbers of serial killers. Serial killers are no more or less intelligent than their non-murderous counterparts. Within the serial killer population there are examples of the intellectually challenged right through to those with genius IQs. Women can be serial killers, although to a much lesser degree.

But overwhelmingly, the evidence shows, serial killers do not appear strange or menacing in any meaningful way (presumably until the point of realisation that you are the intended victim). They have jobs, families, hobbies. They hide in plain sight; they blend in. They appear innocuous.

Most of all, however, serial killers do not suffer from mental illness any more than the general population does. They are not normally legally insane. They *do* understand that what they are doing is legally and morally wrong; the truth is they simply do not care. Their compulsion to inflict pain and death on others is what drives them to ignore legal and moral rules. And that is what makes them very dangerous … and compelling. The serial killer is your "Average Joe".

He could be your next-door neighbour.

So how is it that some serial killers are not caught? The answer is simple and obvious. It is because they do not want to get caught. They are highly motivated to remain at large. They commit their acts in secret and often make efforts to keep it that way. Sometimes they completely conceal the fact that a murder has been committed. They hide the bodies so well that no one finds them, at least not for a long time, so long that the trail has gone cold and the evidence is degraded and useless. All that is left is a vague notion that something is awry. The fame-hungry killer is more likely to give himself away.

And that is how the serial killers get away with it as frequently as they do – they are devious. They will have thought about their crime in advance and practised it in their head. They will have stalked their victim for a long time until they feel it is safe to strike. And they do so swiftly and brutally, in cold blood. They are often obsessive and meticulous. Intensely so. And they have to be, for their freedom to kill again and again without detection relies upon it.

- J.G., July 2020

America's Unidentified
Serial Killers

The Servant Girl Annihilator
(active 1884-1885)

AUSTIN, TEXAS, already a large town in the late-nineteenth century, was experiencing a construction boom. Wooden buildings were being replaced with more solid structures, and the Houston and Texas Central Railway had recently opened up the town to increased trading opportunities. Recent consolidation as the region's political capital and educational centre further improved its status. As the large town transitioned towards small city status its population was likewise burgeoning. Immigrant workers were drawn to the work and opportunities that such development inevitably aroused, many of them from European countries. A sizeable proportion of the population, however, were Africa-Americans, newly emancipated following the end of the Civil War; and by the 1880s around a third of the inhabitants of Austin comprised of black settlers, who had congregated around the western residential communities north of the Colorado river.

The local newspapers of the time tended to report the usual stories associated with a quiet mid-American town, with politics, economics, local events and petty mischief-making appearing to be the subjects of the day. Soon, however, this was to change. "The town is fearfully dull," was how one local resident, William Sydney Porter, described the town in a letter to a friend, "except for the frequent raids of the Servant Girl Annihilators, who make things lively during the dead hours of night". Because of the frequency of the attacks, it must have seemed that there must be more than one killer. Surely one man[*] alone could not be responsible for such carnage! Intentionally or not,

---

[*] Throughout this book serial killers are referred to as male in order to ease the text flow. Whenever male-specific terms are used in respect of serial killers, they should be understood as referring to both genders, unless explicitly stated.

Porter (a short story writer better known under his own pseudonym, O. Henry), had penned the sobriquet of the first of a new breed of killer.

However, because of the killer's apparent weapon of choice (it was thought that an axe was used to inflict violence upon the victims) he was also referred to as the "Austin Axe Murderer". Later the killer would leave a blood-stained hatchet at the scene of his crime, thus confirming the deadly weapon. No matter. Whatever the moniker given to this monster, seven decades before the term *serial killer* had even been coined, the Servant Girl Annihilator had been gifted the dubious honour of being referred to as America's first serial killer.

Over the period of a year, between late 1894 and Christmas Eve 1885, the unknown killer conducted a series of brutal murders. The murdered victims were seven females, the youngest fatality being an 11-year-old girl. One male also died. Additionally, six women and two men suffered grievous injuries. The serial nature of the horror understandably left local citizens paralysed with uncertainty and trepidation, for the attacks crossed racial identity groups, and all of the victims had been struck whilst indoors, asleep in their beds. Inevitably, the frequency of the occurrence of the attacks – and the attacks themselves, so shocking, irrational and perplexing – had come to render the townspeople simply insensible with fear, terrified to close their eyes at the end of the day. At the time, these same townsfolk would have been aware of the overseas reputation of Jack the Ripper, a frenzied multiple-killer of prostitutes, who had recently stalked the backstreets of London's Whitechapel. Three years later, Austin, Texas was to gain the unenviable reputation of the first city in America to produce a serial killer – indeed, to deliver the first serial murderer in the country.

The grisly remains of Mollie Smith, a 25-year-old black cook, were found outside her home. Smith had worked for the Walter Hall residence on Sixth Street (then named Pecan Street). She was struck about the head with an axe as she slept on the night of 30 December 1884. Her body was dragged outside and placed in the snow, next to her employer's outhouse. She had been raped *post mortem*, and when her body was found it had been severely hacked – "hacked to pieces", as a witness at the time described. She had died as a result of the slashing axe wounds to her head and stab wounds to her abdomen, chest, legs and arms. She had lost such a substantial amount of blood during the process of dying that she reportedly appeared almost to be floating in a pool of it. Her head displayed a gaping axe wound. No effort had been made to conceal the body. A black male, Walter Spencer, Smith's boyfriend, had been seriously wounded, but miraculously survived the attack.

This set the pattern for the murders that followed. All of the victims were attacked whilst sleeping in their beds. Five of the victims, still alive after the initial attack, were hauled outside only to be killed outside. Three victims underwent catastrophic mutilation after having been taken outside. Six of them had a sharp implement inserted forcibly into their ears. All of the victims suffered the indecency of being posed after death.

Clara Strand and Christine Martenson were two Swedish servant girls. On 19 March 1885, they were wounded but survived the severe assault.

Eliza Shelly, on 6 May 1885, was not so fortunate. A black cook, Shelley became the Annihilator's second murder victim. She was found the next day with her head having been split nearly in two, such was the savagery of the attack. The axe was the killer's tool of the trade.

Two weeks later, on 23 May, Irene Cross, another serving woman, was the third victim to die a gruesome hacking death. She too was black, and she too had been stabbed several times. Her injuries included being almost completely scalped *post mortem*. The killer's *modus operandi** had become apparent to

---

* In the context of criminal profiling the *modus operandi,* or *M.O.,* is a perpetrator's particular method of operating. It consists of the actions used by an individual to execute the crime, prevent detection and facilitate escape.

all by now, including William Sydney Porter, whose writing of the terror in a letter to his friend, Dave Hall, unwittingly lent the Servant Girl Annihilator his bloodcurdling epithet.

The next victim to be "annihilated" was Mary, the 11-year-old daughter of Rebecca Ramey. Rebecca Ramey, a servant, survived the 30 August 1885 attack, suffering serious wounds. Her unfortunate daughter, however, was killed. Mary, a mixed-raced child, was pulled from her bed, dragged outside into an outhouse where she was raped and stabbed through the ear. Records do not indicate if the girl had been alive during this ordeal.

Porter's epithet for the Annihilator proved to be a misnomer with his next two victims, a pair of sweethearts, Grace Vance and her boyfriend Orange Washington, both black, who were found on 28 September having been bludgeoned to death. The pair occupied a room in a shack on the property of their employer, Mr Willliam Dunham. Two girls were also sleeping in the room at the time of the attack. Orange Washington was the first to be struck. He died instantly, the result of a brutal attack using an axe. His head had been split open. That same axe was used to knock the two girls senseless, whilst Grace Vance, according to the *San Antonio Light*, "was dragged out of the window, thrown over a fence and then dragged over a vacant lot fully a hundred yards from the cabin, where she was found lying the weeks with a brick alongside of her all besmeared with blood".

The grisly aftermath was clearly witnessed and able to be described by a newspaper in graphic detail:

> *Blood stains could be seen on the widow [sic] sill and fence, and the trail was plainly seen where the women [sic] had been dragged. Her head was literally covered with gashes inflicted with the brick, and she presented a horrible scene after death.*
> (*San Antonio Light*, San Antonio, Texas, 1885)

In the vernacular of the time, it was noted that "the woman[,]

Vance, was the only one who was outraged [i.e. killed]". The _Light_ reporter went on to mention that Sergeant Cheyenville and his posse soon gave chase to a negro, and "fired eight shots after the fiend but he made good his escape". The reporter speculated that the perpetrator would no doubt be caught, "as he is known".

Time has shown this to be an inaccurate prophecy. Although there were many suspects and several theories evolved, the true identity of the serial killer remains unknown.

Up until this point all the victims were black. The final two murders occurred on Christmas Eve of 1885. Sue Hancock was the penultimate victim. She was to be found in her backyard by her husband. Hancock was described as "one of the most refined ladies in Austin". And finally, mere hours later, Eula Phillips, described as "one of the prettiest women in Austin", was found in her in-laws' backyard. Both spouses of the two women were accused of their murders – this even despite Jimmy Phillips, Eula's husband, having himself sustained severe wounds in the attack – though each was subsequently found to be not guilty. Sue Hancock and Eula Phillips, the Annihilator's final victims, were white. It was an aberration of the killer's _modus operandi_, and prosecutors claimed that Jimmy Phillips had used the murders of Austin's black working-class women as a cover to kill his unfaithful wife, Eula. Jimmy Phillips' initial conviction and sentence to seven years imprisonment was overturned within six months. Nevertheless, following this late escalation in the attacks, the violence stopped. Austin's Servant Girl Annihilator simply discontinued, and the orgy of death stopped as suddenly as it had started. The total body count was eight.

Apart from the husbands of the two final victims there _were_ other suspects. In fact, 400 men were questioned. All, however, were released and to date the identity of America's first serial killer remains unknown. The stain of suspicion, though, does blemish a few of the names provided by history. Nathan Elgin, a 19-year-old black cook, was a strong suspect. He had worked in the vicinity of the crime scenes and he knew the small city's streets well. Elgin himself died in February 1886 as a result of injuries sustained after being shot by police. Elgin had, at the time, been in the process of attacking a girl named Julia as she screamed for help. Police had attempted to pull the man away from the girl as it seemed that he had been attempting to beat her to death, and he simply could not be subdued. The uncontrolled man was eventually shot after brandishing a knife at the police officers. The source of the man's frenzied rage against Julia could not be explained at the time and remains lost to history. Perhaps coincidentally, after Elgin died the killings also stopped.

It was discovered after Elgin's death that he was missing a little toe. Footprints believed to have been left by the Annihilator at the crime scenes indicated that the killer may have held a similar defect – a missing toe. Elgin was a likely suspect, and his footprint was certainly strong circumstantial evidence. However, a dead man could no longer be interrogated, it should go without saying, and no confession would be forthcoming. Little could be done with the material evidence now.

Maurice, a Malaysian cook, whose last name is not known, appeared to have had connections to many of the Annihilator's victims. The spree ended after the Malay had left Austin, several weeks after the final Christmas Eve murders, drawing theorists to surmise that he was the killer. Maurice was bound for London, and it was suspected by some that he may also have been "Jack", the so-called ripper murdering prostitutes even more ferociously on the other side of the Atlantic.

The Englishman James Maybrick has also been mooted as a suspect in America's first serial killer case. Maybrick, a Liverpudlian cotton trader, had been in Austin on the days of the Annihilator murders. Maybrick died in May 1889, possibly after being poisoned with arsenic and strychnine, perhaps administered by his wife. His journals contained confessions that he had killed prostitutes, as well as a page signed "Jack the Ripper". It is unlikely that both Maurice the Malaysian cook and Maybrick the cotton merchant were responsible for two separate killing sprees.

All we have now is speculation and, given the time that has lapsed since the end of the murders, it is unlikely at this stage that historians will arrive at a conclusive answer. Whoever the Annihilator was, his identity more than likely will remain unknown. He was, however, the first to usher in the modern age of the serial killer. Many others were to follow; and like the Annihilator, many others remain unidentified.

The Denver Strangler
(active 1894-1903)

TODAY, MARKET STREET, in downtown Denver, Colorado is a fashionable thoroughfare containing desirable apartments and duplexes, modern office buildings and upscale retail establishments. At the turn of the 20th-century, however, the neighbourhood's reputation was rather more downbeat. Colorado, in that pioneering era, could easily be described as male-dominated, and consensus lists at the time indicate that men outnumbered the fairer sex at a ratio of twenty-to-one. And men being men, there soon developed the need to avail of services that only a woman could supply. What happened in Denver was no different to what has happened countless times the world over. Noticing the gap in the market, resourceful opportunists and paying customers came together in order to fill that hole in the spirit of a mutually beneficial entrepreneurial endeavour: Denver's skin trade began to develop and flourish.

As might be expected, drinking saloons thrived alongside the railroad tracks where visitors might while away a few hours during their travels. Brothels inevitably sprung up in the same areas, serving the needs of lonely travellers – miners, fortune-seekers, businessmen and railroad employees alike. Railroad employees, quite sensibly, would deposit their lamps outside the brothels as they visited so that they might be easier found in an emergency. In time, the red lantern came to be an identifier of the brothel itself and so the term *red-light* came to describe districts where it was known that prostitution thrived.

Despite early laws prohibiting prostitution in Denver the practice flourished. Indeed, some of the establishments – the House of Mirrors, the Hotel Richelieu, the Walhalla Club Rooms, Schlitz – became well-known bordellos, inducing neighbourhood tongues to wag and arousing the jealousy of competing madams. Many of the brothels in Denver, however, were not upmarket establishments. Many could be called "two-bit houses", reflecting the payment that changed hands for the service, and the girls would sometimes have to turn as many as fifty tricks per week just to pay for their accommodation. Market Street –first known as Holladay Street, then known as McGaa Street – was also known as The Row; it was Denver's notorious red-light district, teeming with parlour houses, _maisons de joie_, brothels, dancehalls, hurdy-gurdy houses and lowly cribs. In the year 1894, Market Street was informally renamed yet again: it became known as "Stranglers Row".

The Row's wares were advertised in a pocket-sized publication known as the "Red Book". It listed the attractions of Market Street, where gentlemen would be extended "a cordial welcome to strangers" and promised "all the comforts of home". A rival publication advertised premises where the lady of the house would assuredly "discuss with Yourself and your friends the Political Aspect of the day". The thinly veiled insinuations would have been lost to few. The whereabouts of the local bawdy houses were clearly advertised and they did good business.

Lena Tapper, a German prostitute (some sources claim she was French), was aged 37 when she came to her demise on 3 September 1894 in a house at 1911 Market Street, one of the so-called "lowly cribs", tucked in between the saloons and gambling dens of the street. Tapper had the unenviable reputation of being "unchaste", a "soiled dove". A surviving photograph shows a hefty lady with a plain countenance. Tapper had previously lived in Fulda and Heron Lake, both Minnesota, before moving to Denver as the mistress of Richard Demady. Both individuals here operated within the order of the _Macquereaux_, a French term which translates as "pimp" or "procurer", itself later bowdlerised to "Mack". In other words, Tapper and Demady functioned as sex workers in the roles of pimp and prostitute. Little else seems to be known of Tapper other than the fact that she had been found choked to death on her bed, the first victim of the Denver Strangler. Demady, charged with first-degree murder, was ultimately acquitted, the trial later referred to as a "high-priced fiasco".

Twenty-three-year-old Marie Contassot, a French national, was killed on 28 September 1894. The coroner described her death as unknown, despite the decedent having a swollen purple face, eyes bulging from their sockets and the presence of a rope nearby. Like the previous murder, just over three weeks earlier, there had been no sign of a forced entry, and a towel had been forced into the hopeless victim's mouth. It was assumed that the girl had succumbed to the ministrations of one of her customers. Contassot's beau, Tony Saunders, a man leading a double life as both a police officer and a pimp on the Row, came under scrutiny for the brutal murder. However, after repeated questioning he was released without charge. Contassot's own pimp, Charles Chaloup, also came under suspicion, as well as her sister, Eugenie, who had come to America with Marie. The motivation for the crime, it was claimed, was financial gain: Marie and Eugenie had been the beneficiaries of a recent inheritance, and suspicious minds had concluded that Eugenie and Chaloup were in collusion to keep the large sum of money for themselves and leave Marie nothing. In the end, though, neither party was charged with the crime. Marie ended up buried in a grave decorated by a large tombstone arranged by her sister Eugenie.

Alternatively, a sailor, Alfonse LeMarie, a homeless French sailor, was reported to have indicated that he had knowledge of a large sum of money in Contassot's house, saying, "I will kill her to get that money."

Understandably, the working girls of the Row had now become frightened and security was doubled. It was at this time that the Row was dubbed "Strangler's Row" and iron bars were installed on the windows of several brothels.

Despite precautions, Kiki Oyama became the third victim of the Denver Strangler. The *New Castle News* announced it thus:

> *About fifteen minutes past 1 o'clock No. 1957 Market Street was visited by the fiend whose strange hobby is to choke women to death, and when he left the place, Kiki Oyama, a Japanese girl who ran the place, was a*

corpse with the marks of the strangler's work upon her throat.

This morning's murder was committed in the same row of houses in which Lena Tapper and Marie Contassott were strangled. The mode of her death, too, was extremely similar. After partially choking her, the job was completed by tying a towel around her neck and tightening the noose until life left her body.

The only difference between Kiki Oyama's case and the strangler's other jobs is that she was discovered while her pulse was sill beating and the breath yet in her lungs.

(_New Castle News_, New Castle, Colorado, 1894)

Oyama had last been seen alive on 13 November 1894, some two weeks following the preceding murder. She had spoken to her friends, returned home, drawn her curtains, and, it was assumed, fallen asleep. During this time her lover, a Japanese called Imi, had gone out for a walk. Upon his return he found his luckless paramour lying on the bed, gasping for breath, on the verge of death. Panicking, he ran across the road to seek the aid of another Japanese woman, Hana. Their disturbed behaviour, however, had attracted the attention of a police officer who joined their return to the scene of the crime, only to discover that Oyama had, by now, already expired.

A heavy struggle had clearly occurred within the room. The bedsheets had been disturbed and were stained with blood; a damp towel had been laid upon the washstand; and it appeared that the drawers in the room had been rifled, as if someone had been searching for loot. Moreover, Oyama had been battered around the head and clear to see were the red marks of bruising around her windpipe. It was evident that a towel had been used in order to garrotte the poor woman. There had been no forced entry. The Denver Strangler had struck again, the third time in as little months.

The victims had all been women of differing in age and

ethnicity. In none of the cases had there been forced entry. All victims had been sex workers, working within the same vicinity a few blocks apart. Had the killer simply gone from door to door, seeking to find an unlocked entrance? Had he been looking for a random women to attack, their choice of profession being the only common denominator?

After Oyama's death, police began to take more seriously the goings-on in the red-life district of Denver. However, the deaths ceased as quickly as they had begun, but not before some of the more upmarket bordellos ceased trading, or at least shortened their business hours for a while. Could the Strangler have simply moved on? Or had he died, become incapacitated or imprisoned? Perhaps the answer will never be known.

But perhaps the Strangler *may* have killed again. Julia Voght, was a clairvoyant. She claimed that whilst in a trance spirits had given her a description of the murderer. Voght was discovered dead, strangled by a towel, on 7 October 1898. It may be that the killer believed the woman's claims and killed again in order to silence her supernatural murmurings. And a second possible victim, Mabel Brown, died in 1903, after having been found murdered in similar circumstances – lying on her bed, strangled.

In 1894, three other murders invited speculation that they were the work of the Denver Strangler. These deeds, however, were committed much further afield, in Ohio and New York, and a man, Alfred Knapp, was electrocuted for the Ohio crime as well as other unconnected ones.

As an interesting aside, it was reported in the *Chicago Tribune* in 17 November 1894, that a lady escaped the clutches of the Strangler with barely her life:

> *Marie Andrews, an inmate of the district known as Strangler's Row, thinks she escaped tonight the fate which befell three of her sisters within the last two months. At 11 o'clock an Italian called and assaulted her as soon as he entered the place. Her outcry brought the score or more special police who are doing their*

*duty in the threatened district. On his person was found
a dirk and stiletto and a razor was in his hands. Officer
Peterson rushed this man off to the county jail as it was
feared a lynching would ensue if the police waited for
the patrol wagon of the district, which was out on another call. The prisoner registered as H. Moeller from
Italy.*

Marie Andrews' profession is not recorded, although her "sis-
terhood" to the three known victims of the Strangler had been
noted, and it can be assumed that she also had been involved in
prostitution. If her story is to be believed, Andrews had the great
fortune to escape a very close brush with death.

Or perhaps the Strangler actually *had* killed before. Due to the
speed and killings, the cunning of the murderer and similarity of
the victims – known prostitutes – it was thought that there could
be a connection between Denver's Strangler and London's Ripper. Certainly, writers in newspapers of the time seemed to draw
their own conclusions:

*Denver's strangler must be a near relation of London's
Jack the ripper.*
    (*Salt Lake Herald*, Salt Lake City, Utah,1894)

*Jack the Ripper is abroad in Denver, and there is terror
in the hearts of the women, who seem to be the victims
of his taste for blood.*
    (*Evening Express*, Denver, Colorado, 1894)

*The fiendish crimes of the Market Street Strangler will
be rehearsed in the criminal court here. Richard Demandy will be placed on trial for the murder of Lena
Tapper. Whether or not this Frenchman is guilty of
murders that resemble the work of Jack the Ripper in
the Whitechapel district of London will be decided by a
Jury. The district attorney claims to have startling*

evidence that will prove as conclusively as is possible that Demandy at least strangled the first victim.
(*Deming Headlight*, Deming, New Mexico, 1899)

The Dayton Strangler
(active 1900-1909)

THE HORRIFIC MEMORY of the English serial murderer Jack the Ripper was evidently still afresh in the mind of a reporter for the *Wilkes-Barre Times Leader* newspaper when writing, in 1909, of "five beautiful young girls, all of good and unsullied reputations, struck down by the same hand":

> *Another series of murders of girls, the victims being added to from time to time as in Dayton, Ohio, occurred in 1888, in the Whitechapel or slum district of London. Three murders were committed evidently by the one brutal hand and followed each other at brief intervals between April and September of that year. The crimes were laid by popular theory to an unknown degenerate referred to as Jack The Ripper, all the bodies being frightfully mutilated. Guilt was fastened upon no one, but a strong suspicion exists that a man executed in 1903 at Melbourne for crimes in Australia was Jack The Ripper. All the London victims were women of much inferior character to the girls who have been slain by a fiend in Dayton. all of whom have been struck down unawares.*
>
> (*Wilkes-Barres Times Leader*, Wilkes-Barres, Pennsylvania, 1909)

Not long before this article appeared, between 1900 and 1909, a series of rapes and murders were committed around the Dayton, Ohio area. Five of the victims were vital, attractive females, of ages ranging from 11 to 19. One man was also a victim. The *modus operandi* of the killer was similar in each case.

Eleven-year-old Ada Lantz, when found, had been bruised, badly mutilated, strangled and then raped. The fun-loving girl had been playing with her friend at a parent's birthday party.

Her body was found in the slurry pit of the outhouse that evening, hours after she went missing. "This deed was one of the foulest in the local annals of crime," said the local coroner, "and the barbarity evidenced knew no bounds. The fiend, intent upon his brutish deed, considered the life of an innocent child no more valuable than that of a dumb animal."

Dona Gilman, 19, had been returning home from work. She got off at the trolley stop near to her home. Her body was later discovered in a field some 200 metres from her home. Authorities quickly determined that she had been murdered in a nearby house and dumped in the field. Her gloves and umbrella were found presumably where she had dropped them after being attacked.

Bertha Markowitz escaped the attacker, but her sister, Anna, and Abe Cohan, Anna's gentleman friend, were not so fortunate: Abe had been struck from behind with a baton and then shot in the stomach, later dying from his wounds, and Anna's body was found in some bushes, where it appeared that she had been brutally raped after putting up a struggle. Anna, a serious and shy young woman, had been strangled.

Mary Forschner, an unusually pretty 15-year-old had been making her way to the bank when she disappeared. When she failed to return a search party was organised. Her stepfather, noticing some disturbed soil, followed the trail, eventually finding Mary's lifeless body in a barn. Her body, still warm, had been sexually assaulted and manually strangled to death.

Lively Elizabeth Fulhart, the killer's the sixth victim, was 18 years old. She came from a large family and had many friends and acquaintances. She had been travelling from Vandalia, Ohio seeking employment. It was believed that she was lured into a vacant house by the killer where she was strangled and otherwise abused. After having not been seen for a month, her body, wrapped in a gunny sack, was found at last; it had been dropped into a cistern behind the building. The coroner was unable to tell if Elizabeth had been sexually assaulted such was the degree of decomposition. When she died, it was thought that the girl had been in the possession of about15 cents.

The _Wilkes-Barre Times Leader_ journalist stated that:

> _While comparing with the infamous White Chapel murders of 20 years ago, the Dayton girl murders have no parallel in American crime annals._
>
> _Altogether it appears five young women were mysteriously murdered and the police theory is that all were struck down by the same fiendish hand. This may or may not be true. It is a fact, however, that five young women of about the same age and social condition have been mysteriously murdered in the Ohio city and there are various tangible circumstances which seem to connect the crimes._
>
> _The police call the supposed murderer, Jack The Strangler, from the fact that all of the girls were apparently killed by the clutch of a monster's hand upon the throat._
>
> (_Wilkes-Barres Times Leader_, Wilkes-Barres, Pennsylvania, 1909)

Thus the third of America's unidentified killers also drew comparison with England's Jack the Ripper, and like London's East End marauder, the Dayton Strangler's identity remains unknown. In a twist of fate, Brian Forschner (Mary Forschner was his great-aunt), has uncovered evidence that suggests the killer may have been Hick White, a janitor at the local synagogue, near to where Elizabeth Fulhart's body was found. White, the author believes, attacked another young woman, who managed to escape. The woman, Bessie Stickford, was able to identify White. Forschner believes that he can tie White to the murder of four other girls in Cincinnati. He has written a full account of the case in his book, _Cold Serial: The Jack the Strangler Murders_.

The Man from the Train
(active 1900-1912)

AT THE TURN of the 20th-century the concept of a single individual, travelling interstate whilst committing multiple murder, was unheard-of and not even considered as a possibility. There were, around that time, a number of murders of entire families, comparable in many respects, but which seemed unrelated due to the distance between the crime sites. Undeniable similarities linked many of the attacks: (i) the families lived in small communities with little or no local law enforcement; (ii) the families lived within short distance of a railroad junction; (iii) the families had a barn from where they could be observed unnoticed for long periods of time; (iv) the murders happened at the weekend; entire families were slaughtered by the killer; (v) the families had no dog to provide warning of imminent attack; (vi) the killer's weapon of choice was the axe, favouring the blunt edge, and leaving the murder implement in plain sight; (vii) it was a weapon of opportunity, belonging to the owner of the house; (viii) the killer covered the inside windows of the murder rooms with sheets or towels (presumably to prevent being witnessed); (ix) the killer covered the victims with sheets prior to the assassination (presumably to minimise blood spatter); (x) the fact that the bodies were moved after death; and (xi) the apparent absence of robbery as a motive. Underpinning the similarities was the practised nature of the crimes, as if the killer had gained some expertise and experience. Additionally, there is evidence that the killer on occasion had attempted to attack a second group of victims, entering another nearby house to begin the onslaught again.

Despite these similarities, though, the crimes were only considered locally, and only local suspects were questioned. Usually these suspects were released upon the lack of evidence; other individuals, however, were convicted (possibly unsafely) and executed or, in the case of some black suspects, lynched without trial. Mostly the crimes were considered unsolved and, although they received considered attention from contemporary media, the passage of time caused them to fade from memory and has rendered them unsolved or unsolvable cold cases.

One notorious unsolved crime, however, drew the attention of writer Bill James and his daughter Rachel McCarthy James. Working together, the team investigated researched the infamous Villisca Axe Murders, and in their investigation of the case – the slaughter of eight individuals on the night of 9 June 1912 – they uncovered evidence of the murders of several entire families, committed between 1898 and 1912, in such far-flung places as Arkansas; Colorado Springs, Oregon; Ellsworth and Paolo, both Kansas; Monmouth, Illinois; Florida and Nova Scotia. The James duo claim to have uncovered an elusive, previously unknown serial killer who transgressed the USA, with up to 100 victims to his name. Due to the proximity of the killer's murder sites to railroad junctions, they called this individual The Man from the Train, writing up their discoveries in a book of the same name.

Villisca in 1912 was a small community of a few hundred citizens in south-western Iowa. The Moore family consisted of parents Sarah and Josiah, aged 39 and 43 respectively at the time of their deaths, and their four children, Herman, aged 11; Mary, aged 10; Arthur, aged 7; and little five-year-old Paul as the youngest of the brood. Two visitors to the family home, Ina and Lena Stillinger, aged 8 and 12 respectively, had been invited by Mary to spend that Sunday evening at the Moore household, and they were also present when the killer made his presence known and left his mark.

The next day, Monday, horses neighing in the barn at the Moores' house alerted a neighbour who then became concerned after noticing that the family had not begun their morning chores. Mrs Mary Peckham knocked on the door and, receiving no response, tried to open it, only to find it was locked. Alarmed, she contacted the father of the household's brother, Ross. Upon rapping the door and shouting, he too received no response.

With his own copy of the front door key, he unlocked the house and went into the parlour and then into the guest bedroom. There he discovered the bodies of Lena and Ina lying on the bed. Moore and Peckham sought the Villiscan law enforcement officer, Marshal Hank Horton, who arrived at half-past eight and made a search of the house, only to learn that in addition to the two Stillinger girls the entire Moore family had been slaughtered. The weapon, Josiah's own axe, was found in the same room as the Stillinger girls. Reportedly, when Marshal Horton came out of the house, having witnessed a grisly sight, he said that there was "somebody murdered in every bed". His face was etched with sheer terror and drained of colour. The children had been battered, apparently, with the blunt edge of an axe; Mr and Mrs Moore were administered both the blunt and sharp edges of the axe, between 20 and 30 times, their faces bludgeoned and hacked to beyond recognition.

An examination of the property commenced immediately. The discovery of two cigarette butts in the attic suggested that the killer had remained there for some time, waiting patiently until it was safe to come out. With the Moores and the two Stillinger girls sleeping, the killer chose first to inflict his violence upon the two elder Moores in the master bedroom. It was said that Josiah Moore's face had been cut to the extent that he no longer had his eyes. It was thought by the coroner that the attacker first killed the parents, ferociously attacking them, quickly but quietly, in order to avoid awakening the children. He then made his way to the four Moore children, dispatching them all by the same method, before going downstairs to complete his mission by executing the two Stillinger girls. "Brains of Parents, Children and Visitors Beaten Out With Ax By Fiend," was how the local paper reported it. Lena, the elder girl, it is believed, was awake at the time of the attack upon, as there was evidence of defense wounds. There was no evidence found on any of the bodies of sexual assault, either before or after death.

Certainly, parallels between this gruesome murder scene and

the Burnham-Wayne murder in Colorado Springs were beginning to be noticed:

> *Police authorities here [Colorado Springs] are not inclined to think there is any connection between the murder of the Moore family at Valisca [sic], Ia., and the Burnham-Wayne murder mystery here of September 17 last, in which six persons lost their lives.*
>
> *It is admitted, however, that there is a striking similarity in the crimes. Local authorities will make a careful investigation of the Villisca mystery in the hope of finding some clew in the crime here.*
>
> (*Bayard News*, Bayard, Iowa, 1912)

And in some places the suspicion that a multiple murderer was afoot seemed to be growing stronger:

> *During the last two years, a madman murderer has killed four whole families in the West. In each case he used an axe. The murders have been at Colorado Springs, Ellsworthy, Kan., Guilford, Mo., and Villisca, Ia. The last, that of the Moores at Villisca, occurred this week. The slayer shows a terrible ingenuity in making good his escape.*
>
> (*The Day Book*, Chicago, Illinois, 1912)

During analysing and comparing the *modus operandi* of violent killings around the time of the Villisca Axe Murders, the James duo found strikingly similar features that are shared by other crime scenes. Their case, reasoning that the Villisca murderer was a serial killer, has been strengthened by the similarities between many of each case's distinctive elements, and these have been listed above.

However, there are also strong *psychological* features that link many of the murders. The first of these is that the killer had not been sufficiently stimulated by his initial slaughter and so had immediately moved to seek further victims; and in Villisca a te-lephonist, Xenia Delaney, reported having been awoken from a light slumber by the sound of an unknown person walking through her rooms, only to be frustrated by the lock to her bed-room door. Delaney then heard the intruder retrace his steps to the street again. This incident reportedly occurred at 02:10 on 10 June 1912, the same night that the Moore murders took place.

The second psychological feature is that there may have been a sexual connotation to the attacks. Many of the families had young girls within their composition. Newspapers of the time reporting events alluded, in thinly veiled terms, that there had been ejaculate left at the crime scenes. Oftentimes the victims were posed *post mortem*; undergarments were removed or dis-turbed; limbs were moved to expose genitalia; foreign objects inserted into the vaginal or anal cavities. There may have been sexual molestation, or at least attempts made to do it. The killer is believed to have had a sado-sexual attraction to prepubescent girls, accounting for the fact that it was only they who exhibited defence wounds. The detail of the covering of the victims' faces (and by extension their vision) may also be psychologically im-portant in the killer's motivation, as is the circumstance that whole families, and only whole families, were wiped out. This undoubtedly must have been psychologically significant to the killer also.

This arresting 1911 account in the *Colorado Springs Gazette* serves as a remarkable comparison:

Two Whole Families Almost Completely Annihilated; Henry F. Wayne, Wife and Infant; Mrs. Alice Burnham and Two Babes the Victims; A.J. Burnham, the Surviv-ing Husband, Taken Into Custody.

The most fiendish murderer this city has ever known stalked red-handed in Colorado Springs Sunday night, and all his victims, six in number, were killed as they slept, their heads crushed with an ax.

The dead: Henry F. Wayne, aged 30 years; his wife,

Blanche McGinnis Wayne, aged 26, and their baby daughter, Blanch, 2 years old, 743 Harrison place.

Mrs. Alice May Burnham, 25 years, wife of Arthur J. Burnham, a yardman at the Modern Woodmen sanatorium, and her two children, Alice, 6 years, and John, 3 years old, of 321 West Dale street, but a few steps from the Wayne house.

Little Alice Burnham, judging from the position in which her body was found, was awakened and tried to escape. But the murderer struck her down and she fell partly across the body of her mother. With the exception of the little girl, all the victims were evidently killed either before they awoke or before they had a chance to move.

Burnham was brought to Colorado Springs from the sanatorium an hour after the wholesale murder was discovered, shortly before 2 o'clock yesterday afternoon, and is being held at the county jail.

He is not charged directly with having committed the brutal crime, but the authorities are working on clews that may make it extremely difficult for him to disprove their theories.

At the county jail last night Burnham declared to newspaper men:

"You will have to look elsewhere for the murderer."

In the absence of any clews Burnham will be called upon to tell where he was between 7:30 o'clock last Sunday evening and 5 o'clock the following Monday morning.

The crime, committed Sunday night, as nearly as can be determined, was not discovered until about 2 o'clock yesterday afternoon. Mrs. Nettie Ruth, 931 South Sierra Madre Street, a sister of Mrs. Burnham, and Miss Anna Merritt, 730 North Pine Street, were the first to find the bodies in the Burnham home.

An odor of decayed flesh greeted them as they opened

the back door of Burnham's house with a key secured at the home of Miss Merritt, half a block away.

"Oh, suppose we find May and her babies dead in the house," exclaimed Mrs. Ruth as she and Miss Merritt neared the Burnham home. "It would be terrible, terrible!"

Together the two women unlocked the door in the rear of the house. The lock caught and it was a minute or two before they could turn the key. On a table in the little rear room, used jointly as a kitchen, dining room and bedroom, were the remains of Sunday evening's supper, "just the same," Mrs. Ruth declared last night, "as when I left my sister's house Sunday night a quarter after 9."

The bed in the rear room had not been disturbed. The women pushed open the door leading to the front bedroom half expecting to see some signs of a tragedy, but little suspecting the shocking sight that confronted them.

Over on the bed there appeared to be a pile of bed clothing, but Mrs. Ruth declared she did not at once see the dead forms upon it. She first – the great splotches of blood on the wall and then the body of her little niece, lying on the edge of the bed with her skull crushed.

The women did not look further, both ran screaming from the house. Two men who were passing the house went in while the women waited – moments later they rushed out and the story of the triple murder spread like wild fire.

Many men were accursed of the murders, including one, Paul Mueller, an immigrant, possibly German, who had been employed as a farmhand and itinerant lumberjack. Mueller had been the sole suspect of the murder of a family in West Brookfield, Massachusetts in 1897, sparking a yearlong manhunt. The James duo believe Mueller to be the serial murderer of 59 people in 14 families in separate incidents over the span of more than a decade and they have convincing evidence to back up their case. They also suspect that he was responsible for the slaying of 25 further families, totalling 94 victims. They considered his involvement in the 1922 Hinterkaifeck murders in Germany (having possibly fled there when the local heat became too great), which bore some notable similarities to the American murders and during which six members of the same family died. If Bueller *was* responsible for a transcontinental series of killings then he was one of the most prolific of his breed. However, officially all cases remain unsolved at this stage and unless and until further evidence comes to light they are unlikely to be solved conclusively. It is not known what eventually became of the nomadic Mr Bueller.

The Cincinnati Streetcar Murderer
(active 1904-1910)

IN THE 1990S, Cincinnati, the second largest city in the state of Ohio, was a bustling, vibrant, densely populated metropolis of some 300,000 inhabitants. It had hospitals and public libraries, and venues for music, art and sports. And to transport its citizens there was a 220-mile track electric streetcar system, on which passengers made in excess of 100 million journeys per year.

Cincinnati – "Queen City", "The Paris of America", "The Queen of the West". The city itself at the turn of the century was a cultured, free-spirited place, prosperous, unspoiled and restless. Its inhabitants thought of the town as chained the past. But if they were restless for change, they were just as content to settle down for the ride, for Cincinnatians considered themselves hardworking, easy-going, decent folk.

The district of Cumminsville is centred around the intersection of Spring Grove Avenue and Hamilton Avenue, and the development of the Miami Canal in the 1820s brought many workmen to the area. Its murky mesh of narrow lanes and back alleys were host to a throng of working-class men and their families, all living cheek-by-jowl in overcrowded housing alongside a diverse population of bohemian students and artists. The district was further swelled by the laying of the Cincinnati, Hamilton and Dayton Railroad in 1851 and the workhands that such industry attracted. Many of the immigrants flooding in from Europe were German, and with them they brought their culture and customs. Numerous taverns sprung up prior to its annexation by the city of Cincinnati in 1873 and, due to its reputation for rowdy drinking dens which heaved with an array of eccentric characters, Cumminsville was dubbed "Helltown". That exuberant moniker, with its dubious undertones, would seem much more appropriate later in 1904.

Thirty-one-year-old Mary McDonald – known as "Mamie" to her kith and kin – had been involved in an ill-fated relationship with her sister's widow. He had promised to marry Mary, but instead he reneged on this agreement and eloped with another woman. Mary, ever hopeful, then followed him to California, only to return to Cincinnati disappointed, where she quickly turned to drink, easing her despondency by roving from bar to bar in the company of "disreputable men", becoming in the process what the *Cincinnati Enquirer* was to call a "pathetic moth on society's fringes".

It seemed that Mary's luck had changed following her next betrothal to a government employee stationed in Alabama. However, this luck was short-lived. After a brief drinking spree, moving between taverns with a man called Charles Stagman, Mary was put on the College Hill streetcar at 01:30. Her drinking partner of that night later claimed that he could not remember a thing about his movements around this time, having himself collapsed in a drunken stupor shortly thereafter.

Mary's luck had run out. She was found on 4 May 1904 near the Dane Street railway tracks unconscious. Her head had been smashed in and a leg had been severed. She passed away a few hours later.

The coroner wished to record the cause of death as accidental, that she had been hit by a moving trolley car. However, engineers who had been working at the time insisted that this would have been impossible: the trolleys would simply have not been moving fast enough. And no doubt, they maintained, if a trolley had hit Mary the operators would have heard a noise. Furthermore, detectives claimed that given Mary's intake of alcohol that night she could not have reached the place her body was found without the help of another. Indeed, drag marks and footprints near the body pointed to another person being involved in its removable. Police later shifted to the view that Mary had been attacked and pushed under the trolley car and a verdict of death by murder was recorded by the coroner. Mary had become the first victim of the killer who came to be known as the Cincinnati Streetcar Murderer.

The second unfortunate victim of the killer was Louise "Lulu"

Mueller. She was found in a "lovers' lane" a short distance from rail tracks, resting in a clump of weeds. She had taken a shortcut across a field whilst walking in the dark to a friend's house. She was snatched just yards from safety and suffered a sustained attack to her head. Such was the ferocity of the brutal onslaught that mercifully the first blow would have been enough to render her senseless to further blows or to extinguish life completely. Lulu had died on 1 October 1904.

Her head, it was said, was riven to pulp, with deep wounds to the side that might have been inflicted by a hatchet or club. Next to her body, onlookers observed a partially dug grave, freshly unearthed. It seemed that the murderer had been disturbed amidst his exploits. Incredulously, it later transpired that a passing policeman had heard the screams of a woman the previous night but had not investigated their cause. Additionally, the next day observers noted a thickset, dark-complexioned man in the vicinity repeatedly saying, "It was an accident," before disappearing from the scene.

Lulu was considered a woman of "easy virtue". She had had a number of beaux on the go at the same time, and she had been, it appeared, on good terms with each of them. Nevertheless, suspicion fell upon one individual, 30-year-old Frank Eastman who was, by all accounts, a handsome, dapper rogue of sizeable proportions who had been going steady with Lulu for over two years. That she had been found a few hundred feet from his place of abode, and the fact that he had attempted to have her life insured, seemed reasonable enough circumstantial evidence and he was questioned by investigators. The tearful lover asserted his innocent and insisted that the police look elsewhere for their man. His shaky alibi proved sound in the end and Frank Eastman was discounted as the prime suspect.

Whilst police investigators favoured an "accident" verdict, declaring that a train could have caused Lulu's injuries, the coroner, however, disagreed, citing the extent of her injuries, the distance from the track where she was found and the fact that there appeared to be the traces of strangulation bruising on the victim's neck, and his view won the day.

In addition to Frank Eastman a few other suspects were questioned: Theodore Salmon, a one-legged peddler; William Wilson, a womanising painter accustomed to making idle threats; Mellie Alledon, another girlfriend of Frank Eastman, who, when quizzed, remembered that a mysterious blond woman had gone to Lulu's house in search of her. None was charged with the attack on Louise Mueller.

Alma Steinigewig (Steinway), an 18-year-old, highly respected telephonist of unblemished moral fibre, was the next victim of the killer, the third in seven months. Alma attended church regularly and sang in the choir. She had been returning home from work by train with a colleague, leaving the car at around 21:40. Earlier that day she had declined to go to a dance with her boyfriend, stating that she was tired and simply wished to return home to go to bed.

Alma's body was found some 130 feet from the trolley stop. Drag marks and large footprints were testament to the fact that she had been hauled there by another individual. It was supposed that she had been dealt a blow to the head which incapacitated her and that she had met her death in the place to where her body had been dragged. In her bloodstained hand she clutched a train ticket. Like the other victims, her head had been smashed in, and she had a gash deep enough to penetrate the brain, which the coroner asserted could have been caused by an axe. And in strong corroborative evidence, the wounds were made by a left-handed killer – as they also were in the case of the murder of Louise Mueller.

Two suspects quickly came to the fore: "Jack the Pincher", a molester whose pleasure it was to grab women's bottoms; and the same thickset man who had been seen by the death-scene of Louise Mueller, exclaiming, "It was an accident." The latter had been mulling around near the scene. However, as before, this individual slipped away before he could be detained by police.

This time no one claimed that the victim had been hit by a train. The multiple blows to the head, drag marks, and microscopic evidence showing that she had been raped – all pointed to the fact that a serial murderer was operating within the darkness of a "murder zone" next to Cumminsville's railroad corridors.

Also attacked during this 1904 spree were at least nine other women, who all lived to tell the tale. Commonalities to many of these incidents were: (i) all occurring within the same district of Cumminsville, (ii) their proximity to rail tracks, (iii) the attacker suddenly springing from a hidden place, (iv) the use of an axe as the weapon of violence, (v) the brutality of the assailant, and (vi) the flight of the would-be assassin when disturbed by others. Several of the women described their attacker as a short, rough-looking man. Several other women came forward to describe having been subjected to pestering and harassment. Due to the similar nature of many of the incidents reported at the time it is likely that the same individual was responsible for these attacks as well as the three murders; however, this has not been conclusively established.

The attacks abated for a period of over five years. Then another killing interrupted the hiatus. On New Year's Eve 1909, Anna Lloyd, a 43-year-old secretary, was walking home along Hopple Street, a thoroughfare that overpassed the Cincinnati, Hamilton and Dayton Railroad – an area within the notorious "murder zone". When Anna was found, her mouth had been gagged, her head staved in, her throat slashed, and numerous defensive wounds pointed to the physical strong Miss Lloyd having been involved in a sustained confrontation with an attacker of brutal and lethal intent. When her lifeless body was found, she held a single black hair in her hand, which was of little use due to the less-advanced forensic tests of the day.

Theories abounded about the motive for the murder – including one that she was the victim of a paid assassin, and another that a meat cleaver had been used and thus the killer had been a butcher. Two men had the blanket of suspicion cast upon them: one, C.H. Thomas, an apparently slovenly co-worker whom Anna had deemed "quite unbearable"; and another, Henry

"Dude" Cook, who had been seen skulking in the area on the night of the murder, and whose responses under questioning had been considered "untruthful and evasive". These two proclaimed their innocent vigorously and no viable links could be made towards either man in this crime.

Inevitably suspicions flared (within the press) that this and the three previous track-side murders were connected, and investigators soon came on board with the idea that they were all connected by the same unidentified slayer. No charges were brought upon any individual.

Mary Hackney was the fifth and final victim attributed to the killer. Mary ran her home as a boarding house. On 26 October 1910 the partially disabled 26-year-old lady had been found in the property by her husband, Harley, and a teenage lodger, Charles Ekhert. It seemed that she had been struck in the kitchen and then dragged into dining room, where her throat was slashed from ear to ear and her head subjected to two severe blows, apparently from an axe. There were also numerous vicious slashes to her body and face, specifically to the right cheek.

Charles' alibi, after the initial suspicion of the authorities, proved sound. Further suspects were also discounted after investigation. Clues suggesting that the crime belonged to Cincinnati's serial slayer were clear: the victim had been of the same type (a lone white female); the killing had been within the city's "murder zone"; the excessive brutality of the murder pointed to the same individual being involved; and the killer seemed to be left-handed, in similar fashion to previous murders.

Other women were attacked within the "murder zone" towards the end of 1910, and in the same area a black lady was beaten to death in July 1911. Police, however, did not link this murder to the other crimes. Coroner Coe was not optimistic in his summation: "This is going to be a very difficult case to solve because of the absence of clues indicating even a motive for the crime. Nothing was stolen, the woman was not assaulted, and the only reason seems to have been a lust for blood." A woman claimed to have seen the face of the killer in a dream; and a medium held a séance which proved unproductive. In the end, this crime, like the others, was to remain unsolved. Inevitably, as with the nation's previous serial attacks, comparisons were made with the slasher who had stalked London's Whitechapel area a decade earlier; the *Williamsport Sunday Grit* declared in print writ large: JACK THE RIPPER STILL ACTIVE!

Despite the similarities, however, this theory gained little traction and it soon dissipated.

The lapse of time between the third and fourth murders *may* be accounted for by the killer having been imprisoned or otherwise incapacitated. From modern knowledge of the habits of serial killers, it is unlikely (but not impossible) that the Cincinnati Streetcar Murderer simply took a break from his activities between the years 1905 and 1910; and likewise it is improbable that after the fifth murder he simply discontinued his crime spree, satisfied that he had achieved his desires and that there was nothing left to gain from their continuation. Furthermore, it is possible that the crimes may have been the handiwork of more than one individual. What *is* certain, however, is that investigation into the cases reached to a dead end. Whilst interest has briefly revived in the intervening years – there were the dubious puzzlements of a deathbed confession and a second-hand confession – this mysterious series of cases remain to this day unsolved.

The Atlanta Ripper

[active 1911-1912]

COME THE 1900s, Atlanta, Georgia was a thriving centre of commerce. The importance of the manufacturing industries exploded, business was booming and workers flooded to the city for its employment opportunities. As a consequence, the population nearly doubled in the new century's first decade, and competition between the working-class blacks and whites for housing and jobs was fiercely fought. The rivalry between the racial factions became more intense, giving rise to increased fear and tension. Antebellum Atlanta was far from an idyllic place for its black population. Racial prejudice was rife. Segregation was not just a choice, it was enshrined in law. It was a time when the lynching of black men and women was still a common reality. In 1906, unsubstantiated hearsay about the alleged rape by black men of white women stoked up racial tensions in the print media, triggering a series of notorious race riots during which at least 27 people died, 25 of them African-Americans. Many others were injured.

It was in the context of this scenario that 20 black or mulatto (mixed-race) women were murdered with horrific regularity. Newspaper editors wrote to their readership's interests, who happened mostly to be whites. The reporters and editors were exclusively white. They were concerned about white issues, and the crimes they wrote about were crimes that affected white people. Crimes against blacks were ill-reported. One murder, that of a respectable black woman, was buried seven pages deep in a short article in the *Atlanta Constitution* on 29 May 1911, a Monday. Mary "Belle" Walker, the paper reported, "was found with her throat cut near her home". Belle was a negro woman. She had been found by her sister the previous morning, a Sunday, after she failed to return home from her employment as a cook. Her body had been horribly mutilated.

It was not until two weeks later when the body of Addie Watts was discovered that the question began to arise of a solitary prowling killer of black women. The *Atlanta Journal* published a speculative question deep inside the paper: "BLACK BUTCHER AT WORK?" Addie had been walking home when she was viciously attacked. She had been bludgeoned with a coupling pin (a metal tubular bar) and her throat had been slashed from ear to ear. That was the sum of the brief report.

The death of Lizzie Watkins made it to the front page, and now journalists began to notice links between these and other murders of young black women. They had all been strangled, had their throats cut and violated in the same area of their bodies. Diplomatically, the papers reported that the killer seemed to have a knowledge of anatomy. The discerning reader of the time would have inferred that there had been sexual mutilation.

Emma Lou Sharpe, 20 years old, was attacked when she became concerned by the failure of her mother (40-year-old Lena Sharpe) to return to the house after she had left to fetch groceries. On 1 July 1911, Emma was approached by a "tall, black, broad-shouldered" man who blocked her path, saying, "Don't be afraid. I never hurt girls like you." It was a soon-to-be-broken promise; the stranger immediately stabbed Emma in the back, compelling her to flee to safety. Unbeknownst to Emma, her mother by that time was already dead, slain by a nameless assassin. Lena Sharpe's head was almost detached from her body such was the savagery of the attack upon her body. By now the papers were commenting upon the undoubted "insanity" of this killer whilst making comparison to London's "Jack the Ripper".

The papers had noted that it was the pattern of this dealer of death to strike on a Saturday. "WILL THE 'JACK THE RIPPER' CLAIM EIGHTH VICTIM THIS SATURDAY?" was the spicy headline splashed by the *Atlanta Journal*. An unnamed police veteran predicted: "The negro will kill another woman before midnight Saturday."

Nearly. A "negro man, tall, black and well-built" whistled at Mary Yeldell as she walked past an alley on Saturday, 8 July 1911 upon her return home from the home of Mr W.M. Selcer, where she was employed as a cook. The stranger approached her stealthily. Mary screamed and ran back to her employer's house. Selcer grabbed his revolver and ran to the alley, finding the man still standing there. Selcer ordered him to raise his arms, but the man instead dashed down the alley and disappeared.

The deaths did not stop. Perhaps perturbed by his close shave, the killer now chose a different day of the week upon which to act. And the attacks became increasingly frenzied. One woman, Sadie Holley, had her throat cut so savagely she was nearly decapitated. Another woman, Mary Putnam, was disembowelled "by someone skilled with a knife", and her heart removed after death. This was found placed beside the still warm body upon its discovery. Mary Kates, the killer's latest victim, had been grievously defiled:

> When he lured [her], a comely nineteen-year-old mulatto girl, into an alley, cut her throat from ear to ear, and then mutilated her body about the breast and below the waist, Atlanta's Jack the Ripper had his nineteen victim. The girl's body was found today. The murderer had entirely disrobed her after cutting her throat. The clothing was nearly piled by the body. The mutilation of the girl's body was evidently done with a surgical instrument and the slayer had some anatomical knowledge, as one of the organs was deftly removed.
> (*Evening Star*, Franklin, Georgia, 1912)

A substantial reward was offered for information leading to the capture and arrest of the elusive criminal. The reward lay unclaimed. Public outrage was fuelled by the upstanding character of the victims who were, without exception, "hard workers and generally respected by both races alike. The character of the victims is largely responsible for the indignation at the murders, which has been so evidence among the better class of Negroes."

There were at least 15 corpses by the end of the reign of terror. All the victims were black or mulatto. They had been sexually assaulted. Interestingly, in some of the cases the victims' shoes had been removed and taken from the scenes of the crime.

The pace of the murders slowed and finally discontinued. The official body count stopped at 20, the last tragic victim being a 19-year-old "comely yellow girl" who remains unnamed to this day. Her lifeless body was discovered on 10 May 1912.

The next year, in March, notes were found pinned to fireboxes around Atlanta, on which the author threatened to "cut the throats of all Negro women" who were to be found on the streets after dark. However, this appeared to be an idle threat, for the promised murder spree did not recur. Although a grand jury indicted two men for the crimes no one was successfully prosecuted. The police focused their concentrations on black men, and even arrested one black man, Henry Brown, putting him through "the third degree" until he confessed. The case went to trial. Another black man, however, gave evidence that this confession had been beaten from Brown and the jury wisely found the confession unsafe and on 18 October 1912 acquitted the defendant.

Memories of the Atlanta Ripper have faded over time. No one stepped forward with information pointing to a suspect. The crimes appear to be those of a serial lust killer with a vicious rage and deft ability to blend into his surroundings. Despite this, not even the ethnicity of the killer is conclusively known and the crimes remain unsolved. It is likely that the unidentified, unpunished killer may forever be relegated to the footnotes of Atlanta's dark history.

The Axeman of New Orleans
(active 1918-1919)

THE EDITOR OF A LOCAL NEWSPAPER, the *New Orleans Times-Pica-yun*, received a letter sent from "Hottest Hell", dated 13 March 1919, purportedly written by "The Axeman" of that same city:

They have never caught me and they never will. They have never seen me, for I am invisible, even as the ether that surrounds your earth. I am not a human being, but a spirit and a fell demon from the hottest hell. I am what you Orleanians and your foolish police call the Axeman.

When I see fit, I shall come again and claim other victims. I alone know who they shall be. I shall leave no clue except my bloody axe, besmeared with the blood and brains of him whom I have sent below to keep me company.

If you wish you may tell the police not to rile me. Of course I am a reasonable spirit. I take no offense at the way they have conducted their investigation in the past. In fact, they have been so utterly stupid as to amuse not only me but His Satanic Majesty, Francis Josef, etc. But tell them to beware. Let them not try to discover what I am, for it were better that they were never born than to incur the wrath of the Axeman. I don't think there is any need of such a warning, for I feel sure the police will always dodge me, as they have in the past. They are wise and know how to keep away from all harm.

Undoubtedly, you Orleanians think of me as a most horrible murderer, which I am, but I could be much worse if I wanted to. If I wished, I could pay a visit to your city every night. At will I could slay thousands of your best citizens, for I am in close relationship to the Angel of Death.

Now, to be exact, at 12:15 (earthly time) on next Tuesday night, I am going to visit New Orleans again. In my infinite mercy, I am going to make a proposition to you people. Here it is:

I am very fond of jazz music, and I swear by all the devils in the nether regions that every person shall be spared in whose home a jazz band is in full swing at the time I have mentioned. If everyone has a jazz band going, well, then, so much the better for you people. One thing is certain and that is that some of those people who do not jazz it on Tuesday night (if there be any) will get the axe.

Well, as I am cold and crave the warmth of my native Tartarus, and as it is about time that I leave your earthly home, I will cease my discourse. Hoping that thou wilt publish this, and that it may go well with thee, I have been, am and will be the worst spirit that ever existed either in fact or realm of fantasy.

– The Axeman

The missive was published in all the local papers of the time and it was enough to strike renewed terror into the hearts of the city's citizens towards whom it was directed. On the night of 13 March, every one of the dance halls of New Orleans was filled to capacity, and jazz bands – professional and amateur – performed at hundreds of residences across town, undoubtedly playing not out of love for the music but due to fear. If the Axe Murderer had wanted to hear jazz music that night he must surely have been satisfied, and the people were rewarded for their efforts. No Orleanian was murdered for the lack of a rag-time tune to dance to.

The Axeman of New Orleans had been active since 23 May 1918 when he broke into the combined barroom and grocery premises of Joseph Maggio and his wife Catherine and cut both their throats with a straight razor as they slept. So deeply had

Catherine's throat been cut that her head was nearly removed from the shoulders. She had died instantly. Her husband died a short period after having been discovered by his two brothers, Andrew and Jake. Both the victims' heads had been obliterated by an axe in what may have been an attempt to conceal the true cause of death. Investigators found the killer's bloodstained clothes within the apartment, and the bloodied murder weapon in an adjoining garden. The motive for the attack was clearly not financial gain, for valuables in plain sight had been left untouched. Andrew, the brother, was questioned – he owned a barber shop and admitted that the razor had belonged to him. However, he was eventually released uncharged.

Just over a month later Louis Besumer and his mistress Harriet Lowe were attacked in similar circumstances. They had been in bed together sleeping in the early hours of 27 June 1918.

They were discovered the next day, unconscious, profusely bleeding from hack wounds, but still alive. Both survived the assault, but scandal followed them. The unmarried pair were castigated by the press. Besumer's true wife arrived to the scene, further inflaming the drama. Lowe, the mistress, blamed the police chief for leaking details to the press and refused to cooperate with their enquiry. She eventually left hospital and returned to the home she had shared with Besumer, her face partially paralysed. She did not survive surgery to repair her face, dying on 5 August, the third lethality of the mad Axeman. Prior to her death she informed authorities that she believed her attacker to have been her lover Besumer. The scandalmongering woman might well have been in a state of delirium caused by her injury. Nevertheless, Besumer was charged and served nine months incarcerated before his eventual acquittal. That he himself had suffered a fractured skull in the attack assuredly pointed to the man's innocence. Latter day writers, however, dismiss this exculpatory consideration, believing that Lowe had not been attacked by an intruder, that her assailant was a familiar rather than a stranger.

The next attack was upon an eight-months pregnant woman

called Anna Schneider, aged 28. She awoke in the early hours of 5 August 1918 to find herself being bashed in the face by a dark figure. She suffered partial scalping. However, she survived the attack and two days later gave birth to a healthy baby girl. An ex-convict who had run from police was arrested but later released when no evidence supporting his guilt could be found. It was around this time that investigators publicly speculated a connection between the attacks.

Five days later, Joseph Romano was the next to suffer a violent death. Romano, an elderly man of 80 years, suffered two blows to his head that night. His two nieces, who had been asleep in an adjoining room, were awoken by the commotion. They investigated its cause, only to find a dark-skinned, short and pudgy man fleeing the scene. Whilst Romano was able to walk to the ambulance, he died of his wounds two days later, the fourth fatality of the Axeman's spree. A retired detective, John Dantonio, pondered upon the motiveless nature of this and the other crimes. It was known that the killer had rummaged through drawers in Romano's bedroom, seizing his trousers and a watch. Had the crime been a botched burglary, or had the robbery been an attempt to disguise a planned murder? In an amazingly prescient analysis, Dantonio described the killer as "likely a Jekyll and Hyde personality, like Jack the Ripper. A criminal of the dual personality type may be a respectable, law-abiding citizen when his normal self. Then suddenly the impulse to kill comes upon him and he must obey it." His perceptions pointed to a specific *modus operandi*: the victims resembled Italians, most of them grocers with businesses in the same vicinity; robbery did not appear to be a motive for the killings; the manner and mode of the physical attacks were strikingly similar.

Dantonio did not seek to reassure. He warned that a killer of this type was very hard to catch, that police were unlikely to bring him to justice and that he would be very likely to kill again. Unfortunately for the Cortimiglia family this proved to be an accurate analysis.

Charlie Cortimiglia was a hulking, heavy-set, swarthy

businessman. His robust, darkly pretty wife, Rosie, was what the newspapers called "a pronounced Italian type". They had a daughter, Mary. On the night of 10 March 1919, a 69-year-old local grocer, Iorlando Jordano, heard screams coming from across the street and rushed to investigate. He was greeted at the Cortimiglia residence by the vision of Rosie standing bleeding in the doorway clutching little Mary. Charlie lay inside on the floor, also bleeding. The parents were rushed to hospital. Nothing could be done for young Rosie; she was now dead, having succumbed to the injuries on her head. The family had been attacked as they lay sleeping in their beds. The intruder had removed a panel from the door, thereby gaining access. The same method of entry had been used in the previous murders..

In time, both Mr and Mrs Cortimiglia recovered. Rosie quickly accused the man who had rushed to their aid, Iorlando Jordano, and his 18-year-old son Frank, of the attack. Charlie vehemently countered his wife's claims. Despite the elder Jordano being too frail and his son too large to have squeezed through the door panel, the two were convicted of the crime. It was only after a year had passed that Rosie admitted she had given false evidence out of jealousy and spite and the Jordanos were able to gain their release from prison.

Three days after the attack on the Cortimiglia family, the infamous letter from "Hottest Hell" was published. And the city was spooked. The newspapers did little to dispel the tension. No detail was too salacious to be published. Cartoons lampooning sleep-deprived residents hiding behind doors with shotguns or frantically playing jazz music were printed. Theories abounded about the killer and his apparent love of jazz.

For five months all was quiet, although people still lived fearfully, sleeping little. Then, on 10 August 1919, Steve Boca, a grocer, was attacked as he slept in his bedroom. Nothing was taken from his home. Likewise, Sarah Laumann, a 19-year-old woman who lived alone, was attacked. She suffered head wounds and several of her teeth were dislodged. Nothing was stolen. Despite their injuries both survived.

Mike Pepitone was not so fortunate. He was brutally hacked to death on 27 October. When Mike was found by his wife his attacker was escaping the scene. The room was entirely spattered with blood. Mrs Pepitone could give no details of the killer although she would say that she had seen two men departing from the scene. Other than this, these details of the crime were unchanged from the other Axeman attacks. This was the sixth murder attributed to the Axeman at the time; however, closer examination suggests that the attack may have been part of a longstanding vendetta.

There may have been other murders connected to the spree. In December 1920 Joseph Spero and his daughter were killed in Alexandria, Louisiana; in January 1921 Giovanni Orlando was killed in DeRidder, Louisiana; and in April 1921 Frank Scalisi was killed in Lake Charles, Louisiana. In all cases the victims were grocers and their families who had been attacked with their own axes. After this, the killings suddenly stopped.

The killer was both organised and disorganised. He must surely have spent considerable time scoping his victims, choosing specific homes that were easy to enter. He took the trouble to remove door panels carefully, without making noise to disturb the inhabitants. His weapon was the axe, which he found on the victims' property. And yet the attacks were blitz-like, messy and violent, appearing to release inner compulsions and rage. He liked to "overkill", and enjoyed the thrill of killing – yet he left as many victims alive as he dispatched.

It is not known for certain that it was the Axeman himself who sent the taunting jazz-promoting letter. If it was he, then the action points to a narcissist who craved power and excitement, whose aim was to confound the police investigators whilst revelling in the attention. Equally, references to himself as "a fell demon from hottest hell", "His Satanic Majesty" and "The Angel of Death" point to an individual of unsound mind, perhaps one undergoing a schizophrenic break.

History will probably never know why the killings stopped so abruptly. The Axeman may have been killed himself by another, completed suicide to escape his torments, succumbed to the rampant influenza pandemic currently aflame, or been arrested in his tracks for another, unrelated crime. Certainly, however, the Axeman would not have stopped his spree due to a guilty conscience.

The Cleveland Torso Murderer
(active 1935-1938)

THE NUMBER OF MURDERS attributed to an inhumane butcher that shocked Cleveland, Ohio in the 1930s officially totals twelve. However, some investigators would increase the number by an additional 15, bringing a possible total of 27 victims. The gruesome details of the murders horrified the nation. All of the victims were beheaded, most of them whilst they still lived, the abruptness of the action mercifully causing immediate death. Their bodies were defiled after death in the most grotesque fashion: they were variously subjected to emasculation, dismemberment or the removal of internal organs; often the bodies were severed clean in half, and occasionally they were burned by fire using oil as an accelerant or denatured by use of acid or other chemicals. The heads were always removed from the kill site, often never recovered.

The Cleveland Torso Murderer (he was also called the Mad Butcher of Kingsbury Run) operated in a city that was expanding rapidly. The city was on the rise after the Great Depression. Cleveland, a manufacturing base for the steel industry, was a lure for labourers needing employment. Kingsbury Run in the city was a dank and dangerous place in the 1930s; it was to this dire place that itinerant workers moved, settling down – at least for a while – alongside their dispossessed neighbours. They lived in appalling conditions amongst the grime and trash of a makeshift shanty town on natural river flats. Kingsbury Run was not a welcoming setting.

In September 1934 a young man found the lower half of the body of a woman, estimated to have been in her thirties. Her thigh remained intact but the legs had been amputated at the knees. A few body parts were found nearby although some could not be recovered. The head was never located. A chemical preservative had been applied to the body, rending the skin tough and leathery. This unidentified lady would subsequently be referred to as "The Lady of the Lake". She would later be included in the number of victims attributed to the Cleveland Torso Murderer and she would be known as victim no. 0.

One year later, on 23 September 1935, the body of Edward Andrassy, a handsome 28-year-old white male who had worked as a hospital orderly before turning to drink, recreational drugs, pornography and petty crime. His head and testicles had been removed. He was naked except for his socks, and his body had been drained of blood. The victim had had an arrest record and he was identified by his fingerprints. He was rumoured to have been a homosexual who frequented the local area of ill-repute known colloquially as "The Roaring Third", a home to gambling dens, brothels and flophouses. Even in death, a police report noted despondently, the young man managed to retain his good looks.

Another man, who remains unidentified, was found nearby at the base of Jackass Hill in the Kingsbury Run. He too had been decapitated and emasculated, and his body had been treated with a chemical in the same manner as that of "The Lady of the Lake". The second man's death appeared to have predated Andrassy's by several weeks. Investigators referred to him by the multiple-use name John Doe[*]. As the bodies piled up he would become known as John Doe I.

The murderer now became bolder. On 26 January 1936 the decapitated and dismembered body of Florence Polillo was found neatly wrapped in newspaper and packed in baskets and left to be found outside the Hart Manufacturing Building on Cleveland's Central Avenue. Forty-two-year-old Florence had been a waitress, barmaid and prostitute plying her trade in "The Roaring Third". She was identified by her fingerprints. The head was never recovered.

---

[*] John Does is a commonly used codename for a male whose identity is unknown. The female equivalent is Jane or Janet Doe.

The next victim was found by two boys aged 11 and 13 who had been truanting from school to go fishing. They spotted an object tucked into a bush, wrapped in a pair of trousers. To their shock they discovered the ghastly content within: a severed head. As a direct affront to police investigators, the remainder of the body was found dumped behind the local police department. Noticeable on the body were several tattoos, which were photographed and circulated to tattoo parlours nationwide, to no avail. It was hypothesised that the blue-eyed man had been a Scandinavian sailor. John Doe II is sometimes also referred to as "The Tattooed Man".

The skull of John Doe III was next recovered some fifteen feet distant from the body. This victim had been dismembered whilst still alive. Wild animals had eviscerated the body, which was in an advanced stated of decomposition when found. And all that remained of John Doe IV, the sixth body found, was the upper portion of the torso – minus the head, which was never found.

By now police investigators were admitting that the reign of murder was more than likely the work of one man. The *Cleveland News* prophesised that the killer was an addict who was powerless to halt his rampage:

> *Why these dead? Why this darkest of all Cleveland murder mysteries? He kills for the thrill of killing. He kills to satisfy a bestial, sadistic lust for blood. He kills to prove himself strong. He kills to feed his sex-perverted brain the sight of a beheaded human. He must kill. For decapitation is his drug, to be taken in closer-spaced doses. Yes, he will kill again. He is, of course, insane.*
> (*Cleveland News*, 1936, Cleveland, Ohio)

Theories from the press, their imaginations running riot, included: (i) that the killer was a wealthy doctor who hunted the lower orders for sport, (ii) that a religious fanatic deemed ridding the city of prostitutes and homosexuals God's work, (iii) that an outwardly normal person would occasionally lapse into a madness which opened up an impulse to cause blood-crazed slaughter. Detective Peter Merylo offered an opinion to the press:

> *"The murderer is a sex degenerate [who] may have worked in the pathology department of some hospital, morgue or some college where he had an opportunity to handle a great number of bodies, or may have been employed in some undertaking establishment and ... had a mania for headless nude bodies."*
> (*Cleveland News*, 1936)

Jane Doe I was found on 23 February 1937 at the same location "The Lady of the Lake" had been dumped. Her head was never found. The only black victim, Jane Doe II, was found four months later. The petite woman was missing her head and a rib. The head was later recovered. It was estimated that the body had been undiscovered for a year after death. Unofficial dental identification suggested that the eighth victim of Cleveland's mass murderer was Rose Wallace. If this *was* Rose, the information availed the police little and they were able to develop no new leads pointing to a suspect.

Four further bodies were found between June 1937 and August 1938 – two males and two females, all unidentified. The body of John Doe V, a male in his thirties, was pulled from the waters of the Cuyahoga River. He had been gutted and his heart ripped out. His head was never found. Other parts of Jane Doe III's body were found under a bridge in a sack. One month later the remaining parts of the killer's 10th attributed victim were fished from the river. Hers was the only body to have had drugs in the system.

Although it was considered that the pair had been killed on separate occasions some months prior, Jane Doe IV and John Doe VI were found on the same day at the same location. The torso of Jane Doe IV was found on a city dump. It had been wrapped in a man's suit and then covered again by an old quilt.

The limbs were found close by, held together by elastic bands, wrapped in brown butcher's paper and stored in a box. The victim's head had been treated similarly. Only yards away the body of a male, John Doe VI, was found. This was to be the murderer's final canonical victim. As a final insult to the body, its head was found dumped in a trashcan. Both Jane Doe IV and John Doe VI had been placed in plain view of the office of Eliot Ness. Ness, the city's recently appointed Safety Director, had become heavily involved in the case. Police were confounded. Their quarry, who taunted but evaded them, was intelligent and wily; this was not doubted.

Two suspects are worthy of note. Dr Francis E. Sweeney was a World War I veteran who had worked in a unit that conducted field amputations. He was interrogated by the aforementioned Eliot Ness, overseer of the official investigation, and was said to have failed two polygraphs (so-called "lie-detector" tests). Dr Sweeney later committed himself to a psychiatric hospital, from whence he sent taunting postcards to Ness well into the 1950s. Factors pointing to the involvement of a man of medical knowledge were (i) the lack of hesitation marks, (ii) the confident disarticulation of the joints and (iii) the killer's apparent familiarity with human anatomy, and Sweeney certainly would have fitted this description. However, an individual employed in the butchery of animal carcasses would also fit these criteria.

Suspicion also fell upon a second man, Frank Dolezal, 52, a brick-layer. Little else is known of this individual other than that he produced a rambling, incoherent "confession", replete with precise, detailed information. He himself died under suspicious circumstances in jail before his trial could go to court. An autopsy revealed six fractured ribs, all of which he had obtained whilst in custody.

Interested parties may be keen to learn that some investigators have suspected a connection between the Cleveland Torso Murderer and another notorious murderer who had killed in Los Angeles in 1947, suggesting that the perpetrators were one and the same man. Elizabeth Short, who became posthumously known as the "Black Dahlia", was found severely mutilated and severed at the waist, her body drained of blood. It seems that fresh evidence uncovered in 1980 implicated a former suspect in both cases, Jack Anderson Wilson, and that he had been close to being placed under arrest when he died in a fire in 1982.

It is clear that the Cleveland killings must all have been committed by a single individual. There was too much similarity to be coincidental. A motive for the crimes, however, has not been readily identified. Both men and women were the targets of the killer's murderous rage, but all were poor or homeless citizens of Cleveland*. Did the killer have a grudge against these people in particular? Or were they simply a more freely accessible means (easy prey!) by which to taunt the police, against whom the true target of his revenge lay? And what can be made of the killer's compulsive need to decapitate his victims?

The answer may never reveal itself.

Neither the Cleveland Torso Murderer nor the "Black Dahlia" killer was apprehended. In 1992 a biographer of Eliot Ness, Oscar Fraley, suggested that in both cases Ness was convinced he had the name of the killer but was declining to divulge it. Although both cases continue to perplex criminal historical investigators and to stimulate public interest, they remain unsolved, the killers unidentified.

---

* "Every one of them was a bum," Detective Merylo told the *News-Journal*, Mansfield, Ohio in 1955. "The women were prostitutes. And the men – something worse."

The Phantom Killer
[active 1946]

THE CITY OF TEXARKANA – "Twin City" – is bisected by the Texas-Arkansas state line, its twin halves seamlessly presenting a single cohesive façade. On the Texas side is Bowie County; on the Arkansas side, Miller County. Jurisdictionally each side operates as a separate city, each having its own police forces, governing bodies and its own mayor. However, expediency dictates that responsibility is shared for many public service utilities, and a federal building – the post office – straddles both states on the appositely named State Line Avenue, a pragmatic monument to unity.

The fortunes of the city rose at the turn of the century but declined in the wake of the Great Depression. The Second World War boosted its economy again when major munitions plants took residence in the city. Texarkana attracted business-people, criminals and drifters alike, and the population doubled quickly. The small-town American city became a bustling metropolis existing in a state of duality: "Twin City", on one hand, was an idyllic suburb of unlocked doors and neighbourly ideals; on the other it was a grimy, crime-ridden den known for its brothels, jazz clubs and barroom brawling. In more ways than one Texarkana was split down the middle.

On the night of 22 February 1946 the first of a series of murders and violent attacks on citizens of Texarkana began. The attacks happened on four occasions, at weekends, during the night. The killer – dubbed the "Phantom Killer" or "Phantom Slayer" – targeted two people during each assault. The news media termed the ten-week crime wave the "Texarkana Moonlight Murders".

Twenty-five-year-old Jimmy Hollis and his 19-year-old paramour Jeanne Larey had been out locally on a double-date with Jimmy's brother. After dinner and a movie, Jimmy dropped his brother and his brother's date off first, thinking this would give him some time alone with Mary. He stopped at a secluded lovers' lane, parking at the quiet, desolate track at around 23:45. After about 10 minutes a presence suddenly appeared alongside the car – a man, pointing a flashlight into the car. Although blinded by the disorienting light, both Jimmy and Mary could make out a man wearing a white cloth mask, later recalling that the garment looked like a pillowcase with cut-outs for the eyes and mouth.

Jimmy initially treated the visitation as a prank, but it was not so. The stranger brandished a pistol, ordering the couple out of the parked car, which they reluctantly did. The masked man then directed his attention to Jimmy. "Take off your goddamn britches," he demanded. Jimmy hesitated, but did as bade, afraid of the consequence should he refuse.

At that point the man suddenly stepped forward and delivered Jimmy two savage blows to the head with a heavy blunt instrument, instantly fracturing the skull in several places. Mary was next. She was served a blow to the head which brought her to the ground. She stood up, dazed. The masked man then ordered her at gunpoint to run. She complied with his wishes, running towards a stand of trees.

The man, at this point, shouted after Mary, telling her instead to run along the road. It appeared that he wanted her out in the open. As she ran he followed her. It seemed that he was hunting her.

As Mary approached a parked vehicle she stopped. Unfortunately there was no one in the car. The man caught up with her at that point, demanding to know why she had run, and then becoming unfathomably annoyed when she informed him he had told her to do so. The man shoved Mary to the ground and then proceeded to sexually assault her with the barrel of his gun for several long seconds.

Jimmy, now having come to his senses, noticed that both Mary and their attacker were no longer around. He struggled to his feet and groggily made his way a short distance to another road where he was able to flag down a car. The masked man, meanwhile, seemed to have become unnerved by the headlights of a passing vehicle and fled, disappearing into the gloom. Mary herself also fled, running nearly half-a-mile seeking assistance. A passing car ignored her attempts to flag it down. Mary was eventually able to arouse the resident of a nearby house, who agreed to contact the police.

The two victims spent some time in hospital but they had lived to tell the tale, which was both vague and contradictory. One thing they both agreed on – the attacker was around six feet tall. No one was detained for questioning over the attack. It was reported as a by-line in the local press. Jimmy's pants were found 100 yards from his parked car.

At another lovers' lane, one month later, a motorist noticed an Oldsmobile parked at the side of the secluded gravel road. Thinking this was unusual, the motorist stopped to investigate. He peered inside. A male was in the front seat as if resting with his hands crossed on his lap, whilst a female was in the back seat, sprawled face-down. At first, the motorist thought the two individuals inside were sleeping. It quickly became apparent, however, that the situation was much more serious. There was blood visible on the inside of the vehicle. The man and woman had been shot and lay dead from their injuries.

Richard Griffin, aged 29, and his girlfriend, Polly Moore, aged 17, had been sweethearts for a mere six weeks. The age difference did not trouble them, and indeed, in the 1940s it was much more socially acceptable for an older man to date a younger woman.

On the evening of 23 March, a Saturday, the two had spent some time at a downtown café before going to visit Richard's sister. Leaving at around 22:00, they drove to the lovers' lane where they became the victims of a cold-blooded execution by being shot once each in back of the head. Griffin, a discharged naval construction worker, had been working as a self-employed painter and carpenter. His identify would be confirmed by the vehicle the two were found in. Moore, having left school the previous year, had been employed as a checker at the Red River

Arsenal. Friends described her as "homey". Polly was wearing a class ring when she was found, and the initials engraved on it would help police identify her body.

A couple of .32-caliber shell were found at the scene, but other forensic evidence proved to be inconclusive. Frustratingly, a heavy rainstorm the next morning washed away the footprints observed near the car that might have advanced the case. However, a patch of blood-stained soil some 20 feet from the car pointed to an alternative narrative: one or both of the victims had probably been killed outside the car and then later moved back to the vehicle and posed after death. Griffin's pockets had been turned inside-out. Rumours began to circulate that Polly had been raped. An article in that week's Wednesday edition of the *Texarkana Gazette* edition warned that:

Texarkana residents can help in this investigation and at the same time, if they are not careful, they can hinder the investigation and cause the officers to spend many hours following blind trails. Persons who have information which might furnish a clue to the identity of the slayer or slayers or which might indicate a motive for the crime should not divulge such information on street corners or at cold drink stands but should immediately make it available to the officers. Do not spread rumors regardless of how many bases for the fact there is in them. Do not say "I heard" or "they say" because the chances are that the person listening will repeat your information and enlarge upon it. Before long the story grows to such proportions as to necessitate a detailed investigation by the officers, thereby perhaps pulling them off the true trail and sending them up a blind alley. Stick to facts that you know of your own personal knowledge and relay those facts as quickly as possible to the officers.
(*Texarkana Gazette*, 1946)

A substantial reward was offered for information but this only generated false leads which led nowhere.

A second double murder occurred on Sunday, 14 April 1946. Betty Jo Booker and Paul Martin were the hopeless victims. They had been friends from childhood, attending Kindergarten together. Sixteen-year-old Paul was a high school junior who had lived in Kilgore, Texas. He had made the two-hour drive to Texarkana to meet up with friends the previous Friday. The next day he met up with Betty, spending the afternoon with his 15-year-old friend. Betty was a straight-A student who enjoyed swimming and music. She had a regular Saturday night gig playing saxophone with her band, The Rythmaires. She was picked her up after the gig by Paul, who had agreed to drop her off at a slumber party on the other side of town.

Unfortunately, neither of them made their destination.

Paul Martin's body was discovered by a family at 06:30 the next morning. He had been shot four times – through the nose, the back, the right hand and the back of the neck. Blood further down the road suggested that there was another victim. Betty Brooker's body was found almost two miles away. She had been shot twice – through the chest and in the face. The weapon had been a .32 Colt pistol, the same as used in the double-murder three weeks prior. She was fully clothed when found, but it seemed to investigators that she had been staged: the buttons of her coat were fastened all the way up to her chin, and her right hand appeared to have been placed in the pocket of the coat. It also became apparent that Betty had been sexually violated. She, as well as her friend Paul, appeared to have put up a ferocious struggle against her attacker. The car they had both been travelling in was found some three miles distant from Betty's body and therefore police could not be sure of the order of the events that had befallen the two victims.

All three of the Texarkana attacks up until now had been on the Texas side of the state line. The final crime crossed the border. And broke the pattern.

Virgil Starks, aged 37, and his 36-year-old wife, Katie, lived in a modest house on their small farm around 10 miles northeast of Texarkana in Arkansas. At some time before nine o'clock on the evening of 3 May, a Friday, Virgil was resting his sore back in the sitting room whilst listening to the radio. Katie, who had been lying on her bed, heard a noise outside and asked Virgil to turn down the radio. Seconds later, she heard the noise of breaking glass and went into the sitting room to check on her husband. There she observed him attempt to stand up and then slump forward. She rushed forward, lifted his head, and knew immediately that he was dead.

As she rang for the police she was shot twice – the first shot entering her check and exiting behind her left ear, the second entering her face just below the lip. Hearing her attacker attempt to enter through the window she turned and ran back into her bedroom. Her face was a ruined mess, and she later recalled her difficulty seeing due to the blood in her eyes. The killer then rounded the house and tried to enter via the kitchen window at the rear. In a frantic state, Katie ran through the house leaving blood and teeth in her wake. She exited by the front door, escaping across the road to a neighbouring house, barefoot, in her nightgown, blood-soaked, missing numerous teeth and severely injured. The second bullet was still lodged underneath her tongue. Whilst her husband had been slain, Katie was to survive the last attack of the Phantom Killer ... but only just.

"MURDER ROCKS CITY AGAIN; FARMER SLAIN, WIFE WOUNDED," the *Texarkana Gazette* announced, sending its readers into a state of increased panic and hysteria. Inhabitants equipped themselves with guns. Many of those who had avoided firearms in the past now stocked up with protective weapons. Stores found themselves sold out of much of their ammunitions supplies. Vigilantes patrolled the streets, or laid in wait, seeking to bait the Phantom into revealing himself so they could dispatch the fiend and put an end to his career. They waited in vain, for the Phantom would not trouble them again.

Similarities between the first three attacks were self-evident. The killer attacked couples in lonely places, at night, at weekends, three weeks apart, using a gun. Robbery was not the motive. Sexual assault occurred on one occasion (the first attack) but not conclusively affirmed on subsequent incidents (although rumours of the time suggested otherwise). The killer wore a hooded mask on the first occasion of his spree. If he wore the same mask again in later attacks this could not be reported; the victims were either dead or, in the case of Katie Starks, blinded by her own blood.

The case has never been solved. Some believe that the Phantom Killer and the Zodiac Killer (another unidentified serial killer who surfaced in California 22-years later) were one and the same. Both individuals wore a white hood and used a firearm as their weapon. In 1976, 30 years after the murders, *The Town That Dreaded Sundown*, a low-budget slasher-type movie, was released. The movie, shot in Texarkana, was inspired by the true events that unfolded there. It is shown in the same city every Halloween, to the delight of local teenagers. However, many of the older residents of the town disapprove of the film that turned a real-life tragedy into entertainment. Nevertheless, even they cannot disagree that the film is aptly named; for a while the city of Texarkana *was* the town that dreaded sundown.

IT WILL SEEM STRANGE to see an account of the Boston Stranger in a book purporting to be about the subject of unidentified serial killers. Even well-read students of the subject may ascribe the name Albert Henry DeSalvo to the rapist-murderer in the early 1960s who killed 13 women in eastern Massachusetts. However, although he confessed to the murders, giving extraordinary detail to investigators examining a separate case, the man was never charged for the offence of murder, and his lengthy confession could not (at the time) be substantiated by physical evidence. For this reason DeSalvo was indicted for burglary and sexual offences unrelated to the murders, and it was for these crimes that he was sentenced to life in prison in 1967.

There were 11 "official" murders accredited to the Boston Strangler's canon, and a further two "probables". Eight of these murders actually occurred in the attributed downtown playground of the killer, whilst two were committed in the suburbs – Cambridge, Lynn and Salem – and further afield in the Massachusettsan town of Lawrence, 30 miles north, where the killer struck twice. Thirteen women are thought to have been the victims of a single killer. They were all single, respectable, quietly-living ladies. The youngest was 19-years of age; the oldest (who died from a heart attack) was 85. Most were sexually molested in their apartments and had their lives snuffed out by a strangler using articles of their own clothing. Two were stabbed to death. There were no forced entries into the properties. Either the victims let their attacker into their apartments voluntarily or he had prior knowledge of the means by which to enter unlawfully.

In 1962 Anna Šlesers was an attractive 55-year-old divorcée, the mother of two children, a boy and a girl. She was a devout churchgoer. Ten years earlier she had escaped Latvia, coming to the USA with her children. She settled in a third-floor apartment in a subdivided house in the quiet Back Bay area, working as a seamstress. On the evening of 24 June, the petite lady was due to be collected by her son, Juris, as she had planned to attend a memorial service at the Latvian church. To accompany her whilst she ran the bath she put some classical music on the stereo – a favourite, Wagner's *Tristan und Isolde*. She donned her blue taffeta housecoat.

Just before seven o'clock, Juris arrived. He knocked the door but received no answer. He knocked again, louder, but there was still no response. The door was locked. Now he pounded the door, increasingly nervous. At last, in desperation, he shouldered the door, eventually making an entrance. The site that greeted Juris was shocking. His mother lay outstretched on the floor next to the bathroom. Though she still wore the housecoat it was spread open, as if deliberately arranged that way. She was naked, her legs splayed jarringly apart and her womanhood crudely and shockingly exposed. There was no saving Anna Šlesers; she was already dead, strangled by the cord from her housecoat which had been pulled tightly around her neck. To add gross insult to injury its ends had been tied into a pretty bow.

The apartment had been ransacked – drawers pulled out, rifled and left open; a wastebasket knocked open, its trash spilled over onto the kitchen floor; the contents of a purse strewn about the floor. However, a set of colour slides had been placed onto the floor with some care; and the music on the record player had been turned down. Some valuables had been left untouched. Later police would recognise that this was an attempt to disguise the scene as a botched robbery. Murder had been the motive. Anna had been strangled and her vagina had been violated by a foreign object.

The Boston Strangler had taken his first victim.

Just under three weeks later, the body of 85-year-old Mary Mullan was discovered in her home. In contrast to Anna Šlesers, the death of Mary was not a homicide. The fright of happening upon an intruder in her own house was too much for Mary, and she died from a heart attack there on the spot. The intruder then carried Mary's body to the couch and carefully covered it with a blanket. The name of that intruder, it would later come be to learned, was Albert DeSalvo, aged 29 at the time. When he confessed to the accidental death, he would express great remorse for it and shed tears when speaking of the experience.

Nina Nichols, a retired physiotherapist, was the next to die, some two weeks later on 30 June 1962. Her apartment also looked as if it had been burglarised but inexplicably some items of silver jewellery and an expensive camera were left untouched. Her housecoat had been raised to expose the body below the waist; her legs were spread open. Around her neck her own nylon stockings were pulled tight, strangling the 68-year-old woman to death. It appeared to have been a frenzied attack. The killer, apparently content with his work, had finished by tying the stockings in an elaborate bow. Nina had been sexually defiled with an unknown object. In life she had been a quiet, modest lady; in death dignity was denied her.

It was a similar outcome for Helen Blake. That very same day, 15 miles away in Lynn, the body of the matronly, bespectacled 65-year-old nurse was found. She had been strangled with her own nylon stockings. Her brassiere had been removed and tied around her neck in the jaunty bow that had now become the killer's signature. She was discovered lying facedown on her bed, naked, spread-eagled. There were lacerations found in her anus and the vaginal vault. Investigators concluded that she had been killed in the kitchen and carried to her bed and there sexually assaulted with an unknown object. Only a powerful man, the police surmised, could have picked up and carried the 165lb woman.

There was no evidence of forced entry. Could Miss Blake have opened the door and herself unknowingly admitted her attacker? Did this mean that she had known the killer? The similarities were stacking up. In contrast to the previous murders, however, it seemed as though the attacker had had burglary on his mind: unsuccessful attempts had been made to access a metal strongbox and a footlocker, and two diamond rings had been removed from Helen's fingers.

By the next morning there was no doubt that a multiple murderer was stalking Boston. The headline of the city's *Globe* screamed "ANOTHER SILK-STOCKING MURDER", stating that "a Lynn nurse was found strangled in her apartment under circumstances almost identical with the slaying of a Brighton woman 48 hours earlier". Two weeks later the same paper made a speculation: "STRANGLER OF TWO A MOTHER-HATER?" It suggested that "a paranoid killer, obsessed with a mother-hate complex, was sought last night for the sex-crime strangulations of two women. All division commanders were ordered to compile a list of men … released from mental hospitals in the past year."

Dr Richard Ford, the medical examiner in the case, said: "The more such things happen, the more are likely to happen because – and you can quote me – because the world is full of screwballs and there are so many around we just couldn't begin to round them all up." Dr Ford was to be proved correct, and on 19 August the "screwball" attacked again, repeating the horrifyingly familiar pattern.

Police Sergeant James McDonald described how he found the death scene of 75-year-old Ida Irga on 19 August 1962:

> *"Upon entering the apartment the officers observed the body of Ida Irga lying on her back on the living room floor wearing a light brown nightdress which was torn, completely exposing her body. There was a white pillowcase knotted tightly around her neck. Her legs were spread approximately four to five feet from heel to heel and her feet were propped up on individual chairs and a standard bed pillow, less the cover, was placed under her buttocks."*

It was, as one journalist graphically summed up, a "grotesque parody" of a gynaecological exam.

Jane Sullivan, a 67-year-old nurse, was found dead in her apartment on 30 August 1962 and it seemed that she had died some 10 days or so before being discovered. Her naked body was found by police as if posed, kneeling in the bath. A hefty woman, Sullivan, like Helen Blake, appeared to have been carried from the kitchen where she had been strangled with her own stockings. It could not be determined if she had been sexually violated, such was the extent of decomposition. Jane Sullivan was the Strangler's sixth victim.

Then the killer took an autumnal hiatus.

It would be untrue to think that the city let out a sigh of relief; instead it held its breath.

> *Like a fog creeping inland from the harbour, a clammy fear pervades much of Boston. It's like the anxiety London knew 74 year[s] ago when Jack the Ripper was on the prowl. Here it's the Boston Strangler. He has already killed half a dozen women, and he may strike again.*

This was how a 1962 *Boston Globe* editorial described the tension hanging oppressively in the air. The fear that the attacker could strike again without any warning was palpable. And then, on 5 December, Bostonians' fears were realised. Just a few blocks from where the Anna Ślesers, the Strangler's first victim, was found, victim no. 7 was discovered.

Sophie Clarke, aged 57, had been a careful woman, and security was very much on her mind in the wake of the horrific murders happening almost on her own doorstep. She had a second lock installed on her front door, and she took the precaution of questioning visitors – even her friends – before letting them into her apartment. She had even had a pact with her roommate: because the roaming fiend was on the lookout for single women, they would try never to be at home alone.

Nevertheless, at approximately 14:40 that afternoon Sophie was garrotted to death by her own nylon stockings, which were left knotted tightly around her neck. She was sexually assaulted, and positioned so that her legs were spread widely apart. And even though there had been a struggle, it appeared that she too had willingly allowed her murderer to enter the apartment.

But there were differences. Sophie was African-American. At 20, she was a young woman. She did not live alone. And, in what was a first, semen had been left at the murder site. Despite these variances, police ascribed this murder to the mounting roll call of the Boston Strangler.

The city froze again in collective horror.

Patrice Bissette was next. When the popular, vivacious, outgoing secretary failed to turn up for work on the last day of 1962 her boss became worried. He went to her apartment to investigate, and gained entry with the assistance of the building supervisor. Searching together, the two found the 23-year-old woman in bed, lying as if dozing. But Patrice was not sleeping peacefully. Hidden beneath the covers were several interwoven stockings that had been tied tightly around her neck. Again, semen was left at the scene. Patrice's rectum had been injured. Both she and the one-month-old foetus she carried were dead.

The police began to make more intense examination of the nutters and weirdos, local and beyond. They questioned many men but progress evaded them.

The new year began quietly. For two months no woman died at the hands of the invading brute. Then, 25- miles away in Lawrence, 69-year-old Mary Brown was strangled, stabbed in the breasts with a fork and repeatedly bludgeoned with a blunt object to the point of death. She had been raped. No bow was found around her neck. The ninth of March had been her final day.

And another two months following that, Beverley Samans, 23 years old, was stabbed in a pattern on the left breast, as well as in the neck, the latter wounds being the cause of her death. After her demise two scarves and a pair of nylon stockings were tied around her neck. A friend found her in her apartment naked, legs spread wide, a cloth stuffed into her mouth, and a bow tied around her neck as a decoration. She had not been penetrated in any way and no semen was left at the site.

Beverley had been an aspiring classical singer with ambitions to try for the MET Opera in New York. As a result of her craft the muscles on her throat were well-developed. This happenstance may have been the reason that her killer resorted to stabbing as a means of dispatch. Strangulation may simply have been too difficult.

Four months elapsed before 58-year-old Evelyn Corbin met her ordeal at the hands of the Strangler. As in the case of Beverley Samans before her, Evelyn, an attractive divorcée, had been gagged by having with her own underwear stuffed in her mouth. Also in her mouth was semen, so it appeared that she had been orally raped. Her vagina was free from the same bodily fluid. When found, she was on her bed, naked, supine. Although her apartment had been rifled neither money nor jewellery had been taken. Left behind, though, was a fresh donut. It had been carefully but inexplicably placed on the fire escape outside her window. Its presence simply confounded investigators.

On 23 November Joann Graff, a pattern designer, died by strangulation. The conventional, conscientious and intensely religious 23-year-old woman's neck was decorated with an elaborate bow fashioned from two nylon stockings. She had bite marks on her breast. Her vagina was ripped and bloodied.

And on 4 January, 1964, Mary Sullivan's two roommates found their 19-year-old friend sitting on her bed, naked, after having been strangled to death using a pair of charcoal-coloured stockings and two pink-coloured scarves. A greeting card was placed at her left foot. It read, "Happy New Year". Sticky secretions oozed from her mouth, dribbling onto her exposed, injured breasts. As a final indignity, a broom had been rammed three inches into the deceased woman's vagina.

Mary had only recently moved into her new apartment, and she had been due to start a new job as a bank teller. She particularly enjoyed the music of Johnny Mathis. Mary Sullivan was the twelfth and final victim of the Boston Strangler.

Or was she?

Here the story becomes strange. In November 1964 the man named Albert DeSalvo was arrested for the sexual assault of a newly married woman. She had been napping on her bed when she was awoken by a man with a knife at her throat who said, "Not a word or I'll kill you." The man gagged his victim by stuffing her underwear in her mouth. He then tied her to the bed, her legs parted widely, touched her sexually, kissed her, and then asked how to exit the apartment. He apologised, said to her, "You be quiet for ten minutes," and made his escape.

The woman made a complaint to the police. They believed that the woman had been molested by a serial sexual assaulter they had called the "Green Man" on account of the green overalls he was said to have worn when assaulting women on other occasions. The woman was able to give police a good description of her assailant's face. The sketch reminded them of another sexual assaulter who had operated in the Cambridge area a few years before the strangling murders. On frequent occasions this man had knocked on the door of various young women. He would introduce himself as Johnson and tell the young woman that he worked for a modelling agency. He said that he had been told the woman would make a good model and that he had been sent to measure her vital statistics. Some of the women, flattered, had allowed the charming man to measure them with the tape he had brought with him. Done, he informed that women that in due course they would hear from Mrs Lewis from the agency. No contact ever occurred, for one obvious reason – neither Mrs Lewis nor the agency ever existed. Some women approached the police with a complaint about this dubious individual.

Eventually, on 17 March 1961, police picked up a man attempting to break into a house. His name was Albert DeSalvo, and he confessed not only to the attempted break-in but to being the "Measuring Man". He received a sentence of 18 months and was released from prison in April 1962, just two months before Anna Ślesers, the first of the Strangler's victims, died.

Police wondered if the "Green Man" and the "Measuring Man" could be the same individual. They picked up DeSalvo, the man known to be the "Measuring Man", and invited the newly married woman (who had been assaulted by the "Green

Man") to observe DeSalvo through a one-two mirror. She was unequivocal: this was the man who has assaulted her. DeSalvo was bailed. Other women who had been assaulted then came forward. DeSalvo was arrested again. The other women clearly identified DeSalvo as their assailant. He was then to admit to breaking into over four hundred apartments, assaulting 300 women, and to committing rape. His confession was detailed and consistent, dating back to the molestation of a nine-year-old girl in 1955.

DeSalvo appeared to be a mediocre sort of man with a wife and two children. He worked as a machinist in various factories and seemed to have been well-liked by his employers. He was described as a decent, gentle man who happened also to be a small-time thief, mostly breaking and entering, for which he was awarded suspended sentences each time. When asked why he had undertaken the "Measuring Man" charade, he gave a desultory reason: "I'm not good-looking, I'm not educated. But I was able to put something over on high-class people. They were all college kids and I never had anything in my life and I outsmarted them." Police wondered at the extent of DeSalvo's confessions. They did not seem plausible. And here lay one of DeSalvo's major character flaws: no matter the occasion he always had to show one-upmanship. DeSalvo was an undoubted braggart.

Now transferred to Bridgewater State Hospital for observation, DeSalvo met an important character in his story: George Nassar. Nassar had been admitted to the same hospital after sadistically murdering a gas station attendant. A highly intelligent man, Nassar was also known to have been highly manipulative. The two inmates became close.

It was in March 1965 that DeSalvo's wife received a call from her husband's attorney, urging her to leave town, warning that Albert's face would be on the front page of every newspaper the next day.

Indeed, this came to pass. DeSalvo confessed to the Boston Strangler murders and the press went wild.

But did DeSlavo commit the murders to which he confessed?

Some think not. Certainly not those who knew him, including many of the police who became familiar with him over his career as a petty thief. Some believe that DeSalvo confessed to the crimes for financial gain. It was known that before being sent to Bridgewater the idea of selling his story to the press had begun to form in his mind. He had even asked his lawyer about it. Some have suggested that Nasser and DeSalvo cooked up the plan together. DeSalvo, believing that he would spend the rest of his life in jail for the "Green Man" crimes, would take the fall for the murders; Nasser would pocket part of the award and later pass the rest of it to DeSalvo's wife. DeSalvo himself was known to have had an extraordinarily keen recall. Indeed, professionals involved in the case described his memory as "phenomenal", "remarkable" and "absolute, complete, one-hundred percent total photographic recall". He could easily have memorised details of the Strangler crimes only to repeat them to police investigators later. What is interesting, however, is that details that DeSalvo got wrong about the crimes were identical to details that the newspapers of the time also got wrong.

DeSalvo's admissions to the strangling murders in Boston were never tested in court. He reached a deal in relation to the "Green Man" rapes in 1967, his lawyer, Francis Lee Bailey, strategizing that his client would be committed to a mental institution. The tactic failed, and a jury found DeSalvo guilty of the crimes of rape, armed robbery and unnatural acts, the adjudicating judge sentencing him to life in prison. Lawyer Lee Bailey pithily summed up his opinion of the verdict: "Massachusetts has just burned another witch."

DeSalvo was never formally charged for the Boston Strangler murders. His own statement of guilt is worthless without hard evidence to back it up. No inculpatory evidence exists that ties him conclusively to any of the murders. There were no eyewitnesses to attest to his presence at any of the crime scenes. Indeed, witnesses were strongly drawn to their attacker having a long, narrow face with almond-shaped eyes, a description that closely resembled Nasser. DeSalvo, by contrast, was dark complexioned and had a wide face.

The _modi operandi_ in the case suggests two separate killers. Could DeSalvo have taken the rap for more than one murderer? Experts never saw the strangling murders as being caused by the same pair of hands. And what of Mary Mullen, the elderly lady who died of fright? This is the only death for which DeSalvo expressed any grief. Experts believe that DeSalvo was certainly responsible for this unintentional death.

One night in November 1973, a frightened DeSalvo made a telephone call to a Dr Ames Robey, urgently requesting to meet him ... and a reporter. That same night, before the meeting could happen, DeSalvo was stabbed to death. He was aged 42.

For the murder of DeSalvo one man was brought to a trial that ended in a hung jury. Dr Robey has since speculated that DeSalvo had planned to reveal to him the true identity of the Boston Strangler. Perhaps an agent had stepped in to ensure that that did not happen. We may never know.

In the 1960s, biological forensic evidence was not sufficiently advanced to identify Boston's infamous Strangler. Subsequent breakthroughs in DNA analysis technology have been used to demonstrate a definitive link, to an unprecedently level of certainty, between DeSalvo and Mary Sullivan, the woman believed to have been the Strangler's last victim. Previous DNA examination of different samples, analysed by different laboratories, did not match. The results do not point to guilt. On the other hand, though, they do not point to innocence. The questions that remain may never be answered. Officially, at this time, the case of the Boston Strangler is unsolved.

The Cincinnati Strangler

[active 1965-1966]

RACIAL TENSIONS WERE ALREADY HEIGHTENED in Cincinnati, Ohio in the 1960s. Nearly 30 percent of the population were black, yet public representation in government, law enforcement, education and the like was not proportional. Opportunities for blacks were more limited than for their non-black counterparts. Laws were seen as oppressive, public areas remained defiantly segregated, discrimination was rife. Housing and school for blacks was substandard, and the police were still seen as indiscriminately brutal towards the Afro-American population. A broadly racist culture pervaded the city and provoked resentment and disharmony. The city was a pressure-cooker.

On 12 October 1965 a 65-year-old white woman was sexually assaulted. Outside her apartment in the pleasant Walnut Hills part of town she had been approached by a man asking to speak to the building superintendent. She led the man to the basement whereupon he overcame her, raped her and attempted to choke her with a clothesline. She barely survived the attack with her life. She reported that her assailant had been black.

Within two weeks, three further white women were attacked. All in similar circumstances, by a man seeking assistance with something, all the victims claiming that their attacker had been a black man.

A month later, on 2 December 1965, the attacker became a killer. He had used strangulation to end the life of Emogene Harrington in the basement of her apartment building. Before dispatching the 56-year-old lady he raped her.

Lois Dant, 58 years old, died next by the same means on 4 April 1966.

Then 56-year-old Jeanette Messer died on 10 June. She had been walking her dog in the park. Her body had been dragged into some bushes. When Jeanette's body was discovered, her fox terrier was sitting quietly not far off, tied to a tree.

Alice Hochhausler, aged 50, was found in dead in her garage on 12 October, strangled using the belt of her bathrobe. She had been a mother and the wife of a surgeon. Her murder, in the affluent segregated Gaslight district, sent the entire city atwitch. "My God, this is getting awfully close," one neighbour said to a *Cincinnati Post* correspondent.

Eighty-one-year-old spinster Rose Winstsel was bludgeoned, raped and strangled like all the others. The nearly blind woman had been dragged from her bed with the covers still about her. She died on 19 October 1965.

Understandably, Cincinnati women were petrified. None felt safe. The killings of seven women had happened apparently at random. They were spread over a wide area, from Price Hill to Clifton. As fear gripped the city the police were overwhelmed with reports of strange men in their neighbourhood; door locks and dead bolts sold out quickly in hardware stores. Women stayed indoors. The period the media called "the long hot summer of dread" had begun. A serial killer was on the loose.

Police were frustrated. They expanded their investigative team and stepped up examination of incoming tips, logging in more than 100 hours of overtime. They vacillated on whether or not the same individual had committed all of the attacks. In the end the similarities were just too great. "NEGRO KILLED THREE WOMEN, POLICE SAY," the *Cincinnati Enquirer* eventually announced on 25 June 1966.

Another murder occurred on 14 August. At 02:30, Barbara Bowman, a pretty 31-year-old secretary, suddenly left the taxi she had been travelling in and ran through the pouring rain. The driver gave chase in the stolen cab and mowed her down. He approached the woman, who lay helpless with a fractured ankle, and stabbed her in the neck. She later died of her wounds without making a statement. There was ligature bruising on her neck.

The killer had been sloppy. There were numerous witnesses, including another taxi driver who later reported having picked up a breathless, rain-sodden black man a few streets away.

There were further reports by women of being followed. The

man was described as "slender", "slightly built", "very drunk". In all cases the women said their follower had been a black man.

Then a welcome break in the case! On 9 December 1966 a woman was followed home by a black man in a brown-and-cream car. He parked, then followed her into her apartment building. She woman ran upstairs and into her home, slamming the door shut after her. A curious neighbour peeked out and saw a short black man, "grabbing his crotch and panting like a dog", who ran off as soon as he saw he had been spotted, nearly over-balancing the neighbour's husband in his efforts to escape. The husband noted the peculiar man's license number and reported it to the police.

The next morning, the seventh and final victim was discovered by a relative. The crumpled body of Leila "Lula" Kerrick, an 81-year-old lady who had been strangled using a stocking, was found in the elevator of her apartment building. She had been returning home after having gone to mass at the Cathedral of St Peter in Chains. She had not been raped.

Police, following up on their license number tip, traced it to a 29-year-old man called Posteal Laskey Jr. When picked up he did not resist. He was immediately identified by the couple who had given police his license number, and more tentatively by witnesses of the Bowman murder. Whilst the suspect was in police custody, arrested for that murder, another assault took place: 79-year-old Anna Scales was attacked in her apartment by a short, slightly built black man who had reportedly been looking for the caretaker.

Laskey was indicted, it was said, by an all-white grand jury. He was sent to trial for the first-degree murder of Barbara Bowman on 27 March 1967. His attorneys petitioned for a change of venue but this was denied. He was convicted solely on eyewitness testimony, despite opposing testimony from relatives who swore that Laskey had been at home that 14 August night. "LASKEY GUILTY, MUST DIE", the *Cincinnati Post* harangued. In May 1967 he was sentenced to death. Laskey's cousin, peacefully protesting this sentence, was arrested and for his trouble he also was given the maximum available sentence.

Tensions inflated rapidly. Young black people, already disillusioned with the limitations of nonviolent protest, rioted. The Long Hot Summer now descended into many days of violence and destruction.

Cincinnatian prosecutors expressed their full belief that they had their man, but there is room for doubt. Blood evidence showed that Laskey's type did not match the killer's. He was charged with the "similar" crime of the murder of Barbara Bowman. Eyewitness accounts of the Bowman murder were inconsistent. Defence witnesses' accounts appeared to have been ignored. There was no corroborating evidence.

But the Cincinnati Strangler case has been indelibly linked to the name of Posteal Laskey, and many assume a guilt of the remaining cases that was never tested in court. And perhaps because of this association the full imposition of the criminal justice system was levelled at him.

Eventually Laskey was spared the electric chair – the death penalty was ruled unconstitutional for a period in the 1970s – and his sentence was commuted to life in prison. He was consistently denied parole. He remained in prison for the rest of his life until he died of natural causes on 29 May 2007 aged 69. No relative came forward to claim his body.

Neither Laskey nor any other person was ever charged with the six other violent deaths of elderly ladies. The identity of the Cincinnati Strangler officially remains unknown.

The Michigan Murderer
(active 1967-1969)

TOWARDS THE END of the 1960s a series of murders of young women studying at university rocked Michigan to its core. At the time the unknown perpetrator was dubbed the "Michigan Murderer" by the press. He was also known as the "Co-Ed Killer" – that is, however, until the admission to the annals of American crime of another serial killer, upon whom the catchy epithet also came to rest. Being the more infamous of the two, California-based Edmund Kemper would claim the title and be forever be known as the "Co-Ed Killer".

Like Posteal Laskey a couple of years before him, John Norman Chapman was convicted for only one of the murders with which he is associated. He was convicted and sentenced to life imprisonment for the final murder ascribed to the Michigan Murderer. He remains incarcerated in prison at this time.

Mary Fleszar, a 19-year-old Eastern Michigan University accountancy student, had gone for a walk to take the air on the hot summer evening of 9 July 1967. She was returning to her apartment when a neighbour noticed that the bespectacled woman was being followed by a young man in a bluish-grey car, who twice slowed down to speak to Mary. Twice Mary shook her head and walked on, apparently keen to distance herself from her pursuer.

Just under a month later her body was found by two teenage boys in a dumping ground near a former farm. They had thought they heard a car door slam and went to investigate. Initially they believed the foul-smelling blackish-brown object before them was a decomposing animal: the rotted head was shapeless but it appeared to have a human ear. No car was to be seen. The boys drove straight to the police.

Mary had been stabbed in the chest several times, brutally beaten about the legs (several bones were fractured) and she was missing her fingers and feet. She was formally identified by dental records. She was found naked, and because of this police speculated that she had been sexually assaulted. However, due to the advanced state of decomposition this could not be determined for certain.

A year later, Joan Schell's roommate became concerned when Joan did not return on the night of 30 June 1968. The 20-year-old student had been hitchhiking near the Eastern Michigan University student union after missing the bus she had planned to catch to meet her boyfriend. The next day the roommate contacted the police to report the uncharacteristic disappearance of Joan. Construction workers found her body one week later, in a bleak spot four miles from where the body of Mary Fleszar had been found. Joan had been stabbed five times and her throat slashed. She had been raped. Her boyfriend, initially questioned by the police, was later released, no longer considered a person of interest.

Just before Mary's funeral, a dark-haired young man in a bluish-grey Chevy arrived at the funeral parlour. He asked to see the body so that he could take a photo for the family but this was denied him. "You mean you can't fix her up enough so I could just get one picture of her?" he asked in incredulity. When told a second time that this would be impossible the young man scowled, turned and wordlessly departed. He had not appeared to have been carrying a camera.

Another co-ed to die was Jane Mixer, studying at the University of Michigan law school. On or around 21 March 1969, 23-year-old Jane was shot twice in the head with a .22 calibre pistol. Her body was found in a cemetery. Until 2002, Jane was thought to be the third victim of the Michigan Murderer, al-though a "cold case" review of handwriting and sweat stains, the discovery of a Polaroid photo of a drugged girl lying on a bed, together with more persuasive DNA analysis, now casts some doubt upon this theory, pointing instead to a man called Gary Leiterman.

Sixteen-year-old student Maralynn Skelton went missing on 24 March 1969. She had been hitchhiking at the front of a mall.

Her badly beaten body was found a mere quarter-of-a-mile from where Joan Schell had been found. It was believed that she had been whipped with a leather belt and strangled with a garter belt. Her face and head had been brutally pounded to the extent that her skull contained multiple fractures. When found, her shoes had been placed neatly by the side of her body.

Reported missing by her mother on 18 April 1969, the following day produced a fifth victim (or fourth, if the murder of Jane Mixer is discounted). Dawn Basom's body was found on a desolate road. There was evidence of strangulation and slash wounds across her buttocks and breasts, caused by a razor-sharp blade, and a handkerchief had been stuffed into her mouth. As with all the previous murders, Dawn's body had been dumped at the side of the road where it could be easily found by any passer-by. She was missing her trousers. At aged 13, Dawn was to be the youngest of the Michigan Murderer's victims.

Alice Kalom, a 23-year-old University of Michigan arts graduate, died next. On the evening of 7 June 1969, Alice had been at a rock music bar where she had been dancing with a long-haired youth. That was the last time she was seen alive by anyone other than her killer. She had been raped, shot once in the head and stabbed twice in the chest. Her body was then dumped near to a derelict farmhouse to the north of the city. Bloodstains found later suggested that she had been murdered elsewhere and the body moved after death.

With the recent case of their own Strangler echoing in the collective mind of its horrified readership, the *Boston Herald* questioned the similarity of the case: "Strangler Still Loose?"

In scenes similar to those which occurred only recently in Boston, public tension ratcheted alarmingly. Female students armed themselves with knives and tear gas. Security locks were quickly installed. Hitchhiking no longer occurred with such freedom. Women only walked in public in pairs or with trusted males. The town was now on high alert, few going easily about their business. Nerves were shattered.

Eighteen-year-old Karen Beineman was the next victim. She

had gone to buy a wig, and whilst in the store the proprietor overheard her say that she had done two stupid things in her life: the first was to buy a wig; the second to accept a lift from a stranger on a motorcycle. After she left the store she was seen getting onto a motorcycle with an unknown man.

Karen's naked, battered, strangled body was found the next day in a ravine. The _News and Observer_ stated that "[it] appeared as if the girl's body was taken to the wooded, isolated area by car on a narrow dirt road and then was dumped or pushed from the vehicle and rolled down the steep gully".

A later report noted that:

> _Six of the eight victims, including Miss Beineman, had pierced ears and an earring was missing from the ear of each of the five others, said Washtenaw County Sheriff Douglas Harvey. Harvey would not say if one of Miss Beineman's snowflake-shape earrings was missing when her body was found._
>
> (_News and Observer_, Raleigh, North Carolina, 1967)

Had the killer been collecting trophies?

Now the police developed a carefully constructed plan. Announcement of the discovery of the body was withheld in an agreed news blackout. With minimal fuss, the body of Karen Beineman was taken away and replaced with a tailor's mannequin. It was believed that the killer had returned to the bodies of at least two of his previous victims. Detectives arranged an undercover stakeout at the dumping scene and waited through the night.

Close to midnight, the following Saturday, a lone male came walking through the isolated area during a downpour. This seemed unusual. It was late, dark and raining, and there were no obvious amenities nearby. With the detectives watching, the man entered the ravine and made his way towards the spot where the mannequin lay. Upon discovering that it was not the body of a dead woman, the man immediately bolted though the woods, with detectives pursuing on foot. Though they searched the area, they could not locate their quarry. It seemed that the man might had run through a marsh and escaped by swimming across a river. The press, upon hearing of the incident, roundly lit upon the police, comparing them unfavourably to the "Keystone Kops" of silent film fame. The disgruntled police were forced to point to a series of unfortunate factors impeding the stake-out that night: the difficulty of the terrain; the dark night and driving rain, which diminished visibility; the failure of a walkie-talkie; the requirement to limit the number of detectives at the scene so that they would not be spotted; and, not least, the fitness and athleticism of the jogging man making his escape.

The case was to take a strange but serendipitous turn. Police corporal David Leik, having returned home from vacation, noticed patches of black paint on the concrete floor of his basement, and that some containers of detergent and ammonia had gone missing. Whilst away on vacation he had left the house under the charge of his nephew who had been looking after the family dog. Leik then came to learn that his nephew was a possible suspect in the Michigan murders, and that he had been asked to take a lie-detector test, agreed, and then backed down. Realising that something was amiss, Leik asked for the paint on his concrete floor to be forensically examined. It contained blood. Leik's nephew, a handsome, part-time factory inspector, was currently majoring in elementary education at Eastern Michigan University. His name was John Norman Collins, then aged 30 years old. Acquaintances would come forward to describe him as a chronic thief who was polite around females, but short-tempered and oversexed, with a propensity to violence towards women who resisted his advances. Ex-lovers recalled that he had been into bondage activities and that the female menstrual repulsed him intensely. One girl who had been accosted by a man in a car who looked like Collins remembered that he had told her he did not like girls who wore earrings "because they left holes that defile the bodies".

The incriminating evidence found by investigators in Leik's

basement included numerous hairs and blood, both of which matched samples taken from victim Karen Beineman. In his haste to cover up his tracks, Collins had inadvertently led the investigators straight to the evidence that would prove to be his undoing. Despite his protestations that he had never known or met Beineman, she had been in Leik's basement around the time of her murder. Collins was arrested, charged and arraigned for this murder alone.

After the apprehension of Collins, on July 13 1969, the nude, badly decomposed body of Roxie Phillips, aged 17, was found in a Californian canyon by a pair of fossil-hunting boys, lying amidst a patch of poison oak. A friend recounted that Roxie had talked of meeting a motorcycling man called "John" who attended college in Michigan who had been cruising near to her house. John Collins had received treatment in California that same week for a rash caused by poison oak.

The dumped body of Eileen Adams, aged 13, from Toledo, Ohio was found one month later in Michigan. After being kidnapped, she was raped, viciously beaten with a hammer, strangled, and a three-inch nail driven into her skull. Eileen had apparently left willingly with her killer. Her body, stuffed into a sack, was found in plain sight by the side of the road. At some time during her attack she had been hogtied.

These last two victims were officially linked to the case of the Michigan Murderer, making eight in total.

Collins was tried by a jury of his peers only for the first-degree murder of Karen Beineman. On 19 August 1970 the jury foreman stood to say, "We find the defendant guilty as charged." It was a unanimous verdict, the climactic end to the longest trial in the history of Washtenaw County. On 28 August Collins was sentenced to life imprisonment with hard labour in solitary confinement with no possibility of parole. He rose to protest his innocence:

> *"I have two things to say: I think they [the jury] consci-
> entiously tried to give me a fair trial. The jury did not*

take its task lightly, but, I think things were blown out of proportion. The circumstances surrounding this case prevented me from getting a fair trial. It was a travesty of justice that took place in this courtroom. I hope someday it will be corrected. Second, I never knew a girl named Karen Sue Beineman. I never had a conversation with her; I never took her to a wig shop; I never took her to my uncle's home ... I never took her life."

Judge Conlin then informed Collins that if the verdict of the jury were wrong that error would be corrected in due course.

Defence Counsel Neil Fink, however, said that there were "obviously" several members of the jury who had felt his client had been innocent. "The others wore them down," he said to the *Ann Arbor News*. He said that Collins had been tried "not only for the Beineman murder, he was being tried for all seven murders. There was prejudice."

Despite subsequent court appearances, the final appeal of the jury's finding was exhausted and the conviction stood. At the time of writing, Collins remains in prison. serving his life sentence in Administrative Segregation at Marquette Branch Prison. He vehemently continues to maintain his innocence of the brutal rape and murder of Karen Beineman and the other attacks associated with the Michigan murder spree. He is renowned as an unpopular, troublesome prisoner who has dealt in drugs and repeatedly flouted prison rules. It was said that two attempts to escape failed. He was unable to participate in a first successful attempt due to a broken foot. The second, by means of a tunnel, was thwarted before it could come to fruition.

To date, the ruthless organised killer of the other Michigan Murder victims has not been charged with those crimes. It may be (and it seems likely) that that same serial killer is currently incarcerated for a single crime committed in the same spree, for which he is serving a life sentence. However, at the time of writing, the Michigan Murderer remains officially unidentified, and the victims' earrings – trophies that may have inflamed a killer's searing sexual rage – have not been recovered.

Zodiac

[active 1968-1974]

OF ALL THE CODENAMES linked to America's unidentified serial killers perhaps the most infamous is that of The Zodiac Killer – or simply Zodiac, as he called himself. It was a self-proclaimed nickname; and so great was (and still is) the notoriety of the killer's actions that he inspired numerous books, documentaries, blogs, films (including the acclaimed mystery thriller *Zodiac*), conspiracy theories ... and even two copycat killers. Not many murderers can claim to have achieved that! The names of various suspects abound, but none has been conclusively identified as the elusive killer.

Zodiac is confirmed to have murdered five times, and confirmed to have attempted to murder once. He is suspected of murdering at least 12 other times. The killer himself claimed to have taken 37 victims. Three people are thought to have escaped Zodiac's endeavours to murder them.

The first murders occurred on the night of 20 December 1968 on a quiet road a mile or so outside the small town of Vallejo, California. High school students Betty Lou Jenson,16, and David Faraday, 17, were on their first date. They had planned to attend a Christmas concert. After visiting a friend and stopping at a local restaurant, David drove the pair to a well-known lovers' lane and parked. A journalist, Robert Graysmith (upon whose fascinating account the film *Zodiac* is based) postulated that another car soon joined Betty Lou and David. Betty Lou appeared to have left the car first, via the passenger door, whereupon she was shot in the back five times as she fled, some 28 feet from the car. David was shot once in the head at point-blank range as he attempted to exit the same passenger-side door. The weapon was a .22 calibre pistol. There was no indication of sexual molestation or robbery and the killer simply drove off.

The killer waited for over half-a-year before making his next move, four miles distant from the first murders. Accompanied by 19-year-old Michael Mageau, Darlene Ferrin, aged 22, had pulled her car into an isolated parking area to talk. It was 5 July 1969. Immediately upon their arrival a light brown car pulled up alongside them, waited a few moments, then drove away. After approximately 10 minutes the same car returned, this time parking directly behind Ferrin's car. No other cars were present in the parking lot.

The driver of the second car exited his vehicle, carrying a torch and a pistol. Thinking this was a police officer the couple started digging for identification. Without warning the man fired five shots into the car, wounding the couple. The man turned and walked slowly back to his car with his head down. Mageau screamed and thrashed out with his legs, at which point the man turned back to resume shooting, firing an additional two bullets into each victim. Darlene Ferrin briefly gasped and died at the scene. Mageau, who survived the attack, got a good look at the man and was able to describe the shooter's appearance to the police. He was white, of stocky build, weighing about 160lbs, around 5'8" to 5'9", 25-30 years old, with a full face and wavy or curly brown hair. He wore a blue shirt or sweater. He did not speak during the deadly encounter. "The slayer drove away rapidly, making some gravel fly, Mageau said [to the _Vallejo Times-Herald_], but 'he didn't really gun it or burn rubber'."

Around 30-45 minutes later an anonymous man used a payphone to contact the Vallejo Police Department, claiming responsibility for the attack, correctly identifying the weapon used in the attack and also taking credit for the slaying of Jenson and Faraday the previous December.

An investigation into the murder of Ferrin gained no traction and stalled. Then, on 1 August 1969, three newspapers, Vallejo's _Times-Herald_ and San Francisco's _Examiner_ and _Chronicle_, received letters claiming to be from the killer of Faraday, Jensen and Ferrin, including details that only the true killer could have known. Additionally, each letter contained one-third of a strange 408-symbol cryptogram that, once broken, would reveal the identity of the killer. The killer demanded that the letters be printed in full on the front page of each of the newspapers to which he had sent it, otherwise he would "crus [*sic,* cruise] around all weekend killing lone people in the night then move on to kill again, until I end up with a dozen people over the weekend". Vallejo Police Chief Jack E. Stiltz was quoted in the paper saying, "We're not satisfied that the letter was written by the murderer." In response to this another letter was sent to the *Examiner*. "Dear Editor This is the Zodiac speaking," it began, the first time that the killer used this identification. The letter contained further details that would not have been known to the public as well as a message to the police that once they had cracked the code "they will have me". It was the start of a five-year letter writing campaign containing deadly threats that would horrify and frustrate in equal measure.

The killer did not make good on his threats to murder a dozen people that weekend and eventually all three parts of the cryptogram were published.

Within about a week the code was cracked by a schoolteacher and his wife. Bettye Harden is credited with reaching the solution after discovering two cribs. She had correctly guessed that the attention-craving murderer would use the words "I" and "killing" somewhere in the letter. The sinister message, reproduced here, complete with its spelling errors, seemed to refer to a short story or film called *The Most Dangerous Game*:

```
I like killing people because it is so
much fun it is more fun than killing wild
game in the forrest because man is the
most dangeroue anamal of all to kill some-
thing gives me the most thrilling exper-
ence it is even better than getting your
rocks off with a girl the best part of it
is thae when I die I will be reborn in
paradice and the I have killed will become
my slaves I will not give you my name
because you will try to sloi down or atop
my collectiog of slaves for my afterlife
ebeorietemethhpiti
```

The killer had made his intentions known, as well as giving some indication of his state of mind. Killing, to him, was a thrill. References to "paradice", "collectiog of slaves" and "afterlife" pointed to a psychotic schizophrenic mind harbouring narcissism, self-aggrandisement and resentment. It was theorised that Zodiac copied his symbols from a watch with the brand name "Zodiac". Profilers noted similarities to the Texarkana Murderer of 1946 and wondered if that killer had moved further afield. Film buffs wondered if the killer had been inspired by the movie _The Most Dangerous Game_, then showing at some venues in downtown San Francisco. The jumble of letters at the end of the message, investigators supposed, hinted at a clue to the killer's name, but all attempts to decipher it failed.

On 27 September 1969, students Bryan Hartnell, aged 20, and Cecelia Shepard, aged 22, were picnicking on a small island in Lake Berryessa which was connected to the mainland by a narrow sandspit. Approaching them through the trees was a white man, around 5'11" in height and 170lbs in weight, with combed greasy brown hair. He wore a black executioner-style hood with clip-on sunglasses over the eyeholes and a type of bib across his chest with a cross-circle akin to a gun crosshair sight symbol.

The sinister-looking man approached Hartnell and Shepard pointing a gun. He explained that he was an escaped convict and that he needed a car and money to continue his getaway. The man had brought pre-cut lengths of plastic clothesline, and he now ordered Shepard to bind her friend. Shepard proceeded to do so, but when the man checked the bonds he found them loose and so tightened them more to his satisfaction. Believing this to be a robbery, the two friends complied with the hooded stranger's requests, offering money and help, but the man was not content until both of them were hogtied and incapacitated. "Your hands are shaking," Bryan had noticed. "Are you nervous?" "Yes, I guess so," replied the assailant. The interaction pointed to a man who had pre-planned the attack, who was shaking with either nerves or excitement, but who was also composed enough to be able to change tack under pressure.

Suddenly the man viciously began to stab at Bryan, inflicting six wounds until he feigned death, and then at Cecelia, dealing her 10 wounds. After this, the man hiked the quarter-of-a-mile to the couple's white Volkswagen car and drew a cross-circle "signature" on the door with a black felt-tip pen, adding beneath it a taunting validation: "Vallejo/12-20-68/7-4-69/Sept 27-69-6:30/by knife". It seemed the Zodiac wanted no doubt to remain about the provenance of *this* deed. He had even thought to bring a well-chosen colour of felt-tip pen.

At 19:40, Napa police received a call from a payphone. "I want to report a murder – no, a double murder," said a man with "a young voice". "I'm the one who did it." When the officer pressed for further details the telephone receiver was dropped. When the phone was found minutes later at a car wash on Napa's Main Street, only a couple of blocks from the sheriff's office, it hung off the hook.

At Berryessa Lake, some 27 miles away, a man and his son out fishing had heard screams for help and sought the help of park rangers and law enforcement officers duly arrived. Cecelia Shepard, in extreme agony, was able to give a detailed description of the attacker before she lapsed into a coma and died two days later in hospital. Bryan Hartnell survived and it was through his story that Zodiac's menacing disguise came to be known to the world.

Paul Stine, a 29-year-old taxi driver, was the seventh victim to be attacked by Zodiac, and his fifth and last officially confirmed kill. On 11 October 1969 a passenger entered Stine's cab and requested to be taken to an intersection near to San Francisco's Union Square. At Cherry Street, the passenger shot Stine once in the head, took his wallet and car keys and tore some cloth from his bloodstained shirt. Before leaving, the passenger wiped down the vehicle.

Three teenagers who had heard the shot immediately called the police, and a dispatch was issued informing responders to be on the lookout for a black male suspect. Two officers who were in the vicinity made towards Cherry Street, passing a white male on their way. Having been led to believe they were looking for a black suspect, the two officers' suspicions were not aroused and they paid little attention to this individual. When the misleading description of the suspect was corrected the two officers came to believe that the white man may have been the suspect. They were later able to describe him as 35-40 years of age, 5'10', barrel-chested, having light-coloured hair styled in a crew cut, wearing heavy-rimmed glasses. The reason for the dispatcher's incorrect description was never explained.

The crime was thought to be a robbery gone wrong, but then the *Chronicle* received a letter from Zodiac on 14 October claiming responsibility for the murder and bragging about the failure of the police officers to apprehend him on the night of the murder. The envelope contained a blood-stained swatch from Stine's shirt:

> *This is the Zodiac speaking.*
> *I am the murderer of the taxi driver over by Washington St & Maple St last night, to prove this here is a blood stained piece of his shirt. I am the same man who did in the people in the north bay area.*
> *The S.F. Police could have caught me last night if they had searched the park properly instead of holding road races with their motorcicles seeing who could make the most noise. The car drivers should have just parked their cars and sat there quietly waiting for me to come out of cover.*

The letter also threatened to kill schoolchildren as they alighted from their bus:

> *School children make nice targets, I think I shall wipe out a school bus some morning. Just shoot out the front tire & then pick off the kiddies as they come bouncing out.*

A letter to the *Chronicle* dated 9 November continued in the same taunting tone:

> *So as you can see the police don't have much to work on. If you wonder why I was wipeing the cab down I was leaving fake clews for the police to run all over town with, as one might say, I gave the cops som bussy work to do to keep them happy. I enjoy needling the blue pigs. Hey blue pig I was in the park—you were useing fire trucks to mask the sound of your cruzeing prowl cars. The dogs never came with in 2 blocks of me & they were to the west & there was only 2 groups of parking about 10 min apart then the motor cicles went by about 150 ft away going from south to north west.*
>
> *Must print in paperps. 2 cops pulled a goof abot 3 min after I left the cab. I was walking down the hill to the park when this cop car pulled up & one of them called me over & asked if I saw anyone acting suspicious or strange in the last 5 to 10 min & I said yes there was this man who was runnig by waveing a gun & the cops peeled rubber & went around the corner as I directed them & I disappeared into the park a block & a half away never to be seen again.*
>
> *Hey pig doesnt it rile you up to have your noze rubed in your booboos?*

On 20 December Zodiac wrote to Melvin Belli, a noted attorney, wishing his readership "a happy Christmass [sic]" and asking for relief from his woes:

> *I am finding it extreamly dificult to hold it in check I am afraid I will loose control again and take my nineth & posibly tenth victom. Please help me I am drownding.*

Zodiac continued to send letters throughout 1970. Some of his writings were boastful, claiming that he had killed 10 people, and that "there is more glory in killing a cop than a cid [kid] because a cop can shoot back" (letter dated 20 April 1970). A greetings card sent to the *Chronicle* said that the writer "would like to see some nice Zodiac butons [buttons] wandering about town" (28 April). Later letters expressed sadness because people were not wearing buttons (badges) depicting the crossfire symbol as he had previously requested (26 June, 24 July). Zodiac's letter postmarked 24 July claimed credit for the abduction of Kathleen Johns and her infant daughter on 22 March 1970, recalling "the woeman + her baby that I gave a rather intersting ride for a couple howers one evening a few months back that ended in my burning her car where I found them". During this episode, a man had driven them all around mid-California for around an hour-and-a-half before Johns was able to make her escape.

In a letter postmarked 26 July, Zodiac complained that no one was wearing buttons and threatened that:

> *[...] I shall (on top of everything else) torture all 13 of my slaves that I have wateing for me in Paradice. Some I shall tie over ant hills and watch them scream & twich and sqwirm. Others shall have pine splinters driven under their nails & then burned. Others shall be placed in cages & fed salt beef untill they are gorged then I shall listen to their pleass for water and I shall laugh at them. Others will hang by their thumbs & burn in the sun then I will rub them down with deep heat to warm them up. Others I shall skin them alive & let them run around screaming. And all billiard players I shall have them play in a darkened dungen cell with crooked cues & Twisted Shoes. Yes I shall have great fun inflicting the most delicious of pain to my slaves*

This letter paraphrased a song from the light operetta *The Mikado*, prompting profilers to suggest that Zodiac was a cultured man, or an Anglophile:

As some day it may hapen that a victom must be found. I've got a little list. I've got a little list, of society offenders who might well be underground who would never be missed who would never be missed. There is the pestulentual nucences who whrite for autographs, all people who have flabby hands and irritating laughs. All children who are up in dates and implore you with im platt. All people who are shakeing hands shake hands like that. And all third persons who with unspoiling take thoes who insist. They'd none of them be missed. They'd none of them be missed. There's the banjo seranader and the others of his race and the piano orginast I got him on the list. All people who eat pepermint and phomphit in your face, they would never be missed They would never be missed And the Idiout who phraises with inthusastic tone of centuries but this and every country but his own. And the lady from the provences who dress like a guy who doesn't cry and the singurly abnormily the girl who never kissed. I don't think she would be missed Im shure she wouldn't be missed. And that nice impriest that is rather rife the judicial hummerest I've got him on the list All funny fellows, commic men and clowns of private life. They'd none of them be missed. They'd none of them be missed. And uncompromiseing kind such as wachmacallit, thingmebob, and like wise, well—nevermind, and tut tut tut tut, and whatshisname, and you know who, but the task of filling up the blanks I rather leave up to you. But it really doesn't matter whom you place upon the list, for none of them be missed, none of them be missed.

Profilers were in no doubt, however, that Zodiac was a man of insecure psychiatric standing.

Zodiac is suspected of killing Robert Domingos, 18, and Linda Edwards, 17, who were shot on a beach near Gaviota on 4 June 1963. The circumstances of the killings were similar to the Lake Berryessa attack six years later.

A connection has also been drawn to the disappearance of Donna Lass, 25, from Forest Pines condominiums at Lake Tahoe. A postcard was sent to the Chronicle on 22 March 1971 Pasted to the back was an advertisement for Forest Pines, with the words "Look through the pines" written.

And some consider the Zodiac Killer a suspect in the Santa Rosa hitchhiker murders, a series of seven homicides. After nearly three years of silence, the _Chronicle_ received a letter franked on 29 January 1974. The letter referred to the film _The Exorcist_ ("the best saterical comidy that I have ever seen") and contained a short verse from _The Mikado_:

He plunged himself into the billowy wave
and an echo arose from the suicide's grave
titwillo titwillo titwillo

The bottom of the letter was signed with an unusual symbol what remains unexplained to this day. It concludes with an updated score that was surely designed to taunt the San Francisco Police: "Me = 37, SFPD = 0". If the tally of Zodiac's claims is true he was keen to have this recognised.

Further missives sent to the news media have been deemed inauthentic, unverified, debatable or declared a hoax. The "Exorcist" letter proved to be the final communication officially ascribed to the elusive Zodiac Killer.

There are suspects in the case, and some of the circumstantial evidence is compelling. Arthur Leigh Allen is the prime suspect, and Robert Graysmith names him as a strong potential suspect in his book. He came to the attention of investigators when a friend reported that Allen had spoken of a desire to kill people and use the name Zodiac. Allen, who had been discharged from the US Navy in 1958, was thought to have had a fixation on young children (he was arrested for committing lewd acts upon a 12-year-old boy) and anger towards women. He never had a girlfriend or wife. He had a Zodiac brand wristwatch. Partial

DNA profiling taken from saliva found on the stamps and envelopes of the Zodiac letters does not match either Allen or the friend who initially pointed the finger at him. Allen does, however, fit the description of Zodiac by survivors of the attacks.

In 2014 a friend of Louis Joseph Myers reported that he had confessed to the crime in 2001 after learning that he had terminal cirrhosis of the liver. The friend approached police after Myers' death in 2002 but he said that he had difficulty having his claims taken seriously. Myers, it transpires, attended the same high school as David Faraday and Betty Jenson and worked alongside Darlene Ferrin in the same restaurant. Myers was in the army and during the almost three-year hiatus in Zodiac letters between 1971 and 1973 he was stationed abroad. There are some similarities between Myers and the description of Zodiac by surviving victims.

An apparently lucid seaman approached a lawyer in 1975 and claimed that he was the Zodiac Killer. The story seemed plausible to the lawyer, and in 2007 he took out a full-page advert in the *Vallejo Times-Herald* stating that he could clear the name of suspect Arthur Leigh Allen. The lawyer has yet to do so.

Circumstantial evidence points rather wobblily at a convicted murderer, Edward Wayne Edwards, who spent time in California in the late 1960s, who had been in the US Marines and who had been in the habit of attacking couples. Edwards died in 2010.

Several people have come forward to claim that their fathers were the elusive killer. Deborah Perez, Dennis Kaufman and Steve Hodel each claim that they are the offspring of the Zodiac Killer, pointing to the less-than-compelling evidence of hired handwriting experts and tenuous circumstantial indicators. They cannot all be correct.

The identity of the Zodiac Killer – who changed and perfected his *modus operandi*, who killed for sport, who craved attention and control – continues to attract the speculation and debate of criminology enthusiasts. It is certainly possible that his true identify will never be known.

The Texas Killing Fields
(active 1970s-2000s)

SINCE ITS CONCEPTION and through its evolutionary reconstructions and modifications, Interstate 45 has suffered somewhat from an identity crisis. Contrary to its name, this major highway does not cross state borders; it is not "interstate": the I-45 is located entirely within the US state of Texas.

It is a relatively short highway, stretching just short of 285 miles over the range of its broadly north-south span. It stretches from Dallas, Texas to Houston, Texas – and beyond, terminating at Galveston, Texas, next to the glittering Gulf of Mexico.

Travelling south of Houston the horizon opens up, becoming a vast, desolate stretch of swampland and hardscrabble. These are the central plains of Texas, where the skeletons of long abandoned oil rigs and refineries stand petrified against the wide-open sky. The land itself is as flat as pancake. The predominant colour is a brownish bracken. The climate on a typical summer's day is hot and humid. Winters are relatively mild.

The I-45 cuts through this landscape in an unveering line, passing by an abandoned oil field known as Calder 3000. This 68-mile stretch of asphalt has been dubbed the "bloodiest road in America", for it bisects a 25-acre patch of land known as The Texas Killing Fields, where the bodies of scores of missing young women and girls have been found dead, or where females (and sometimes males) have simply vanished, never to be seen again.

It has been happening since the 1970s. At least 27 young women and girls have been found, mutilated or dismembered, having been dumped in lakes or canals or on undeveloped land. Possibly as many others have mysteriously vanished. It is thought by law enforcement officers that whilst many of the cases are linked, others are not. By the time the victims' bodies are found they are no longer intact: some have been scavenged by animals; many are skeletonised. Most of the cases of the slaughtered females remain unsolved to this day. The ages of the victims range from 12 to 34.

The register of victims is a grim list.

Brenda Jones went missing on 1 July 1971. She had been walking to hospital to visit an aunt. Her body was found the next day floating in Galveston Bay. She had been killed by blunt force trauma to the head. Her slip had been crammed into her mouth, presumably before death.

Colette Wilson, aged 13, was dropped off at a bus stop after band practice on 17 June 1971. Her naked body was found some 35 miles from where she disappeared. She had been shot in the head.

When last seen by someone other than their murderer, Rhonda Johnson, aged 14, and Sharon Shaw, aged 13, had been walking along the Seawall Boulevard in Galveston on 4 August 1971. Their skeletons were recovered alongside from a marshland near Clear Lake. They had been deposited beside each other. Investigators could not determine the cause of death of the two girls.

Gloria Gonzales, aged 19, was reported missing by her roommate on 28 October 1971. Her bones were found next to those of Colette Wilson. Blunt force trauma to the head was the cause of her death.

Alison Craven, 12, went missing from her apartment near the I-45 on 9 November 1971. Early on, two hands, some bones from an arm and some teeth were found 10 miles from her home. The remaining parts of her body were found over three months later in a nearby field. She had been bound and shot in the head.

A week later, on 15 November 1971, Debbie Ackerman and Maria Johnson, both 15, went missing. Their partially clothed bodies were found after two days, floating together in Turner's Bayou. Both girls had been bound and shot in the head twice before being dumped.

Nearly two years passed before Kimberly Pitchford, 16, went missing on 3 January 1973. Her strangled body was discovered in a ditch 30 miles from the driving school where she had last been seen.

It was to be nearly six years before the skeletonised remains of Brooks Bracewell, 12, were found, alongside her best friend, Georgia Geer, 14, under a stump in a remote, wildly overgrown swampy area near Alvin. Both had skipped school and gone missing at the same time on 6 September 1974, last seen at a convenience store near to I-45. They had been beaten or shot to death.

The skeletal remains of Suzanne Bowers, 12, were found two years after she had gone missing from Galveston on 21 May 1977. What appeared to be gunshot holes were observed in her skull.

Michelle Garvey, 15, went missing from her home in New London, Connecticut around 1 June 1982. She had a history of running away and it was thought that she had left to start a new life. Her body was found buried near to two other murder victims, the Harris County Does, a female (est. age 15-25) and a male (est. 20-30) who remain unidentified. Michelle had been sexually assaulted and strangled. Her identity was not confirmed until DNA analysis showed a match to her brother in May 2011. It is unknown how she came to be transported from her home to the Texas Killing Fields, a distance of around 1750 miles.

Fourteen-year-old Sondra Ramber was deemed to be missing due to the circumstances of her disappearance: the front door of her residence was left open, biscuits were baking in the oven and her coat and purse were still at home. It is believed that she may have momentarily gone to the store that day, 26 October 1983, but never returned to the house. Sondra had ambitions to become a model and had just finished modelling school. No body has been found and her disappearance remains unexplained.

Heide Villarreal-Fye, 23, was a cocktail waitress who disappeared on 10 October 1983. Her remains were found in the Calder 3000 after a dog brought her skull to a nearby house. She had broken ribs and may have died from being bludgeoned about the head. Heide had last been seen using a payphone at a local convenience store.

And it was from the same convenience store, a year later on 10 October 1983, that Laura Miller, 16, also went missing. Her remains were found 17 months later, some 60 feet distant from the place where Villarreal-Fye's remains were found.

And discovered on the same day at the same location was Audrey Cook, 30, a mechanic. She had gone missing sometime in December 1985. Her skull showed evidence that she had sustained a bullet wound. Both Villarreal-Fye and Cook had been hidden from view rather than buried.

The disappearance of Shelley Sikes, 19, just before midnight on 24 May 1986 is a presumed homicide. She never made it home after leaving her waitressing summer job and her abandoned, bloodstained car was found the next day, stuck in mud at the side of an I-45 feeder road near the Galveston causeway. Her body remains unfound.

Suzanne Rene Richerson, 22, is presumed to have been kidnapped and murdered. She worked as a night-clerk at holiday lodgings in Galveston, and on the early morning of her disappearance, 7 October 1988, another employee heard a scream and a car door slam shut before the car drove away. Her school books and purse were left behind, and her car and one of her shoes were found in the parking lot. She is still missing. A suspect, Gabriel Soto, 39, was never charged and he has since died of a drug overdose.

Donna Prudhomme, 34, had relocated frequently to escape an abusive relationship. She disappeared sometime in July 1991 and her body was found in a field in the Calder 3000 on 8 September 1991. Injuries to her spine may have contributed to the cause of her death. Her identity was only confirmed in 2019.

Lynette Bibbs, 14, and her friend, Tamara Fisher, 15, visited a teen dance club on 1 February 1996. The bodies of the two black girls were found the next day, side-by-side along a rural dirt road near Cleveland, Texas. Lynette was partially clothed and had been shot to death, twice in the head, once in the thigh. Tamara, fully clothed, had been shot in the head.

Krystal Baker, 13, left her grandmother's house on 5 March 1996 after an argument. Later she phoned from a local convenience store to ask her family to collect her. Her body was found two hours later. She had been raped, strangled and thrown over a bridge. In 2012 Kevin Edison Smith was convicted for this death, but investigators believe that he may have been involved in other unsolved cases of missing or murdered females along the I-45 "killing fields".

On 3 April 1997 Laura Smither, 12, told her mother she was going for a short jog. The aspiring ballerina's body was found in a muddy area near a retention pond 17 days later. It had been decapitated, although this may have been caused by natural disarticulation of the bones, or by being moved by animals or water flow. She was naked apart from one sock. Investigators noted strong similarities between the death of Laura and that of Amber Hagerman, aged 9, in Arlington three months earlier.

A suspect was named for the murder of Smither, but he was never charged. The same suspect had abducted another young girl, who escaped from his fast-moving truck, and he was convicted for the crime of aggravated kidnapped. He is suspected also of the disappearance of Jessica Cain, 17, who went missing after leaving friends at a restaurant at around 00:20 on 17 August 1997. Her body was found 19 years later in a south-east Houston field after the same suspect, William Reece, led authorities to the dumping site. Reece is a person of interest in other unsolved murder cases and several agencies have requested to speak to him.

Tot "Totsy" Harriman, 57, a Vietnamese maid and seamstress, had been planning to relocate to Texas. She was driving to meet a realtor with that in mind when she inexplicably disappeared on 12 July 2001. Neither she nor her vehicle have ever been found. She was last seen around League City, Texas, near the I-45.

One year later, Sarah Trusty, a cleaning lady, went missing on 12 July 2002. The 23-year-old had been riding her bicycle at around 23:00 near her church in Algoa, about 10 miles from the

I-45. Her bicycle was found in the foyer of the church. Sarah's decomposing body was found on rocks at a nearby reservoir two weeks later by fishermen. The cause of her death is undisclosed, but there were no marks or stab wounds on her body.

On 31 October 2006 Teressa Vanegas, 16, disappeared. That Halloween night the black teenager had been visiting friends, and was reportedly going to meet up with a male (three years older than her) that she had met online. It appeared that she did not make it to the man's house for she had been abducted on the way. Her body was found – raped, beaten, cut and murdered – in a shallow drainage ditch three days later. The cause of death has not been released by police although it is likely that she had been strangled using her own belt. No one has been held to account for the murder.

In addition to these cases there have been multiple disappearances, sexual assaults and attempted abductions, from which the victims were lucky to have escaped with their lives.

The identities of various Jane and Janet Does (and less frequently, John Does) continue to be confirmed using the advances of modern DNA analysis. Chillingly familiar patterns have emerged from many of the murders, suggesting that more than one serial killer has been operating in the I-45 corridor. It is an area of wide and open terrain; it has easy access. The remote, desolate landscape is dotted by little more than abandoned oil rigs, low-lying scrubby grass and dirt roads. If a victim runs there is nowhere to escape to; if she screams for help there is no one to hear. The "Killing Fields" has been described by local law enforcement agency officials as "the perfect dumping ground". They believe that many more bodies have been hidden in the area which have never been discovered. And they may never be. Those responsible for the murders – there are undoubtedly more than one – are likely to have roots in the area, but they remain, to this day, unidentified.

The Freeway Phantom

(active 1971-1972)

THE TWENTY-FIFTH OF APRIL 1971 in Washington D.C. was noted to be unusually warm for that time of year, and it was perhaps the desire for a cool drink of soda that led to the untimely demise of a 13-year-old black girl called Carol Denise Spinks.

The Spinks family lived in an apartment just south of the Anacostia River in America's capital city. Petite Carol, scant five feet tall in her stockinged feet, was one of eight children. Their mother, Allenteen, was a strict disciplinarian who could mete out punishments such as hitting with a switch or a belt for misdemeanours. Allenteen expected her children to stay in line and to do as they were told.

That spring Sunday, Allenteen informed the children that the she was going to visit a nearby relative and told them to stay inside. Failure to comply with this would result in severe punishment. Carol Spinks knew this, but she was not deterred. Carol's sister, 24-year-old Valerie, who lived across the hall in the apartment building, needed some groceries. She came to Carol's apartment and asked if she or any of her siblings would go to the convenience store and pick items some up for her. As a reward for going, Valerie said that she would pay for some soda. The store was just down the street, a mere half-a-mile away. Carol agreed to go, and accepted five dollars from her older sister.

She walked the short distance along Wheeler Road towards the store, crossing the state border into Maryland. On the way, she passed her mother who was returning home at that same time. Allenteen spotted her daughter out of the house and spoke to her. Nevertheless, she allowed Carol to resume her journey to the store. Carol, knowing that a severe punishment awaited her when she arrived home, continued with her chore.

A store clerk served young Carol, selling her the items which she had come for – TV dinners, bread … and the keenly desired soda. A local neighbourhood child saw Carol walking back towards her apartment block clutching the bag of groceries.

Carol never made it home. At some stage along the half-mile journey the shy girl simply disappeared. Her mother contacted police and filed a missing person report. She rallied family and friends to search the neighbourhood that evening. There was no trace of Carol to be found. Not yet.

On Saturday, 1 May 1971, less than a mile away from Carol's apartment, a group of children were playing in the grounds of a local mental health facility, St Elizabeth's Hospital. One of the children, an 11-year-old boy, wandered off, ending up on a grassy embankment bordering the Anacostia Freeway. Here he found the body of a girl. He managed to flag down a police officer, and soon detectives were called to the scene. It was quickly established that the body belonged to Carol Spinks, the 11-year-old girl who had gone missing under a week ago.

The body was autopsied. It had undergone around 2-3 days of decomposition before being disposed of along the freeway. Carol, it soon became apparent, had been sexually assaulted (both vaginally and anally). She had been brutalised, suffering blows to the face several times and there were lacerations on her arms, face and torso. Cause of death appeared to be strangulation. It was determined from the contents of Carol's stomach that she had been kept alive for around four days after her abduction. It appeared that her kidnapper had fed her some kind of citrus fruit during her captivity. The shoes were missing from the body.

Two months later another black girl went missing from the same Congress Heights neighbourhood where Carol Spinks had lived in. On 8 July 1971, 16-year-old Darlenia Denise Johnson was walking towards the Oxon Run Recreational Centre where she worked as a counsellor. She was going to be staying the night as the centre was hosting a sleepover for its young members. The walk from Darlenia's apartment to her employment was a short one.

She never made it. Darlenia's absence was only really noted

the following morning, and it was then that a missing person report was filed. One witness reported that Darlenia had been with her boyfriend the previous evening, a lead that went nowhere. Another witness stated they had seen the missing girl being driven in the car of an older African-American male, sometime after her supposed abduction. This lead also turned up nothing.

According to a person familiar with the family, in the days that followed, Darlenia's mother was called on the phone by an unknown taunting voice making a disturbing claim: "I killed your daughter."

An employee of the D.C. Department of Highway and Traffic found the body of Darlenia by chance 11 days later. It had been dumped 15 feet from the site where Carol Spinks had been found. The employee called his discovery in, only to be told that this was the second call they had received about the body that day. A couple of police had, in fact, been sent to investigate, but they made little attempt to locate the remains. Without even getting out of the car, they instead radioed in that there was nothing to be found. The employee later returned to the scene and was shocked to discover the body still there, a week after he had originally reported it. The remains appeared to have been undisturbed by anything other than the action of the hot summer sun. The body of Darlenia Johnson had been discovered … and rediscovered.

Medical examiners were unable to ascertain if she had been sexually assaulted; however, there was evidence of strangulation. Due to decomposition she could only be identified by her fingerprints. Like that of Spinks', Johnson's clothing was undisturbed; only the shoes were missing.

Brenda Faye Crockett was a tiny-framed 10-year-old black girl of 4'5" height and 75lb weight. At about eight o'clock on the evening of 27 July 1971, Brenda and some local children were settling in to watch a film. Brenda's mother asked her to go to a local store to buy some groceries and to bring a friend with her. It seems that Brenda ignored this advice, leaving the house alone, apparently shoeless and with her hair in curlers.

When she failed to return home, Brenda's family organised a search, knocking on doors and making calls to anyone that Brenda knew. Whilst most of the family were out scouring the neighbourhood, Brenda's sister, Bertha, aged 7, remained at home. It was during this time that the phone rang. Bertha answered it. On the other end of the line was her sister Brenda. "A white man picked me up," said Brenda, "and I'm heading home." Brenda then mentioned that she was in Virginia, whereupon the call was abrupted ended.

Around 40 minutes later the phone rang a second time. This time the call was answered by the boyfriend of Brenda's mother. It was Brenda again. She repeated the same information, that a white man had picked her up and that she was returning home in a cab.

Brenda's mother's boyfriend asked Brenda if she was in Virginia.

"No," Brenda replied. "Did my mother see me?"

This response seemed confusing. "How could your mother see you if you're in Virginia?" the boyfriend asked, but Brenda could give no meaningful answer.

The boyfriend then asked to speak with the man. At that point heavy footsteps were heard, Brenda said, "Well, I'll see you," and the call was abruptly disconnected.

The family awaited in the hope that Brenda would walk through the door, exhausted but safe. They were to be cruelly disappointed. Eight hours later came crushing news: the body of Brenda had been found by a hitchhiker – not far away, dumped in plain sight just off the John Hanson Highway. She had been strangled to death and the knotted scarf used to do so was still wrapped tightly around her neck. She was barefoot, although this did not seem unusual, for it was thought that she had left the house without putting on any footwear. However, her feet, it was noticed, were extremely clean – not what one would expect for someone who had been walking outside. She was still wearing the blue-and-white print shorts and matching halter top that she had been wearing before her disappearance. There was a slight mercy – she had not been sexually assaulted.

Detectives would later theorise that the caller had forced Brenda to make the two phone calls in order to feed misinformation to the police: Brenda had stated on both occasions that she was with a white man. Moreover, Brenda had said that she was in Virginia, yet her body was found close to where she had apparently been abducted. Detective Romaine Jenkins would speculate that the killer was someone who knew the family and who had wanted to ascertain that he had not been spotted with the girl. "Did you see my mother?" Brenda had specifically asked. Perhaps Brenda had known her abductor too. "Well, I'll see you," she had said. It is possible that she fully expected to return home. The killer had spent a considerable period of time with both of his previous abductees, and yet he appeared quite keen to dispose of Brenda quickly – within hours, in fact. Perhaps he was worried about an imminent visit by the police. This would imply some connection with Brenda Crockett and the neighbourhood from where she had disappeared.

It was only after the disappearance and killing of 12-year-old Nenomoshia Yates (those who knew her called her "Neno") that the police officially linked the four murders. Neno's stepmother had not long given birth, and her father was toing and froing between hospital, to be with his wife, and home, to look after Neno.

On 1 October 1971, two months since the abduction and murder of Brenda Crockett, Neno went to a local convenience store to buy groceries. The store clerk was later to remember having served the diminutive black girl. She had bought flour, sugar and some paper plates just after 19:00. Those same items were to be found later that evening scattered on the street just outside the store. It seemed like the elusive killer had grabbed her off the street and bundled her hurriedly into a car.

Neno's remains would be found less than three hours after she went missing. A hitchhiker happened upon the body on the shoulder of Pennsylvania Avenue on the Maryland side of the state line.

Neno, like the others, had been raped and manually strangled to death; the girl's oesophagus was crushed from the excessive force of the violence. Her body, still warm, bore little evidence of a struggle, a small scratch on her forehead the only mark. She was almost fully clothed in brown shorts, sweatshirt and white tennis socks; only her shoes were gone, which had been removed and were nowhere to be found. In her pocket was her house key and $2.91 in change.

Police making a door-to-door enquiry were told by a neighbour that they had seen a girl getting into a blue Volkswagen with a Maryland license plate. Nothing more was thought of this at the time as Neno's father's first wife drove a similar vehicle. The initial investigation into this lead led nowhere, and soon it was announced that the FBI intended to become involved in the search for this ephebophilic "repeat offender".[*]

In reporting this murder the *Washington Daily News* seized on the fact that all the victims had been dumped in the grass alongside freeways. It was this newspaper that coined the epithet "The Freeway Phantom". And it would soon become clear that the killer himself was paying attention … for he would come to embrace the name and taunt the police with it.

Brenda Denise Woodard, 18 years old, was a typing student taking night classes in Baltimore, Maryland. On 15 November 1971, Brenda met up with a classmate and the two of them went for dinner at a local restaurant. As the classmate's car was being serviced, the two caught a bus together for a few blocks. When their paths diverged Brenda said goodbye to her friend and got off the bus in order to catch another. That is when the trail turned cold.

Police Officer David Norman happened upon Brenda's body

---

[*] The support of the FBI evaporated quickly in the wake of the Watergate scandal. They would return, but not before many leads had dried and the case grown cold and stagnant.

the next morning, next to a bus stop that her mother herself used regularly. The scene was cordoned off. Brenda's mother, coming to wait at the bus stop herself, unwittingly stumbled upon the crime scene only to learn of her daughter's death.

The scene was extremely gruesome. Brenda had been stabbed six times and in the ensuing struggle she had suffered extensive defence wounds on her arms and hands. She still wore her black boots and her coat had been carefully draped over the body. These facts initially led investigators to believe that this was a separate crime, one unconnected to the previous slayings. However, they were to find a note in the inside pocket of the coat:

> _This is tantamount to insensititivity [sic] to people especially women. I will admit the others when you catch me if you can!_

> _Free-way Phantom!_

It had been written in pencil, on paper from Brenda's own notebook, in Brenda's own handwriting, and the FBI speculated that it had been penned at the killer's behest, dictated by the killer himself. Two hairs were found on Brenda's clothing, one from an African-American, the other from a Caucasian. This lead turned up a blind end.

Investigators struggled with these recent discoveries and wondered if the killing of Brenda truly had been the work of the Freeway Phantom. A number of differences set it apart from the preceding murders: (i) Brenda was older than the other victims; (ii) her shoes had not been taken from her; (iii) she had been killed in a different way by being stabbed; (iv) the dump site was some distance from the other sites; (v) the note seemed unduly timely; no other missives had been offered by the killer. However, the age difference may be explained otherwise: Brenda was petite, which may have led the killer to assume she was younger than she actually was. Another explanation could be that the Phantom simply saw an opportunity to abduct and took it. Even psychopathic killers cannot be too choosy!

Was it possible that Brenda had been targeted by a separate killer who had been keen to take advance of the Freeway Phantom's handiwork and sought to blame him for a crime he had not committed?

Ten months passed since the death of the Phantom's last victim. Then, on the evening of 5 September 1972, the sixth and final accepted victim of the Phantom, Diane Denise Williams, disappeared. A 17-year-old aspiring model, Diane had gone to visit her boyfriend, with whom she was deeply in love. After spending some time together, he walked her to the bus stop on Martin Luther King Avenue, not far from the abduction sites of Carol Spinks and Darlenia Johnson a year ago. Diane got on the bus but she never made it home. Her body was found by a trucker on the verge of Interstate 295. Her shoes had been removed but placed carefully beside her at the scene.

Police quickly concluded that the killer had been the Freeway Phantom, flexing his muscles after a dormant period. It was later determined that she had not been sexually assaulted, even though semen was found on her clothing. Her boyfriend denied that they had had sexual contact that night. In a scandalous twist, despite advances in DNA analysis, the semen stain has never been tested. Bureaucracy and case mismanagement mean that the sample became trapped in a perpetual bottleneck, with neither local nor federal agencies willing or able to test it. The ample is now considered lost, and no agency is even sure who has it in their possession.

It had not escaped the notice of investigators that five of the victims had the middle name Denise. Two had the first name Brenda. Was this more than a coincidence? Could the killer be deliberately stalking girls with these names? If that were the case he must surely have had some connection with them: the fact of an individual's name is not readily known to a stranger.

The recurring name Denise and the letter D are of particular interest and have led one psychiatrist to

> *postulate that the killer, if it is one person, might have*
> *some psychotic hostile association with the name or the*
> *letter.*
> (*The Anniston Star*, 1971, Anniston, Alabama)

Suspects have emerged. Amongst those considered promising were members of a gang called the Green Vega Rapists who were collectively responsible for a spate of sex crimes in Washington D.C. Detectives spoke to each of them individually in prison where they were serving sentences after successful prosecution of their crimes. One inmate gave information implicating another inmate, stating that he would provide details only under the stipulation that he remain unidentified for fear of retribution. This condition was agreed and the first inmate began to provide details[*] not reported in the media. However, the second inmate was able to provide verifiable alibis which exculpated him from suspicion. It was announced to the press that a break had been made in the investigation, whereupon the first inmate declined to be interviewed further, recanted his statement calling it "an elaborate hoax" and then denied having cooperated with the investigation in the first place. Thus the investigation, seeming to have grown legs after a promising lead, once again stalled and evaporated into nothing.

Circumstantial evidence pointed to another suspect, Robert Elwood Askins, a black man who had worked at St Elizabeth's Hospital in the 1970s. Not only had Askins worked at the hospital, he had also been sent to its psychiatric unit in lieu of prison after having poisoned a sex worker who had given him a venereal disease. And not only did Askins have ties to the hospital where one of the victims was found, he also lived in the Congress Heights area from where many of the girls disappeared.

---

[*] These details are referred to as "signature details", facts only known to perpetrators and investigators.

Askins was noted to use the word "tantamount" often, and seemingly randomly. The word had been used in the note found on Brenda Woodard (*"This is tantamount to insensititivity"*).

In 1977, Askins was arrested after he abducted a woman, sexually assaulted and beat her before releasing her. A search of his house by investigators revealed that Askins owned women's scarves, which were described as "soiled". Askins did not live with any women. Also in Askins's possession were many photos of females – unknown girls and young women. A search of his car revealed two buttons and an earring which he could not account for. Neither, however, could the items be linked to any victim.

Askins was later convicted and sentenced to life for kidnapping and rape. He died aged 91 in prison. In correspondence with a detective who had worked on the case, Askins continually denied his involvement in the freeway murders.

Relations between the police and the black population in the US have never been particularly warm. Disdain and distrust between the two parties was endemic, and the Freeway Phantom investigation did not improve matters. To the black community it seemed that the mostly white police force was doing little to solve the case. When the police announced that the man they were seeking was probably from the Afro-American community the animosity of that population grew. In 1980 Leon Williams, father of Diane, the final victim, was to say to the *Washington Post*:

> *"If it was a white girl, the police would have found the person. I don't believe that police followed the leads they had. Why do they think the person was black? Why don't they investigate whites as well?"*

Of course, the statement cannot be held up to objective scrutiny; the answer to Mr Williams' charge is unknowable. However, the truth of the matter is this: police had very little in the way of leads to follow, and they have refuted the assertion that they did not take the investigation seriously. Nevertheless, the slaughter of six young women and girls within a district is a travesty, and the fact that no one has been brought to justice for the crimes will certainly appal and outrage the victims' families and the wider community.

A reward for "up to $150,000" was offered for information leading to an arrest. This has never been claimed. The Freeway Phantom murders remain officially unsolved.

The Alphabet Murders
(active 1971-1973)

NOW AND THEN, a case becomes known that seems so outrageous it could only have been concocted as the plot for a mass-market crime thriller. The Alphabet Murders is just such a case. Unfortunately for the victims and families of the killer's crimes, this was not a work of fiction. Three girls were the targets of the Alphabet Murderer's lust and rage, all connected by similarities in their ages, religion, socioeconomic status, their struggles in school, and – in a bizarre, macabre and tragic twist – the fact that their first names and surnames began with the same letters. Additionally, the girls' bodies were all found in New York towns of the same initial letter: Carmen Colón was found near Churchville, Wanda Walkowiz in Webster, and Michelle Maenza in Macedon. Each of them died at the hands of an unknown serial killer in Rochester, New York between 1971 and 1973. Undoubtedly, this individual, with a penchant for choosing victims based upon their initials, was an intensely focused and ruthless man.

Downtown Rochester, in the early 1970s, was still somewhat a hub for the wider community. It had its own monorail, beautiful movie theatres and small neighbourhood stores. Decentralisation was in its infancy. Some people, wanting to get away from the low-level crime of downtown, started to move to the suburbs. The city itself began to sprawl, and malls and new local amenities were developed to accommodate the downtown migrants. Essentially, though, Rochester was still at that time a pleasant and agreeable place for parents to raise their children.

Carmen Colón was a petite 10-year-old brunette girl with brown eyes. She lived with her doting grandparents in Rochester. Having lived over five years in Puerto Rico, however, she was struggling to learn English. She was bullied in school, but she could fight back to defend herself. Teachers, nevertheless, recalled Carmen as being friendly, happy-go-lucky and never without a smile on her face.

On 16 November 1971 Carmen was picking up a prescription on behalf of her younger sister. The prescription, however, was not yet ready, but Carmen seemed to be in a rush and urgently told the pharmacist that she had to go. A witness recalled that he had seen "a small girl grabbed by the arm and taken into a car, apparently without a great struggle". The driver appeared to have been waiting for her outside the drugstore. It turned out that Carmen had been abducted.

An hour later, she was spotted, unbelievably, on the Interstate 490, naked from the waist down, running and flailing her arms in a desperate attempt to gain someone's attention. Shockingly, no one stopped to help the young girl, and she was abducted a second time.

Two days later, around 18 miles from where she had first been abducted, a grisly discovery was made by two boys riding their bicycles in the village of Churchville. Carmen had been dumped along a little used rural road. The body was clad only in her sweater and footwear. She had been raped and manually strangled; her body was covered in fingernail scratches. An autopsy revealed that she had sustained fractures to her skull and a vertebrae. Two weeks later, Carmen's trousers were found. They had been discarded in a nearby field.

In the aftermath of the murder the city of Rochester reeled in horror. No one could quite believe that not a single one of the hundred-or-so witnesses to see Carmen running semi-naked along a busy freeway had stopped to help.*

A reward of $6,000 was offered for information. A few leads were developed but they amounted to nothing and the suspects

---

* The failure to do so is sometimes called "crowd apathy" by psychologists. Very often people do not even recognise that an emergency is happening; and, if they do, their interest is curtailed at the thought of actually doing something to help. _It's someone else's responsibility_, is a common supposition.

were eliminated. Eventually coverage faded and the townspeople came to think of the murder of Carmen as a single tragic event.

They were wrong.

Nearly 18 months later, eleven-year-old Wando Walkowicz went to buy groceries from a local delicatessen at around 17:00 on 2 April 1973. She bought the groceries, as attested by the proprietor of the store, but after that she disappeared. A search was initiated but this turned up nothing.

Wanda's body was located at the base of a hillside in Webster, around seven miles from Rochester, found by a state trooper. It appeared that her body, like Carmen Colón's, had been pushed out of a moving car. Examination revealed that her fully clothed body had been redressed after death, and an autopsy uncovered traces of semen and pubic hair on her body as well as white cat fur on her clothing. After being raped, the girl had been garrotted from behind with a belt, this action being the cause of her death. Defence wounds showed that she had fought against her attacker. "She's such a tiny thing, I don't think she was capable of putting up much of a struggle," said Dr John F. Edland who performed the autopsy.

Blue-eyed, red-haired Wanda was known to have been a feisty tomboy. She much preferred to kick a ball or wrestle than stay indoors and play dress-up. She could stick up for herself against anyone who tried to cross her, but neighbours recalled an honest, mature girl whom they trusted to clean their houses for extra pocket money.

Wanda was struggling at school, but on the day that she went missing she had been returning home with an improved report card which she could not wait to show her mother. Things seemed to be looking up …

After they found her body the police went into action. A photograph issued to the newspapers for publicity showed a freckled girl with a pixie cut, her smile revealing a chipped front tooth. An anonymous "witness line" was set up and leads came in thick and fast. One witness recalled seeing a red-haired girl with a man next to a light-coloured Dodge Dart in Rochester, whilst another recalled seeing a light-coloured Dodge Dart near to where Wanda's small body was found. Two 10-year-old girls remembered a man with a black coat, a black beard and a mole on his head attempting to lure them into his car. Police recalled an incident that had happened the Saturday before Wanda's disappearance. The mother of a friend of Wanda reported a strange man had followed Wanda and her friend along railway tracks, lurking in bushes and covering his face when the girls looked back at him. Upon hearing this, Wanda's distraught mother had to be hospitalised.

No useful leads were gained. Suspects who had been questioned turned out to have solid alibis, and they were crossed off the detectives' list and let go.

Understandably, the citizens of Rochester were thrown into a heightened state of panic. Parents accompanied their children to and from school and warned them in no uncertain terms to keep their distance from strangers. But despite their supervision and precautions the killer would strike again.

On 26 November 1973 11-year-old Michelle Maenza went missing. She had not returned home from school, and it was considered that she might have gone to a shopping plaza to fetch a purse that her mother had happened to leave behind. She was seen at the plaza by classmates at around 15:20. Around 10 minutes later, a witness observed the weeping child being driven at speed by a man in a beige or tan car. At around 17:30 that day, another witness saw a man and a girl he believed to be Maenza standing beside a beige or tan car near the village of Macedon, approximately 15 miles from Rochester. The car had a flat tyre and so the witness stopped to offer help. However, the man grabbed the girl and pushed her behind his back, also making attempts to obscure his number plate. The man made a rude gesture, and so infuriated had his expression been that the witness felt compelled to drive away.

A missing person report was filed and the search commenced. The police were looking for a white, chubby, 5'1" girl of around

120lbs, with dark hair and dark eyes. She had been wearing a purple coat with silver trimming, purple trousers and black boots. On the day that Michelle went missing she had spent part of the afternoon at school in the nurse's office, crying. She was often the victim of incessant bullying by other pupils who called her "Stinky" and ruthlessly mocked her weight. The taunts had been particularly callous that day.

Two days later the body of Michelle was found, face down in a ditch along a desolate road in Macedon. Her skin was riddled with bruises. She had been brutally beaten, raped, manually strangled as well as garrotted from behind using a thin cord. In her hand Michelle clutched a leaf. It was thought that she had grabbed at foliage during the attack. Her body was fully clothed but for the purple coat she had been wearing. This was later found around half-a-mile from the body. Like Carmen Colón, strands of fur from a white cat were found attached to Wanda's clothing.

The autopsy revealed that in the hour before her death Michelle had eaten a hamburger with onions. The autopsy of Wanda Walkowicz had also revealed the same, that she had eaten before being killed. A credible witness provided police with a description of a white male, very slender, with dark hair and stubble. Police were now certain that all three murders were the evil deeds of this very same man. However, although this lead, and others, were pursued, they all eventually drew a blank, leaving the case to stall.

Suspects include an uncle of Carmen Colón, who had a car similar to the one described by witnesses, and after her death investigators discovered that the car had been scrubbed clean using a powerful cleaning agent. Shortly after Carmen's death he had reportedly wished to leave the area as he had "done something wrong in Rochester". He did, in fact, move to Puerto Rico two days later. The uncle was unable to provide an alibi for his whereabouts or movements on the day of Carmen's death. Miguel Colón committed suicide in 1991, aged 44.

Another suspect was a 25-year-old firefighter who owned a

beige car and committed several rapes of girls and young women between 1971 and 1973. On one occasion he had attempted to abduct a teenager at gunpoint but ran away when she screamed. Another attempted abduction was thwarted by police and he ran away, shortly thereafter ending his life by his own gun. His beige car was examined and found to contain strands of white cat hair. Dennis Termini's body was exhumed in 2007. Comparison analysis of the DNA taken from his body did not match the semen samples found on Wanda Walkowicz's body.

Suspicion has also fallen upon Kenneth Bianchi, the so-called "Hillside Strangler". Bianchi had worked as an ice cream vendor in Rochester at the time of the murders before moving to Los Angeles in 1976 where he killed 10 females between the ages of 12 and 28. It is known that he drove a car similar to the one described as being used in the Alphabet Murder crimes. Bianchi, who currently resides in Washington State Penitentiary, has denied involvement.

Elsewhere, a 79-year-old man was convicted for the murder of four women between 1977 and 1994, all of whom had the same matching first name and surname initials. He had lived in Rochester in the early 1970s. His DNA did not match the semen deposit taken from Wanda Walkowicz's body.

It is certainly conceivable that in the case of Alphabet Murders the matching initials of the girls (and the initials of the towns where their bodies were found) is entirely coincidental. It is supposed that mothers, either consciously or unconsciously, find the alliteration of names pleasing, and so the incidence of girls whose names begin with the same initial may be slightly raised, thus raising the statistical chance of a random attacker taking girls with names such as these.

However, it is also possible that the girls _were_ targeted specifically because of their names. The killer may have worked in a social security office; the families of the victims were all supported by government benefits, and a disgruntled employee may have had access to information about these three families. If this were the case, the murderer was certainly a certifiable psychopath of incredibly driven remorselessness and cruelty.

The killer's motive was undoubtedly sexual, and the lust for power may likewise have been a possible element fuelling his murderous rage. Nevertheless, whoever that individual might have been, his crimes stopped (as far as we know) and they did not recur in the same area utilising the same *modus operandi*. He has escaped justice for his offences, and unless there is a late breakthrough in the case it may well be that his identity will never come to light.

The Santa Rosa Hitchhiker Murders

[active 1972-1973]

AS A MEANS of self-transportation, by the 1970s hitchhiking had
become etched deep into the collective American psyche – ever
since the days of the Great Depression when the practice became
increasingly permissible and common. As a mode of travel it
had become normal and acceptable to see travellers "thumbing"
for lifts at the side of the road, soliciting strangers for a ride to
the next destination, wherever that may be. Indeed, early in the
century hitchhiking became such a popular means by which to
get around that people used to dress up in order to do so. It was
cheap and accessible; it was exciting and liberating. It relied
upon civic cooperation and, despite what the average mother
might have said, in the early 1970s it was actually a very safe
method of travelling.

That is, unless you were a female hitchhiker travelling through
Santa Rosa, California …

Maureen Sterling and Yvonne Weber were two pretty 12-
year-old middle-school girls who wore their long hair parted in
the middle. On the evening of Friday, 4 February 1972, the two
friends from Sonoma County, California were dropped off at a
local indoor ice rink. However, this was a deception. After their
ride had driven off, Maureen and Yvonne would leave the area
in order to hitchhike across town to a park frequented by other
young people. That night a witness stated that he had seen the
two girls hitchhiking on Guerneville Road. It was the last time
anyone – anyone other than their killer or killers – would see
them alive.

Eleven months later, on 28 December, the two girls' disartic-
ulated skeletal remains were found down a steep embankment,
just over 60 feet from Franz Valley Road, north of Santa Rosa.
Some jewellery was found at the scene, but no clothes, which
prompted detectives to speculate that the girls had been naked.
Cause of death was indeterminable. Due to the fact that their

killer had to have lifted the girls across a ditch, it was surmised that he must have been a man of considerable strength.

Before the bodies of the last two victims could even be identified another body was found. It had been tipped into a ravine.

Kim Allen was an attractive 19-year-old student attending Santa Rosa Junior College. She wore her long, light-brown hair parted at the centre. On 4 March 1972 Kim left her job at a health food store to go a night class. She was seen hitchhiking not far away, wearing a three-quarter-length coat and appeared to be carrying two bags and a barrel of soy.

The next day, two 17-year-old boys found the naked body of Kim down a 20-foot embankment in a creek. She had been thrown into the ravine, and detectives speculated that whoever had cast the body over the edge may have taken a tumble himself. From marks and impressions at the scene, it appeared that someone had slipped and fallen at least part of the way down the slope. That person may even have injured himself in the process.

Early coroner reports determined that Kim had been raped and slowly tortured by strangulation with a wire before dying around midnight. She was identified by her sister, who later spoke about Kim's hopes and expectations for the eventual moment of her demise:

> *Annilee Shannon, Kim's sister, mentioned that only the week before, she and Kim had talked about death and Kim had mentioned how joyful an event she wanted it to be – a beautiful ending for a beautiful life.*
> (*Press Democrat*, Santa Rosa, California, 1972)

It is unlikely that Kim's end was how she had hoped it would be. It would surely have been unimagined and unimaginable.

Lori Lee Kursa's mother reported her 13-year-old daughter missing on 11 November 1972. The two had been grocery shopping when Lori Lee apparently ran away. It was speculated that she had been going to see her father in Florida. Eventually, however, it was realised that she had gone to visit friends. She had been wearing blue denim bell-bottoms, a brown leather jacket and brown suede shoes. Her light-blond hair, cut in a shag style, was parted at the centre. She was last seen by friends on 30 November. Lori Lee, reportedly, would occasionally go hitchhiking.

Her naked body was found approximately 30 feet down a steep embankment off Calistogan Road, northeast of Santa Rosa. She was identified by dental records.

It appeared that the body had been thrown over the embankment, although Detective Sergeant John Coffman said that he was investigating the possibility that the girl may have jumped from a moving vehicle and fallen into the ravine. Her fall was broken by several small trees. An autopsy reported that due to the extreme cold (the body was frozen solid) he could only record the date of Lori Lee's death as having happened between 1-8 December. There was no initial evidence of rape, sexual interference or assault. Dislocated vertebrae near to Lori Lee's neck may have caused or contributed to her death. Her clothes were never found.

A young boy came forward to report that on an evening sometime between 3-9 December he had witnessed two men push a girl matching the description of Lori Lee into the back of a van which then sped forwards Calistoga Road.

When the body of a young female was found on 31 July 1973, a mere four feet from where the bodies of Maureen Sterling and Yvonne Weber were found, it was becoming apparent that "[the] spectre of a maniacal killer with an insane sense of humor loomed over Sonoma County" (*Press Democrat*, 1973). The naked body, found by a motorcyclist, was believed to have lain undiscovered for up to two weeks. The pathologist was unable to establish if she had been sexually assaulted before her death.

Carolyn Davis, 14 years old, who had a history of being a runaway, had been dropped off at the Garberville Post Office on 15 July. She was seen hitchhiking on the same afternoon and reported missing at 18:00 that evening. It was the body of Carolyn that was found on 31 July; she was identified by dental records.

A subsequently released photo shows a girl who wore her long brown hair parted in the middle.

An autopsy indicated that Carolyn had died as a result of poisoning by strychnine (a highly toxic pesticide), pointing to a murderer who showed considerable premeditation. The body showed no signs of violence. Again, due to the circumstances of the crime, it was postulated by detectives that a man of some strength had to have been involved.

The oldest known victim in the spate of murders was found on 28 December 1973 by two youths who were kayaking along Mark West Creek, which runs alongside Calistoga Road near Santa Rosa. A young woman's remains were caught in an eddy between a rock and a submerged log. She had been hogtied using a thin piece of nylon clothesline, and her arms and legs were bound tightly against her chest. She had a slip-knotted noose around her neck. It was determined that she had been dead one week before being found. The pathologist reported that the female had been strangled to death, and that a severe blow to the back of the head may also have contributed to her demise. The press described the woman as 18-25 years of age, possibly of Mexican-American descent. She had long dark hair and brown eyes.

It was not until 9 January that the body was identified as that of Theresa Walsh, the 23-year-old mother of a two-year-old son. When last seen on 22 December 1973, she had been hitchhiking from Malibu to spend Christmas with family in Garberville. She had been wearing a lavender blouse, a hooded brown fur coat, and white bell-bottom trousers. Theresa, like the other victims, had long dark hair, parted in the middle.

It is possible that the murderer roaming Santa Rosa killed other girls and young women.

Seventeen-year-old Lisa Smith was last seen hitchhiking in Santa Rosa on 16 March 1971, some months before the first acknowledged murder. If she did die as a result of a chance encounter with the slayer then her body has never been found.

Jeannette Kamahele was a 20-year-old college student who

she was most likely abducted whilst hitchhiking in Sonoma County, California. Skeleton remains found approximately 100 yards from the place where Lori Lee Kursa were initially thought to be those of Kamahele. This victim had worn contact lenses and had reddish hair. She had been hogtied and suffered a fracture of the arm around the time of her murder, which was thought to have been three years earlier. Dental records later showed conclusively that this was not Kamahele. The identity of this person remains unknown.

Francine Trimble and Kerry Graham were aged 14 and 15 respectively when they disappeared in December 1978 after leaving home in Forestville, California to go to a shopping mall. In July 1979, two skeletons were uncovered 80 miles away, buried in plastic bags within an overgrown embankment area. The remains were not identified until 2015 when DNA profiling was able to confirm it was the two girls.

The above-mentioned four females had all had long hair which they wore parted in the middle.

The Department of Justice issued a document, *Unsolved Female Homicides – An Analysis of a Series of Related Murders in California and Western America,* in February 1975. The special confidential report asserted that during a five-year period, December 1969 to September 1974, 14 young women were likely killed by the same person. Amongst the names included in this chilling list were: Rosa Vasquez, aged 20; Yvonne Quilantang, aged 15; Angela Thomas, aged 16; and Nancy Gidley, aged 24. All of them had connections to the San Francisco area; all of them had been strangled.

There has been speculation that the unapprehended Zodiac Killer may have been responsible for these deaths, with Zodiac suspect Arthur Leigh Allen being a leading candidate. Allen, during the time of the murders, owned a mobile home in Santa Rosa. He was convicted of child molestation in 1975 and imprisoned until 1977. None of the murders happened during his incarceration, and Francine Trimble and Kerry Graham disappeared in December 1978, sometime after his release. The timeline certainly fits. Allen died of a heart attack in 1992. He was never charged for these or the Zodiac crimes.

Curiously, a heavyset 41-year-old creative writing instructor, Fredric Manalli, was also a suspect. Manalli died on 24 August 1976 as the result of a head-on automobile collision. An employee of the Sonoma Sheriff's Department recalled learning about the traffic accident, and about certain possessions later found in his van:

> *Amongst the drawings in his van were drawings of some of the seven victims in the Santa Rosa area, which portrayed them in hog-tied positions. Included with these drawings were their names and sexual preferences.*[*]

Manilla had worked at the colleges that some of the victims had attended, but neither his physical description nor his handwriting matches that of the Zodiac Killer, the man whom some have speculated was also the Santa Rosa killer. The circumstantial evidence certainly keeps the waters muddied.

Accusing fingers have also been pointed in the direction of Ted Bundy, a particularly savage and brutal prolific slaughterer of women. Bundy was known to travel extensively in his search for victims. A feature of his *modus operandi* was to keep his victims alive, returning to torture them by strangling them to unconsciousness before reviving them and repeating the action. His targets were brunette girls and women with their hair parted in the middle, just like most of the victims of the Santa Rosa Hitchhiker Murderer. However, detailed credit card records and known whereabouts effectively ruled Bundy's involvement in the killings. It is a chilling coincidence, however.

Suspicion has also fallen upon Kenneth Bianchi and his accomplice Angela Buono, Jr, the so-called Hillside Stranglers of

---

[*] Quote taken from *Zodiac Unmasked* by Robert Graysmith, 1986.

Los Angeles. Bianchi, it has been noted, was also a suspect in the similarly unresolved Alphabet Murders. The involvement of these two has certainly never been ruled out.

The case of the string of Santa Rosa murders now lies cold. There have been no new leads and, despite advances in forensic technologies and techniques, many questions remain unanswered. The bones found in 1979 have not been identified; Jeanette Kamahele has not been found. And the killer who targeted vulnerable female hitchhikers escaped justice.

Charlie Chop-off
(active 1972-1974)

HUMANS HAVE BEEN GOADING each other with creepy tales and spooky anecdotes for centuries. We often have a morbid fascination with that which elicits disgust, and we frequently cannot help ourselves from participating in the gossip and repeating it to our friends, aiming to inspire in them the same degree of horror we ourselves felt upon hearing the tale. Oftentimes the tale suffers (or benefits, depending upon one's outlook) from the odd adjustment to detail. As the tale spreads it becomes creepier or spookier with each retelling – right until the point that the listener is left reeling with an odd admixture of amazement and scepticism.

The urban legend can be thought of as a contemporary version of spine-chilling folklore. It still consists of a story that is circulated from one person to another – usually orally, but sometimes by other means, such as newspapers or social media. The narrator will often claim to have been told the tale by someone else – a "friend of a friend" – and in this respect it is usually an unsubstantiated tale, but one that seems as though it could be underpinned by a degree of truth.

The content of the tale is always something designed to incite horror, disgust or pity – whilst sometimes incorporating humorous elements. But most importantly, the urban legend seeks to promote moral standards, and in this sense, they are no different from the ancient fairy tales our ancestors used to tell their children to keep them out of trouble and to maintain their safety.

A mad bogeyman man roaming the city streets, stalking young boys, dragging them into dark alleyways, stabbing them, hacking off their genitals with a switchblade, might seem like the stuff of a gruesome but fanciful urban legend. However, the reality is that this actually happened. It happened in Manhattan, New York between March 1972 and May 1974 and, due to the method of his madness, the bogeyman came to be known as

"Charlie Chop-off".

Douglas Owens, an African-American boy aged eight, was the first victim. Douglas, a Harlem resident, had been running an errand for his mother on 9 March 1972. It was a rainy day. When he did not arrive home his worried mother notified the authorities who instigated an immediate search of the area.

Douglas' body was found short afterwards on the rooftop of a building on East 121st Street, not two blocks from his home. He had been stabbed 38 times, mostly in the neck, chest and back. The body was fully clothed, although the shoes had been removed and set neatly beside the body. However, alarmingly, Douglas' pants had been slashed open and his penis hacked to the point that it remained attached only by a bloodied flap of skin. Evidence suggested that the boy had also been sodomised.

Investigators initially suspected the family and acquaintances of the attack on Douglas as it seemed to be personal. However, this investigation drew a blank. The police, stymied for the lack of witnesses or evidence, drew the conclusion that the boy had been the victim of random violence.

Six weeks later, on a rainy 20 April, came another grievous assault. A 10-year-old black boy was running errands when a man who introduced himself as "Michael" lured him into a building under the pretext of helping him with a labour task on the roof. Once on the roof the man called "Michael" attacked, stabbing the boy several times, sodomising him and severing his genitals completely from his body. The assailant then carried the boy downstairs and left him in the hallway to be found by a neighbour. It was reported that the boy's shoes had been removed and were located "nearby". The boy's genitals were nowhere to be seen.[*]

Mercifully, the boy, whose name was withheld to protect his

---

[*] The amputated body part was later found in the hands of school children who had been playing with it in a local park.

anonymity, survived the attack. He was able to give investigators a description of his attacker: a slender, olive-skinned man with an obvious mole on his left cheek, who had foul breath and walked with a distinctive limp.

Wendell Hubbard, a nine-year-old black boy, was attacked and mutilated under similar circumstances on 23 October 1972. He had been playing in the courtyard behind the apartment complex where he lived. When he failed to come inside when called, his mother became concerned; Wendell generally would not disobey her requests. She was aware of the recent attacks against black boys and immediately fretted, frantically searching the local area for her son whilst police also cruised the vicinity.

Four hours later Wendell's body was discovered by three boys playing on the rooftop of a 5th Avenue building They straightaway ran to inform the police of their find. Wendell's mother immediately identified her son. Residents of the murdered boy's building denied having seen or heard anything suspicious.

Wendell, like the two other victims, had been stabbed between 18-19 times. His genitals had been detached using a sharp implement and removed from the scene. They were never found. And like the two other victims, Wendell's shoes were removed and placed neatly at his side. The killer was endorsing his crimes with the signature of a distinct and unusual *M.O.*

It was around this time that the children of the local area came up with the dreadful nickname for the bogeyman roaming their streets: "Charlie Chop-off". "Watch out for Charlie Chop-off," they would call to each other in the dwindling light. But this was no plot from an episode of *Alfred Hitchcock Presents* or a farfetched urban legend; this was real, and it was actually happening on the streets of New York.

Charlie Chop-off's pent-up rage and madness exploded again the next year, on 6 March 1973. Luis Ortiz, a 10-year-old black boy, was sent by his mother to buy some groceries, which he was able to do despite not having the full amount required. His mother, worried when he did not return, filed a missing person report. Luis was found the next day in the basement stairwell of a building just two blocks from his residence. He had been stabbed in what amounted to an overkill, 38-40 times, and his genitals had been sliced off, most likely with a switchblade, and removed from the scene. Neither the genitals nor the groceries were ever found. And, as in the other attacks, his shoes had been removed and placed by his side.

The fact that the investigation came to nothing only served to increase local apprehensions: "Search for Boy's Slayer Yields Only the West Side Area's Fear," reported the _New York Times_ gloomily.

Investigators were able to gain a detailed description of Charlie Chop-off from witnesses who had seen him in the company of Luis. The description closely matched that given by the unnamed survivor of the attack – a slender, 5'7"-5'10" tall, dark-complexioned man with acne scars and a prominent mole on his left cheek. A witness also believed that the same man had approached her nine-year-old son with the offer of a free ride on his bicycle if he should help the man with some manual work. The boy agreed to return the next day after he had asked his mother's permission. The next day, the mother arrived at the agreed time and place, confronted the man, and told him to stay away from her son or she would contact the authorities. The mother's description of the man matched that of the surviving victim's, apart from the detail of his voice. She stated that he had a "slight but noticeable Dominican accent". The mother was able to cooperate with a police sketch artist to produce a composite image of the suspect. The police distributed this image locally, and one year after the first death (that of Douglas Owens) they publicly announced that they were treating the murders as related.

Steven Cropper's parents only realised that their son had died after being shown a photo of his lifeless body by detectives who were attempting to identify him. He had been with his parents just one hour before the discovery of his body by a woman walking her dog on the roof of a tenement building. Steven's distraught mother collapsed upon hearing the news.

The murder of Steven was thought by detectives to break the killer's pattern. He seemed to fit the victim profile perfectly – an eight-year-old black boy, found dead on a rooftop close to his home, his shoes placed neatly by his side. However, Steven was not stabbed (he died from a slash wound to his arm) and his genitals were left intact. Whilst Steven's shirt had been yanked up, his trousers undone and he had allegedly been posed in a sexually suggestive position, there was no evidence of sexual assault. Furthermore, an autopsy revealed that a deep 9-inch "X" had been carved into the boy's chest with a rusty razor that was found beneath the body, causing investigators to conjecture that this was the work of a copycat killer. Despite their misgivings, however, investigators eventually decided that the similarities were just too coincidental and they discounted the theory of a second murderer. Witnesses to a strange man seen talking to young boys in the area confirmed that he bore a strong resemblance to the composite image produced earlier, and authorities now added this fourth death to the killer's canon.

An unemployed 22-year-old Hispanic man was briefly suspected of the killings, by virtue of the single fact that he happened to have a similar appearance to the widely distributed composite sketch. Police brought him in for questioning but none of the witnesses could identify him. Despite this, the man's name was printed in the newspapers and an angry, vocal mob gathered outside the police station calling for his execution. He was smuggled out of the station dressed as a policeman and was discounted as a suspect.

Another man, Daniel Olivo, also fitted the description of a 5'7" tall, slender, olive-skinned, pock-marked man who walked with a limp. Thirty-year-old Olivo was indicted on separate charges of sexual molestation, having assaulted a five-year-old boy the previous week in a Bronx park. Despite the promising lead, Olivo's whereabouts during the period of the killings failed to fit the facts of the case and he too was discounted as a suspect.

The only other suspect considered somewhat plausible was

Erno Soto, a Puerto Rican convict and drifter who was also an intermittent psychiatric in-patient who had experienced religious delusions and violence. He fit the physical description provided by some witnesses perfectly, and a background check of the man's past uncovered the fact that his wife, from whom he was separated, had been involved with a black man and had a child from that relationship. At the time, the state of psychiatry would have promoted the interpretation that this affected him so deeply that he would have been unable to restrain his violence. However, despite the logic of the explanation, it is unlikely such a circumstance would spur Soto into sudden paedophilia.

Soto, aged 34, was arrested for attempting to abduct a nine-year-old Hispanic boy. When caught he was walking along holding the screaming boy over his head aloft. He was arrested. However, Soto was exculpated by the differing description of another witness: he was considerably taller at 6'1", he did not have a mole or walk with a limp, and he was left-handed*. Nor did he have the Dominican accent that the witness had detected during her confrontation of the man.

Soto confessed to the murder of Steven Cropper but he was unable to provide details of the attack. He was deemed competent to stand trial for the murder. A psychiatrist giving evidence at the trial referred to him as a "walking time bomb" who suffered from grandiose religious delusions and hallucinations; but nevertheless, doubt was cast upon the confession and Soto was acquitted by reason of insanity. Soto himself was later to say, probably in the midst of a florid psychotic episode, that God had told him to turn little boys into girls. His "confession" may have been a delusion based upon snippets gleaned from the news, although certainly, once he was committed to hospital, the mutilation-murder of young black boys discontinued.

The "Charlie Chop-off" cases remain technically open and

---

* The surviving victim had described being attacked by a right-handed man.

Soto is still an in-patient in the Kirby Forensic Psychiatric Center. According to reports, his stay had not been uneventful: he attempted to slit a psychiatrist's throat and threatened to "jab the eyes" out of a fellow patient. He is terminally ill, according to his lawyers, and confined to a wheelchair. Due to his deteriorated mental state it is unlikely that he will ever be tried for the horrific crimes on black boys in New York in the early 1970s.

The Doodler

AROUND THE SAME TIME that the Zodiac Killer was stalking the San Francisco, California environs, another ruthless killer was operating within the city. Just like Zodiac, the Doodler was never brought to justice for his crimes, but, whilst Zodiac's crime wave was heavily publicised and continues to evoke interest today, the Doodler's spree went largely unreported at the time, and the case is a mere footnote in the annals of criminal history.

The 1970s in the US seemed to be golden age in the Golden State for the multiple murderer. Joseph DeAngelo, the recently confessed Golden State Killer, was terrorising a swath of the state with rape and murder; Juana Corona was hacking to death a number of transient workers; and Ted Bundy is now believed to have encroached Californian turf to audaciously snatch, torture and murder female victims.

And San Francisco seemed to be gaining its fair of attention from this new breed of serial murderer: Zodiac was evading escape for targeting mainly courting couples; the Santa Rosa Hitchhiker Killer was picking off lone girls he found by the side of the road; and the so-called "Zebra Killings" of white men by a number of black assailants were in full swing.

In 1974 the Doodler – also known as the Black Doodler – stepped onto a patch where anonymous killers already seemed thick on the ground. He was believed to have committed 14 murders and three assaults within the gay community of San Francisco. Due to the fact that three distinctive victim types were targeted the police at first thought that they were dealing with three different serial killers. Five casualties were drags queens from the Tenderloin district, murdered by a knife-wielding slasher who appeared to have an aversion to transvestites. The world of sadomasochistic leather bars yielded another six victims, including the renowned attorney George Gilbert. And three of the slain (along with three survivors) frequented the Castro Village bars, where San Francisco's gay community congregated to eat, drink and be merry. However, as the *M.O.* pattern appeared to be consistent the police gradually came to realise that they were seeking a single maniac whose rage was directed towards gay, white males.

The first victim was found on 7 January 1974 at around half-one in the morning after police dispatch received a tip-off from a caller who calmly said, "I believe there may be a dead person, I just wanted to let somebody know. Maybe he needs help or something. I felt it was my duty to report it." The caller declined to give his name, instead hanging up.

Gerald Cavanaugh, aged 49 at the time of his death, is believed to be the Doodler's first victim. The plain-looking, heavy-set, balding man was fully clothed and lying face-up on Ocean Beach, *rigor mortis* already setting in. The coroner determined that he had been subjected to 16 stabs and that he had been alive at the time of the attack. A defence-wound on his finger indicated that he had made at least some attempt to intervene against the assault. Initially unidentified, the authorities temporarily referred to him as John Doe #7. He had been a single man, working in a mattress factory. It was the first of five cases officially attributed to the Doodler.

A popular Texas-born female impersonator was the next of the Doodler's victims. Joseph "Jae" Stevens, aged 27, was last seen on 24 June 1974 leaving the Cabaret Club in the North Beach district. His body was found by a woman walking her dog in the Golden Gate Park the next day. Police conjectured that Jae had driven his killer to the park. He had been stabbed five times (some reports state three times) and there was blood in his nose and mouth, indicating that he had been stabbed in the lungs. His body was clothed. Police believed that he had been killed shortly before being found.

Less than two weeks later Klaus Christmann, a 31-year-old German tourist and employee of Michelin, met his death. A woman walking her dog on 7 July discovered the body of

Christmann on Ocean Beach. He was fully dressed in the fashionable garb of the 70s, although his trousers had been unzipped and opened. The coroner reported that he had been stabbed so extensively in the neck and shoulders that "it seemed as though the assailant had attempted to decapitate the deceased". Unlike the previous victims, Christmann had been married with two children before answering to an inner calling to leave and taste what pleasures San Francisco had to offer. He had been in the city three months prior to his death. Police believed that he may have been a closeted gay man due to the fact that, in addition to the wedding band he wore, when he died Christmann had had a tube of makeup on his person.

By now the police had come to the conclusion that the three killings were connected.

Thirty-two-year-old Frederick Capin was found 10 months later on Ocean Beach on 12 May 1975. Capin, a lithe six-foot tall man was a decorated medical corpsman in the Navy. That night he had clearly coordinated his dress in order to go out and have a good time, but on this occasion, unfortunately, he happened to cross paths with a psychopathic butcher. Capin's body, was found by a hiker behind a sand dune. Cause of death, the coroner determined, was stab wounds to the aorta and heart. The body had been dragged a distance of around 20 feet, presumably by his assailant. It is possible that Capin had tried to escape when he realised the vulnerability of his situation.

The killer did not lie low for long. Within a couple of weeks he had killed again. Harald Gullberg, a 66-year-old Swedish sailor, was the victim. He had the tattooed arms that typically marked those of his profession. His decomposing remains were found approximately two weeks after his death at Lincoln Park Golf Course, 10 yards off the trail. He had been slashed across the neck. When found the zip of his trousers was down and he wore no underwear. Despite apparent dissimilarities in the _M.O._ – Gullberg was considerably older than the other victims – his death was the last conclusively linked to the Doodler.

It is a strange but apt nickname. It was given due to the killer's singular proclivity: he would sketch his victims, using this activity as a means to luring them into the conversation that would inevitably lead to a sexual encounter ... and death. He always met his victims at gay bars and restaurants or nightclubs. The facts were confirmed by three survivors of the Doodler's attacks. These witnesses refused to proceed with criminal charges due to the fear of being "outed", and to the damage to their relationships and careers that would likely ensue.

In the year-and-a-half duration of the Doodler murder case little progress was made by police, despite the release of a detailed composite sketch. The case barely even made the headlines of the mainstream San Franciscan newspapers during the duration of the killings, although it was well-reported by the district's now defunct gay newspaper, *The Crusader*. Tip-offs came in to the police, and there were dozens of suspects at the time. However, these amounted to little, and the case of the Doodler murders almost became lost to history.

Interest in the case has picked up in the wake of the emergence of Internet forums, and in the absence of suspects rumours abound. One account concerns a Los Angeles man who was about to go to bed with a young black man when a knife fell from his coat. The Angeleño made a rapid retreat from the situation, possibly saving himself from a very unpleasant predicament. Rumours fly about the three surviving witnesses: that one is a European diplomat; that another is a high-profile, nationally known entertainer; that the third is a San Franciscan public figure.

Police believe they have a name for the Doodler, a man undergoing "mental difficulties involving sex". They have not released this name, but they describe their Afro-American suspect as a "person of interest" and have released a new composite sketch to show how the killer may look today. They believe DNA profiling may be key to the solving of this decades-old mystery. Additionally, they say that they are keen to confer with a psychiatrist who may have talked to their suspect in 1976. Possibly the Doodler's luck may be about to run out.

The Ann Arbor Hospital Murders
(active 1975)

THE FEDERAL AGENCY, the United States Department of Veteran Affairs, delivers healthcare provision to eligible military veterans at various hospitals and centres throughout the country. The Ann Arbour Veterans Administration Hospital (to give it its full name) in Ann Arbor, Michigan is one of many hospitals that fall under the umbrella of the service. The red- and white-bricked building was built in 1953. It rests on a low rise overlooking a meandering turn of the Huron River, a location that could as easily been chosen for its recuperative properties as any other. Recuperation, however, was the last thing on the mind of at least one employee of the Ann Arbour Hospital during a six-week period in 1975.

In July and August of that year, 35 patients at the hospital were stricken with a mysterious ailment which led to respiratory failure. Veterans would be struck without any warning; they would be apparently recovering well one moment and then approaching suffocation the next. As the illnesses struck without any obvious cause, and with increasing frequency, the hospital staff became more and more unnerved. On 15 August, in a single 20-minute period, three separate patients required lifesaving emergency treatment. Some patients suffered an attack more than once. Some failed to recover. And as patients began to die, taken without warning, others began to fear for their own lives. In total, 11 of the veterans succumbed to the lethal effects of the unexplained respiratory illness and died.

At first the respiratory difficulties raised no undue red flags. This was a hospital and complications, undesirable though they were, were only to be expected. However, it soon became apparent to Dr Anne Hill, the hospital's chief anaesthesiologist, that something was amiss. She was quickly able to rule out environmental factors; after all, none of the nursing or medical staff was affected by the mysterious illness. Dr Anne had no option but to think the unthinkable: the frequency and unpredictability of the illnesses pointed to only one dreadful cause – foul play.

Dr Hill began to investigate. Her diagnostic tests showed that 18 of the affected patients had received unauthorised administration of a medication called pancuranium bromide[*]. Its therapeutic use in medicine is as a muscle relaxant. It is also used in euthanasia, and, in some US states, as a component in the lethal injection given during administration of the death penalty.

Dr Hill noticed a common denominator: all of the affected patients had been receiving intravenous fluids at the time of their unexplained respiratory problems. At the occurrence of next attack, Dr Hill administered the antidote to Pavulon. The antidote had the desired effect and the symptoms were quickly reversed. She did the same following the next two attacks with the same results. Dr Hill became convinced there was a poisoner working within the hospital. She called the FBI that very evening.

The day the FBI arrived the mysterious illnesses stopped. Nevertheless, damage had been done, and the federal investigators commenced an arduous examination of the evidence. Each of the 750 employees of the hospital was questioned. The agents reviewed work schedules, collating and comparing them against the timings of the attacks. Eventually the jigsaw came together and the names of two Filipino ICU nurses emerged as suspects: Leonora Perez, 29, and Filipina Narciso, 31. Both women had worked on all of the shifts during which the attacks took place. Additionally, two of the attacks happened on days not normally on Narciso's work schedule, but on which she had happened to be working additional hours. The FBI believed that Narciso was the culprit. Suspicion fell upon Perez because she was recognised by a surviving patient who had suffered respiratory arrest immediately after she had entered his room. This was enough

---

[*] Trademarked as Pavulon

for the investigators and both nurses were taken into custody.

The two nurses vehemently asserted their innocence. None-theless a federal grand jury indicted them. Despite the evidence being circumstantial, there being no obvious motive, and there being no explanation for how the two nurses could have colluded in a coordinated spree of poisoning, after a four-month trial they were convicted in July 1977 on 10 charges of poisoning, five counts of murder, and one count of conspiracy to commit murder.

Tensions at that time in the US were running high and the trial was marred by accusations of racism. It emerged that the veteran witness who had seen Perez leaving his room himself held ignominious attitudes towards Asians. "Slant-eyed bitches" was how he was known to have referred to the two defendants.

After the verdict, Perez told the _Washington Post_ that she felt the victim of racial discrimination. "I can't believe it, because I was always so confident during the trial," she said.

"I was never so shocked before as [by] what happened today. I had no thoughts of being convicted before today," the second defendant, Narciso, anxiously told the _Post_.

The following December the verdicts were overturned on appeal due to allegations of prosecutorial misconduct. The charges were dismissed and the two nurses were released from prison. The episode undoubtedly affected their lives and careers greatly.

Then news emerged that another suspect was in the frame for the murders. Just before the two Filipino nurses' trial a nursing supervisor committed suicide. Unconfirmed reports began to circulate that the supervisor had left a note confessing responsibility for the hospital deaths at Ann Arbor.

The case remains unsolved. Some feel that the two Filipino nurses literally got away with murder. Others suspect the involvement of another individual who, overcome with guilt, confessed before committing suicide as a means of atonement for the crime. At this stage the truth is unlikely ever to be determined.

The Flat-Tire Murders
(active 1975)

THE TALE IS OFTEN DISMISSED as apocryphal. A young woman finishes shopping and goes back to her car, only to notice she has a flat tyre. As she is taking the jack from the boot a pleasant-looking businessman with a briefcase walks up to her. He tells her that he has noticed her predicament and offers to help. Grateful, the woman accepts the man's help and they chat amiably whilst he goes about changing the tyre. Once done, the man puts the flat tyre and the jack into the boot, slams it shut and dusts off his hands.

After the woman thanks the man profusely he asks her if she would mind giving him a lift to his car at the other side of the parking lot. Surprised the woman asks him why his car is there. He explains that he left by the wrong exit and that as he has helped the woman change the tyre he is now running late for an important business meeting.

The woman feels uneasy. She does not like to tell him "no' – after all, he did come to her rescue and do a good deed – but she also remembers having seen the man toss his briefcase into her boot before asking for the lift. She would be happy to drive him to his car, she tells him, but first she has one final errant to run. She leaves him sitting in the car whilst she hurries back to the store where she informs a security guard what has happened.

The security guard accompanies the woman back to her car, but the man is gone.

They open the boot and remove the briefcase. Inside the brief-case, which has been left unlocked, they find a hammer, a knife, a roll of duct tape and a nylon rope. When they check the woman's tyre they found it was not punctured; the air had been let out deliberately. Whoever the Good Samaritan has been, his motives, to say the least, now seem dubious.

Getting a flat tyre, it should go without saying, is always an inconvenience. And how more inconvenient when it happens on a quiet road away from services in the mid-1970s! The help proffered from a passing stranger would be most welcome ...

Elyse Rapp certainly thought so. The pretty 21-year-old Jewish woman had been shopping at the Hollywood Mall in Hollywood, Florida on the evening of 30 July 1975. The native New Yorker had only recently moved to Miami for the purpose of finding work as an office temp. She was between jobs at the time she went missing, and the manager of Rapp's motel accommodation described her as "a very quiet girl who didn't seem to have made any close friends here yet".

Rapp's naked body was found the next morning floating in the Graham Canal, a rural waterway some distance from the town. She was wearing a gold chain sporting the "chai" symbol, a Hebrew symbol meaning "alive" or "living". She had been struck over the head and subjected to sexual mutilation before being drowned in the canal. Her rental car was found abandoned in the parking lot of the Hollywood Mall. One of its tyres was flat. The case struck detectives as similar to another death which had occurred just the previous week.

Ronnie Gorlin had planned to visit her ill mother at the Parkway Hospital in Miami, Florida on 22 July 1975. The 27-year-old respiratory therapist had spoken with friends about her upcoming wedding before leaving in order to travel to the hospital. She had indicated that her intentions had been to stop at the 163rd Street shopping centre on the way. Police questioned whether she had actually made it to the shopping centre.

The next day, Gorlin's naked body was found in the same rural canal in which the body of Elyse Rapp was found, around one mile away. Apart from minor scratches there were no other mark on the body, and, like Rapp, the death was determined to have been drowning. Also similarly, her rental car was discovered at a parking lot blocking traffic. It too had a flat tyre.

Police were quick to draw a connection between the two similar murders:

A killer may have let the air out of tires on the cars of

*two women and then presented himself as a friend in
need before killing and dumping their nude bodies in a
rural canal, Dada County police investigators said.*
(*Tampa Bay Times*, St Petersburg, Florid, 1975)

"It looks like we have a real sickie on our hands," Sergeant
Doug Taggerty pointed out to the *Fort Lauderdale News*. In the
same article Sheriff Edward J. Stack said, "Naturally, we will
exhaust every resource in trying to determine if the killings were
the work of a maniac, but I see definite differences between
these killings."

However, the similarities were impossible to ignore and the
next day the authorities announced that they were looking for a
single suspect. The cases also drew comparison with a number
of other murders in the area and police now feared that they were
looking for a serial killer.

It seemed to have started when Barbara Stephens, a 23-year-
old married lady, dropped from sight on 12 February 1975. She
had last been seen buying records at the Gold Triangle store.
Her car was still in the parking lot next to the Gold Triangle
store. Her keys were in the car and its doors were unlocked. The
two records she had bought were still in the car, and on the steering wheel of the car were traces of blood.

Stephens' badly decomposed body was found eight days later
in a wooded area behind a shopping mall in Southwest Dade in
Miami, Florida (this had been predicted by a remarkably prescient psychic), approximately one mile from her home. She had
been stabbed.

Then the bodies of two 14-year-old girls were found on a deserted rural road next to a canal in Broward County, west of
Florida. Barbara Schreiber and Belinda Zeterower were discovered on 19 June 1975. They had been shot, more than likely at
the spot where they lay. Reports conflicted as to whether they
had been sexually assaulted. Both slain girls were characterised
as "real sweet" and "nice-looking".

These are the "official" victims ascribed to the "Flat-Tire" murder spree but it does not stop there. Many more victims of murder or unexplained circumstances occurred in Miami-Dade County around that time in 1975.

Fourteen-year-old Joanne Weiss was fished from a drainage canal near to Miami International Airport. A concrete block had been tied to her body.

Renie Tinker, aged 17, a blond, blue-eyed mother, was also found dead in a Broward canal under inexplicable circumstances.

Nineteen-year-old Ann Osterling's badly beaten body was recovered from a canal in Broward County on 26 January 1975.

Robin Losch, aged 14, and Nancy Fox, aged 19, were found in a Broward canal within four days of each other, not far from where Schreiber and Zeterower's remains were found. Both had suffered blows to the head. Losch had more than likely drowned, whereas Fox had been choked before being discarded into the canal.

There were at least nine and up to 17 deaths under suspicious circumstances or unaccounted homicide. All of the victims had long dark hair parted in the middle.

None of these crimes has ever been solved. However, detectives at the time drew comparison to a series of murder victims emerging in the state of Washington and beyond. Detective Charles Mussoline of Dade County told the _Tampa Tribune_:

> _"When you go back to the dates of the killings, it's possible the guy started making his way east, leaving a trail of bodies behind him. But we have nothing concrete, except the consistencies [that link the deaths]."_
> (_Tampa Tribune_, Florida, 1975)

Detective Mussoline seemed to be referencing the serial murderer Ted Bundy, who was known to travel across the country in search of victims, of which he found many with uncannily proficient success. Every single one of Bundy's victims was a young women who had long dark hair parted at the centre. It may be that Bundy *was* responsible for the "Flat-Tire" crimes; it was certainly part of the handsome and charismatic killer's ruthlessly efficient *M.O.* to feign incapacity in order to lure trusting victims into his car. Perhaps he simply reversed this pattern in Florida: women in a predicament were only too grateful to be rescued by the knight in shining armour.

Whilst awaiting execution Bundy confessed to 30 murders, and hinted at many more. Estimates run as high as 100. He finally met his end in the electric chair in 1989, and the answer as to whether or not he duped women by deflating the tyres of their cars has gone with him to the grave.

The Gypsy Hill Killings
(active 1976)

THE FIRST THREE MONTHS of 1976 saw a spate of brutish murders in San Mateo County, California. It was, at that time, still an undeveloped rural area of woodland and chaparral-type scrubland, the perfect dumping ground for a recently-killed corpse.

On 8 January 1976 the first two of the killer's victims were found in Mateo County. Benito "Benny" Navarez was a 43-year-old unemployed man who had been staying at the Casa Mateo Inn. He had been dead three days when he was found with a large knife sticking out of his chest.

Eighteen-year-old Veronica Cascio's partially naked body was found near a creek next to a golf course. The part-time Skyline College student had been sexually assaulted and suffered over 30 stab wounds to the throat and abdomen. She had last been seen waiting for a bus to take her to the Skyline campus. A homeless man was arrested but later released for the lack of evidence.

The remains of 17-year-old Paula Baxter were the next to be found on 4 February. She had been reported missing two days before. Her body was found in some brush amongst a secluded grove of eucalyptus trees behind a church. Like Cascio, Baxter had been stripped and sexually assaulted. However, she had suffered the indignity of being smashed over the head with a large piece of concrete prior to being stabbed to death four times. Police linked the murder of Baxter to that of Cascio.

Tatiana Blackwell, a 14-year-old freshman at Oceana High School, would not be found until several months had elapsed after her disappearance. She had gone out to run an errand but did not return. At first it was assumed that she had run away from home, but on 6 June the mystery of her disappearance was resolved: Tatiana's body was found just one mile from her home, not far from Gypsy Hill Road. She had been stabbed to death. It was around this time that the killer began to be known as the "Gypsy Hill Killer".

Carol Booth, aged 26, was last seen walking home from a bus stop, taking a shortcut that ran alongside a golf driving range. Her husband reported her missing that same day, 15 March. Her skeletonised remains were found in a shallow grave near Kaiser Hospital, south of San Francisco, on 5 May. She had been stabbed to death by an unknown assailant.

When Denise Lampe, aged 19, failed to return home from the Serramonte Mall in Daly City, California her girlfriend became worried and set off to find her. She enlisted the help of a security guard and together they found the slumped body of Lampe on the front seat of her 1964 Mustang. She had been stabbed 20 times in the arms and chest. Newspaper reports announcing the murder linked it to the other "Gypsy Hill" killings.

Whilst the Gypsy Hill murders occurred exclusively in San Mateo County, two other murders have drawn the attention of investigators involved in the case.

In the north of California on 24 February 1976, just after eight o'clock in the evening, 19-year-old Michelle Mitchell's car malfunctioned. A passer-by helped her to push the car into the nearby parking lot of a school. Later that evening her body was found, her hands tied behind her back, her throat slashed. A tantalising clue remained at the scene – a cigarette butt. Three years after the murder of Mitchell a female psychiatric patient in Louisiana confessed to the murder. This would have ruled the murder out of the catalogue of Gypsy Hill murders but for the fact that in 2014 DNA profiling of the cigarette proved that it belonged to someone other than the confessor. The DNA sample, investigators discovered, matched semen samples taken from some of the Gypsy Hill murders. This evidence exculpated the convict and led to her exoneration.

The second murder also happened in San Francisco. Idell Friedman, aged 21, was found stabbed to death on the kitchen floor of her apartment on St Patrick's Day 1976. She had been raped and strangled with a lamp cord before being stabbed to death. Despite some similarities to the Gypsy Hill murders, the death of Friedmann was not officially linked to them.

Rodney Halbower was fingered as a suspect in the Gypsy Hill killings in 2004, 38 years after the San Mateo spree occurred. Born in 1948, Halbower had already spent time in prison in Nevada for burglary, theft, assault and rape, and for fleeing from prison. He was further convicted for rape and assault (stabbing his victim, who survived, several times) and sentenced to life imprisonment in Nevada. Released on parole in November 2013, he violated the terms of his parole and was immediately extradited to Oregon, where he began a 15-year sentence for the earlier crimes of rape and attempted murder. It was there that the DNA sample was taken which led to his extradition to California where, at the age of 70, he stood trial for the murders of Tanya Baxter and Veronica Cascio. He insisted that he was innocent of the crimes but the jury did not believe him and delivered a verdict of guilty.

Halbower, however, has not been connected to the other Gypsy Hill murders, and was ruled out of one of them due to being in prison at the time. But the case takes another twist. New DNA evidence links another convict, Leon Seymore, to the murder of Denise Lampe. The evidence conclusively places Seymore, who is already serving time as an inmate-prisoner for another string of kidnappings and sexual assaults dating back to the 1970s, in Lampe's car at the time she was murdered. Frustratingly, however, there is no evidence to suggest that Halbower and Seymour knew each other. Prosecutors may have to consider the possibility that what looks like a serial murder spree of one man may, in fact, have been the work of two or more killers.

The Oakland County Child Killer

(active 1976-1977)

UNTIL THE FIRST MONTHS of 1976, Oakland County, west of Detroit, Michigan, was a green and pleasant community. The sleepy suburb of Ferndale was serviced by wide, open, tree-lined roads where children laughed, played, and walked or cycled to school. A series of events, beginning in February and continuing for just over a year, put an end to the seasons of care-free innocence. Now parents accompanied their children to school and forbade them from being outside alone. With the demonic presence of the Oakland County Child Killer never far from the everyone's mind, a gloomy pall fell over the area, effectively clearing the streets of children who no longer felt safe to play outside. Alternatively known as "Babysitter", the killer – or killers – remains at large to this very day.

Mark Stebbins, a good-looking blond 12-year-old boy who had ambitions of becoming a Marine, was at a pool tournament with his mother on 15 February 1976. Bored, Mark asked his mother if he could leave to go home and watch a television movie. His mother agreed and at around noon Mark set off on the journey back home, a distance of around three-quarters of a mile. He never arrived.

Mark's mother phoned the house later to check up on him but got no answer. When she arrived home just before nine o'clock she found the house empty. At 23:00 his mother, panicked, called police dispatch and reported her son missing. He had been wearing a blue hooded parka, a red sweatshirt, blue jeans and black boots, she told them.

The initial thoughts of the police were that this was a runaway. They made a wide-ranging check of abandoned buildings across the district of Ferndale, assuming all the while that the boy would turn up sooner or later.

He did. Four days later, on 19 February, a local businessman saw what he thought was a mannequin discarded in the snow next to a dumpster. Upon closer inspection he realised that this was a body – a boy's. He had been placed there carefully and neatly, for the corpse was curled up and looked as if he were sleeping.

Police determined that the boy had been killed less than eight hours before being found. Extraordinarily, he had been washed and his fingernails clipped. His clothes had been laundered and ironed. It was for these solicitations that the killer would eventually gain the nickname "Babysitter".

The body "with rope burns on his neck and hands" was quickly identified as Mark Stebbins by his understandably distraught mother.

> *Police believe the boy had been killed elsewhere and his body dumped in the parking lot of the Fairfax Plaza office building at 15650 W. Ten Mile sometime after 3:30 a.m. Thursday [...]*
>
> *An autopsy was ordered to determine the cause of death and whether the boy had been sexually assaulted.*
> (*Detroit Free Press*, Detroit, Michigan, 1976)

An autopsy *did* confirm that the bound and strangled boy had been sexually assaulted prior to his death.

A psychiatrist attached to the investigation suggested attempting to lure the killer back to the dumpsite by placing a mannequin at the place where Mark's body had been located. This ruse, regretfully, did not catch the perpetrator. Instead, it seemed that the killer was happy to taunt the police. At the dumpsite they found a card from Mark's funeral service at the spot where he had been positioned. It seemed that Mark's murderer had attended the service and been missed. Mark's mother recalled that she had not recognised everyone who had come to the service. "I might have even shaken hands with the killer," she said.

The woman never recovered from the trauma of her son's death, and right up until her own death in 2011 she was tormented by the memories of that chilling day when her son was found murdered.

Then, 10 months later, another 12-year-old girl disappeared. Jill Robinson lived at home with her divorced mother and two sisters. She was a sweet, pretty, precocious girl who could also be challenging to her mother at times.

It was 22 December 1976 and the children's Christmas presents were set under the tree. Jill's mother asked her to prepare some biscuits for tea. Jill had other ideas and an argument ensured. Angrily, Jill's mother told her to go outside and think about her behaviour, a decision she would come to regret ever since.

Jill stomped out of the house, jumped on her bicycle and pedalled away from home. When she left home she was wearing a bright orange parka, blue jeans, a blue wool cap and black boots. A backpack she carried contained a blanket, a hairbrush, underwear, scissors and some cosmetics.

Jill's mother looked for her later but could find neither sight nor sound of her daughter. She called the police and reported her missing. The police initially considered that the youngster had run away and made a perfunctory check with Jill's friends and her father – to no avail. The police carried out no major sweep of the area during the first 48 hours after the disappearance. It was left to Jill's family to continue the search, despite the fact that her bicycle was found that evening outside a local hobby store, the last place she was confirmed to have been seen.

Then, the day after Christmas, a body was found in the snow alongside the I-75 about 20 minutes from Jill's home, and within sight of the local police station. Like Mark Stebbin's body, this too had not merely been dumped. Jill had been set down, carefully and neatly, in freshly laundered clothes. The only difference – Jill had been shot in the face with a shotgun. This major insult had removed half her head, but the cause of death was determined by the pathologist to have been loss of blood. Her body lay in the same location that she had been shot. The autopsy also revealed that Jill had not been sexually assaulted.

The news of Jill's murder stunned the family. "She's just kind of numb," Jill's mother' sister told the _Detroit Free Press_. "I'm just kind of numb right now. Everybody's kind of numb." A family friend summed it up: "Everyone's in a state of shock."

Jill Robinson had been shot. Mark Stebbins had been suffocated, and so also would soon-to-be-found victims nos. 3 and 4. The fact confounded police. However, Jill's mother recounted that her daughter had had a deep-seated dread that she would be shot and even had nightmares that a man would shoot her. Was it possible that her abductor came to discover this fear and in a perversely malignant act of evil made Jill's premonitions come true?

Seven short days after the body of Jill Robinson was found Kristine Mihelich went missing. The pretty, dark-haired girl (who was usually called Kris) was bored that day and wanted to go a local convenience store to buy a magazine. Despite her better judgement, her mother allowed Kris to go, but not before drilling into her 10-year-old daughter how to cross the road safely. After half-an-hour, at around three o'clock, when Kris failed to come home, her mother contacted the police. A store clerk tentatively remembered selling the young girl a teenage movie magazine, but after that Kris, it seemed, simply vanished off the face of the earth.

Kris' frantic mother exhausted herself with worry over the next 19 days keeping 24-hour vigils. She spoke to the media, begging for the safe return of her daughter, and even raised $17,000 as a reward for information.

Then, on the 20th day after Kris' disappearance came the news her mother had been dreading, delivered by a postal worker. The US Postal Service mailman spotted a body buried in snow down a dead-end street in nearby Franklin Village. It had been placed – carefully and neatly – as if laid down for sleep. The arms had been folded and snow had been packed and patted down around the body. The body was Mrs Mihelich's daughter, Kristine.

The autopsy report stated that the cause of Kris' death had been asphyxia caused by smothering, and recorded that the body had not been frozen, indicating that it had probably been left there less than 24-hours. Shockingly, Kris had been kept captive and alive in the days since her abduction. There was no evidence of sexual assault; however semen was found in both her rectum and vagina which could not be accounted for.[*]

Like Mark Stebbins and Jill Robinson, Kris Mihelich's body had been washed and her clothes laundered and ironed. However, Kris' mother believed that she had not dressed herself, pointing to two discrepancies: the blouse had been tied at the front, not the back as Kris would normally have tied it; and the trousers were tucked into the boots, which Kris never did.

Her mother gained some unexpected comfort from knowing that the murderer had not killed Kris straightaway. "Kris was a joy," she said. "This is why whoever took her and kept her so long was enjoying her company. At least this is what we have told ourselves, and I prefer not to think any differently." It must have been cold comfort.

Kris was the youngest victim of the Oakland's cold-blooded "Babysitter".

And he was becoming yet more audacious. With the terrified community of Oakland County on high alert the killer took another child, this time in broad daylight in front of witnesses.

Timothy King, aged 11, was a sweet-faced, reddish-haired boy who loved to skateboard and play sports. Although the youngest member of the family, Tim was sensible enough to have his own paper round and to babysit for other neighbourhood children.

On 16 March 1976, Tim's parents were going out for a couple of hours and they figured that their youngest son would be able to look after himself in their absence, a decision they undoubtedly, like the other parents, came to regret bitterly.

---

[*] A subsequent investigation detected no deposits of semen and it was determined that Kris had not been violated.

Tim's two brothers were already out, and his sister was pre-paring to leave for the evening herself. Before she left, Tim's sister gave him some money for candy and agreed to leave the front door ajar so that he could let himself in again. Then he left, skateboard in hand, heading towards a local drugstore. He was wearing a red jacket, denim shirt, green trousers and white ten-nis shoes.

Tim did not return home. His parents, upon returning home themselves, discovered the front door ajar and became alarmed. After scouring the neighbourhood and phoning his friends they called the police. They were very afraid, and with good reason; the recent abductions had spooked everyone. That night, Tim's brother roamed the neighbourhood with a baseball bat, hoping to deal his own brand of justice to his younger brother's kidnap-per.

Routine investigations established that Tim had made it to the drugstore and bought some candy. A witness reported that on the night of 16 March she had seen a boy wearing a red jacket – a fitting description of Tim – in the parking lot, talking to a shaggy-haired man with sideburns. The witness was also able to give a good description of the man's car. A wanted poster ad-vertising a $100,000 reward for information was issued.

Tim's father wrote an open letter to the abductor which was printed on the front page of the _Detroit News_. His mother prom-ised to get him a Kentucky Fried Chicken meal when he re-turned home safely. To no avail. Tim would not return home safely.

Six days later, in a ditch about one-and-a-half miles from his home, two teenagers spotted Tim's body, his skateboard lying 10 feet from him. He was wearing the same clothes he had worn upon leaving his home; they had been laundered and ironed. He had been set down … carefully and neatly.

The body was identified by his mother.

His death was listed as "smothered" and it was determined that this had happened around six to eight hours before the body had been discovered. The autopsy showed that Tim had marks on his wrists and ankles caused by binding. His body had been cleaned, including his finger- and toenails. There was evidence of anal rape. Troublingly, Tim had eaten a meal of fried chicken about an hour before being killed. Was it possible that his abductor had seen his mother in the press, making a plaintive promise to give Tim the same dish upon his return home? Had the "Babysitter" sought to taunt a mother in her moment of distress?

Experts who studied the murders drew up a psychological profile stating that:

> *... the killer is of above-average intelligence and education, a white man who has a compulsion for cleanliness and who is sot [sic, read "not"] involved with drugs or alcohol. He is believed to be in the white-collar class, possible a professional or someone in a position that suggests authority, someone who children would trust.*
>
> (*New York Times*, New York, 1976)

Certainly, it appeared that there was little or no force was used, and no commotions reported, during the abductions. The four children seemed to have gone willingly enough with their would-be assailant.

The abduction-murders stopped after this final crime and the authorities speculated that the killer had left the area, been arrested or died. However, the family was never to recover. Tim's mother was reportedly broken after the murder, "never the same", and the subject of his death became a "forbidden" topic of conversation. She died herself in 2004 never having seen justice for her youngest son.

In addition to the accepted crimes of the Oakland County Child Killer are three suspected abduction-murders. Cynthia Cadieux, aged 16, was bludgeoned to death on 16 January 1976. Jane Allen, aged 14, accepted a ride whilst hitchhiking in the local vicinity of Royal Oak. She died from carbon monoxide poisoning. Her body was found in a river in Ohio, 230 miles away. Kimberley King, aged 12, disappeared from nearby Macomb County, Michigan on 15 September 1979 and has never been found. Police consider it possible that the case may be a non-family abduction connected to the Oakland County killings. If still alive Kimberley has not come forward, despite appeals for her to do so.

Subsequent investigations into the case have thrown up some shocking theories.

One. A few weeks after Timothy King's death a task force psychiatrist received a mysterious letter from "Allen", who claimed to be the sadomasochistic slave of his roommate, "Frank". "Allen" alleged that "Frank", a veteran of the Vietnam War, had been so traumatised by having killed children during the war that he wanted rich people to suffer for having sent forces to Vietnam by killing their own children. "Allen", having accompanied "Frank" in his mission to find children to kill (although never there at the abductions or murders), was now suffering from remorse, fearing that he was losing his sanity and dreading that he was himself endangered. "Allen" offered to meet the psychiatrist in a bar and to provide photographic evidence in exchange for immunity from prosecution. "Allen", however, did not turn up to meet the psychiatrist at the appointed time. He was never heard from again.

Two. A convicted paedophile, Archibald Sloan, became a person of interest after hairs found in his car matched those found on the bodies of Mark Stebbins and Timothy King. DNA profiling on the hair indicated that they did not come from Sloan. A witness to the abduction of King stated he had seen him being taken by two men, one matching the description of Sloan, the other matching that of John Wayne Gacy, a serial killer of boys and young men who was thought to have been in Michigan at around the same time as the Oakland murders. The DNA of the hair did not match Gacy either. However, it does suggest that Sloan knew or lent his car to someone implicated in the murders.

Three. Ted Lamborgine is considered by investigators to be a suspect. He is believed to have been involved in a child pornography ring in the 1970s. He pleaded guilty to sex-crimes against young boys and is serving a life sentence in prison for those offences. When interrogated about the Oakland murders he is said to have said, "I've been forgiven." He refuses to take polygraph despite being offered a reduced sentence, simply saying, "I didn't do it." Another man is alleged to have made statements to the police that Lamborgine had showed him pornographic photos of a child resembling Timothy King. He is alleged to have stated that he would only give further information if he were to bargain for a deal.

Four. A man called Chris Busch has sparked interest. Busch had been suspected of involvement in homosexual child pornography around the time of Timothy King's abduction. Busch is alleged to have committed suicide by shotgun in 1978 – one shot between the eyes, although four bullet casing were found – one year after the four Oakland killings ended. However, there was no shotgun residue on the body, which incidentally had also been wrapped up beneath sheets … carefully and neatly.

A bloodstained ligature was found in Busch's bedroom. And, pinned to the wall, was a chilling hand-drawn picture of a boy, apparently screaming in agony. The image is such a strong resemblance to the first murder victim, Mark Stebbins, it could almost have been copied from a still image.

A dead body left "neat and tidy". Four spent bullet casings. *Four*. A mysterious drawing of a screaming boy. Had some unknown person dispensed the "Babysitter" a sentence that authorities had not been able to serve?

The case is still open. It is very much active and has not stalled, for the relatives themselves and the wider public are still keen for answers, and they continue to push investigators to bring the guilty to justice.

The four Oakland crimes may have been the work of a single monstrously demented man – the "Babysitter", now incapacitated or imprisoned or dead. Or the crimes could have been the handiwork of a ring of sadistic child pornographers, whose deviant fixations and lusts overrode all other considerations, even to the extent that abduction and murder were seen as not only an acceptable but a necessary price to pay – even though it was the victims, ultimately, who paid that price.

The Skid Row Stabber
(active 1978-1979)

DURING THE 1970s, Los Angeles – so-called "City of Angels" – had become a place where angels feared to tread. The metropolis was gripped by such an unprecedented surge in violent crime that, to stretch the idiom further, even fools hesitated to rush in. As the population grew, so did the rate of crime, with violent crime and homicides more than doubling in the space of a single decade between the '60s and the '70s.

Skid Row, a neighbourhood in Downtown Los Angeles, was established unofficially in 1976. Here, homelessness was tolerated and, although not exactly encouraged, at the very least a blind eye was turned by local government officialdom. Services and missions which fed and sheltered the dispossessed, already in place to a degree, became more organised and established. This became a draw to further itinerant immigrants and people on the margins of society. Although the range of the community was broadly spread by age in the 1970s, around fifty percent of the population was of Afro-American racial makeup.

In 1978 a spate of 11 knife-signature murders in the area defined the crimes of the Skid Row Stabber. It began on 23 October with the apparently random murder of 50-year-old Jesse Martinez, whose blood-soaked body was found sprawled in a parking lot that morning. Initially the case was not reported widely, probable factors being the low profile of victim and the escalating rate of murders within the city. The death of one homeless bum was hardly headline news!

Then, less than a week later, 32-year-old Jose Cortes was killed in an alley, and the following day 46-year-old Bruce Drake was found dead on a sidewalk – both of them knifed to death in the Skid Row area. The next to die was 65-year-old J.P, Henderson on 4 November, whilst on 9 November 39-year-old David Jones was brutally stabbed. Just two days later, on 11 November, 57-year-old Francisco Rodriguez became the sixth victim.

The Stabber's audacity increased. The next day Frank Reed, aged 36, was found and, just 15 minutes later, Augustine Luna, aged 49, was discovered. A double murder – both stabbed, both left sprawled in the spot where they had been sleeping. Now the newspapers were starting to take notice. "Toll Now 8 in Transient Stabbings," wrote a _Los Angeles Times_ reporter who went on to report on the congregation of frightened drifters:

> _Despite the chill rain falling this morning, many transients were standing outside bars and flophouses in Skid Row murmuring to themselves and to anyone who would listen to their concern over the murders._
> (_Los Angeles Times_, Los Angeles, 1978)

On 17 November the body of Milford Fletcher, a 34-year-old Native American, was next to be discovered. Like the others, Fletcher had been ferociously stabbed to death and his remains lay at the scene of the murder.

On 23 November, in the downtown civic centre of Los Angeles, the remains of 45-year-old Frank Garcia were found on a park bench. He had been stabbed to death. All of the other murders had occurred in the still alleys or parking lots of Skid Row. This one was different. Even more shockingly, it had occurred in a prestigious part of the city, within sight of a large crowd. The slayer had simply walked up to his victim, made the killing and left undetected. It could easily be thought that the Skid Row Stabber had wanted to go out in style, for the murdering spree suddenly stopped after the audacious death of Garcia.

In April 1979 Bobby Joe Maxwell was arrested for the Skid Row murders on the basis of palm prints that had been found close to two of the murders. At the time the black transient worker was portrayed as a Satan-worshipping maniac although it is likely that he was not. He was known, in fact, to have been a semi-literate martial arts enthusiast who had moved to the city in 1977 with hopes of becoming a karate instructor. He, like the stabbing victims, had fallen into homelessness himself.

Apart than the palm prints was other evidence, which is now considered "weak". This consisted of a disposable lighter found on Maxwell, which a victim's wife said was similar to one that her husband had owned. The wife was not able to pick out this lighter from an array shown to her. Another witness claimed to have recognised Maxwell's voice at a crime scene. However, the witness was not able to pick the suspect out of a line-up during which he spoke.

Maxwell was tried and convicted of two of the murders, those of Frank Garcia and David Jones. The jury, who had acquitted him on five charges and were deadlocked on the other three, voted to spare him the death penalty. He was committed to life in prison without chance of parole.

The evidence of a frequent recidivist and habitual liar, Sidney Storch, could only be described as questionable, to say the least. Storch claimed that Maxwell had repeatedly claimed responsibility for the crimes. However, unbeknownst to Maxwell's defence team at the time, Storch had made a secret deal with the District Attorney for a reduced sentence in exchange for his testimony.

Other evidence came from witnesses who reported having spoken to the Stabber, who had introduced himself as "Luther", just before killing David Jones. They recalled the suspect having a Puerto Rican accent, which Maxwell, a native of Tennessee, did not have. In a line-up one witness was reported to have said, "You've got everyone up there that *doesn't* look like him."

Three months later, an inscription was found on the toilet wall in a local bus terminal: "*My name is Luther I kill winos and I put them out of their misery*". Handwriting experts were to match the writing to Maxwell's, and this tenuous evidence, it seems, sealed the fate of Maxwell during his trial.

An examination of the prosecution's evidence showed that the case against Maxwell was weak, leading to a Court of Appeals ruling in 2010 that it was "nearly all circumstantial", and some of it, in fact, contradictory.

Maxwell consistently asserted his innocence. Storch, the informant died of AIDS-related complications in 1992 and that eventuality precluded the possibility of a recantation of his testimony. Maxwell's sentence was overturned by the Appellate Court in 2010 and a new trial was ordered. However, in 2017, Maxwell suffered a cardiac arrest. A new trial in 2018 found Maxwell, who had by now fallen into a coma, not guilty of the charged levelled against him. Officially he was exonerated due to false or misleading forensic evidence, perjury or false accusation and official misconduct. He died in a Los Angeles hospital on 28 April 2019, aged 69, without having regained his consciousness. "They stole his life," Maxwell's younger sister said.

The true identity of the Skid Row Stabber may never be known.

The Redhead Murders
[active 1978-1992]

SEVERAL DEFINITIONS of serial murder have been used over the years to describe the acts of this secretive species of killer. Common to previous definitions was the specific number of murders involved, beginning with a body count from at least two victims. However, this did not account for other multiple murderers such as mass murderers, who may have killed several people in the same incident; nor for spree killers, who will have killed many times over a short, unfolding period of time.

Serial murder, however, is generally marked by a different central element: a temporal separation between each of the murders. This "cooling off" period allows the serial killer to return to a level of emotional normalcy following the intense passions associated with the murder event itself. Hence the FBI specified four factors to be included in its definition of serial murder: (i) the criminality of the act, (ii) quantity of murders, (iii) separation of events, and (iv) separation by time. The agency crafted the following definition: "The unlawful killing of two or more victims by the same offender(s), in separate events".

Sometimes a serial killer will revel in his crimes, delighting in leaving bodies where they will be easily found or taunting the authorities with notes claiming ownership of the murders. However, many times it is not always easy to identify that a series of murders *is* the handwork of a single killer – at least not at first. Several factors can work in the serial killer's favour to disguise the fact of the matter. Frequently, they will seek to hide their crimes, leaving bodies hidden in remote, difficult-to-access places. They can repeatedly target victims leading high-risk lifestyles – for example, hitchhikers, sex workers, drug addicts, the homeless. The transient existences of such people can oftentimes hide the fact that a crime has indeed been committed at all. Geographical distance is therefore another element that makes linking the crimes difficult. Serial killers have been known to travel widely in the search for victims. They will pick up hitchhikers and prostitutes and drive long distances before succumbing to their cruel impulses. The victims may not be found for a long time, and the deterioration of the remains can make it difficult to establish that a death has not been by means of suicide, or by natural or accidental causes. And sometimes the bodies of those who have vanished are simply _never_ found, and those looking for them may come to assume that they have run away and do not wish to be found. In some tragic cases the disappearances will not even have been reported at all.

Coupled with these elements is the fact that occasionally there is a lack of communication between different law enforcement agencies, across multiple jurisdictions. These difficulties can and often do impede the linkage of cases to a common perpetrator.

Additionally, sometimes there are differences between the actual crimes themselves – variations between the _modi operandi_ associated with the individual crimes – that delay recognition that they are connected. Sometimes the details just do not match, and an apparently random killing will look just like that – a single, apparently random killing.

This was the case in the series of murders that became to be known as the "Redhead Murders". Spanning many states, using different _M.O.s_, targeting different victim types, at first it was not clear that the deaths were the work of a single murderer. Only one "common" factor linked most of the crimes – the victims had red-coloured hair – and even that was not a true commonality.

Five young, white women have been linked in the case that continues to this day to baffle investigators from several states of the American East – New Hampshire, Pennsylvania, Indiana, West Virginia, Kentucky, Tennessee, Arkansas and Mississippi. Some think that up to 11 are linked. The total is unlikely to become known.

The series may have begun on 13 February 1983, when a pair of senior citizens out walking in Wetzel County, West Virginia noticed what they at first thought was a shop mannequin. They discovered, upon investigation, that this was in fact the body of a naked female. There was fresh snow on the ground, but not on the body, signifying that she had not long been at that site. Tyre tracks and footprints indicated that she had been brought there, most likely transported after death, a fact confirmed by an autopsy which concluded that she had died around two days before being discovered. The woman had not been sexually assaulted. The cause of death could not be determined with certainty although it was believed that she had been suffocated. She had auburn-coloured hair.

The woman's age was estimated to have been between 35 and 45, her height 5'6" and weight 135lbs. At one stage the woman had been a mother – she had the distinctive scar of a Caesarean section. Her legs and underarms were shaven, suggesting the victim had looked after her personal grooming and was more than likely not to have led a transient lifestyle. Witnesses recalled having seen a middle-aged white male – about 5'10' tall, 185-200lbs weight – near the spot where the body was found. The woman's identity remains unknown at this time and she is a suspected victim of the Redhead Murder.

On 16 September 1984 a body wearing only a sweater was found by a hitchhiker along Interstate 40 near West Memphis, Arkansas. She had been strangled. The strawberry-blond victim was not identified until nine months had passed, in June 1985, by which stage a further five bodies had been found. It was further believed that she had been estranged from her family. Her body was identified by a couple from Florida with whom she had stayed for a short period. Her name was Lisa Nichols, a 28-year-old resident of West Virginia. It was believed that she left a truck stop in order to attempt to hitchhike.

The bound, still-clothed body of a woman was found on New Year's Day 1985, down an embankment near Jellico, Tennessee. Although she had been killed only an estimated three days before being found, the remains were in an advanced state of putrefaction. Cause of death was strangulation. Her slight body had been wrapped in a blanket – presumably by her killer – which was later found to have been stained with seminal fluid. The young woman's body was scarred and there was a burn mark on one arm. She carried a foetus of around 10-12 weeks.

The remains remained unidentified until 6 September 2018, when it was announced that her name was Tina Farmer, a native of Indiana, aged 21 at the time of her death. It was said that she had last been seen in Indianapolis, Indiana in the company of a truck driver who was heading to Kentucky. She was never seen alive again. She was survived by a daughter who has since died herself.

In 2019, DNA profiling linked a convict, Jerry Johns, to the murder of Farmer. Johns had previously been jailed for kidnapping and assaulting another woman, two months after the disappearance of Farmer. The other woman had also been bound, strangled using a knotted strip of cloth, and dumped along the I-40. She survived the attack and her testimony helped put Johns behind bars. Like Farmer and other victims, the woman had red hair. Johns died in prison in 2017 at the age of 67. A grand jury ruled that had he been alive he would have been indicted for the murder of Farmer.

The skeleton of a red-haired female was found in the inaptly named Pleasant View, Cheatham County, Tennessee on 31 March 1985. It was estimated that she had died between two to five months prior. Cause of death was indeterminable. She was a petite woman of around five-feet tall; her weight was unknowable. She remains unidentified.

The next day, across the northern state border, the body of a woman was found in a refrigerator in Gray, Knox County, Kentucky. Cause of death was strangulation and she had been dead just a few days. The woman was around 4'9" tall, had hazel-coloured eyes, a few moles and scars on her body, and there were indications that she had given birth to a child. She had long hair, auburn at the front and darkish-brown at the rear. When discovered, the woman was naked, apart from two pairs of socks and two distinctive necklace pendants.

It was these pendants that eventually led to the victim's identification in 2018. After the case was publicised, a woman, having recognised the jewellery, came forward to identify the body as that belonging to her daughter Espy Pilgrim. Pilgrim had, indeed, had a daughter, as well as four older children, and it was from familial DNA that a positive identification was made. Pilgrim had been aged 35 when she died.

On 3 April 1985 partial remains of a girl, aged around 9-15, were discovered four miles southwest of Jellico, where Tina Farmer's body was found. A knotted strip of cloth, similar to that used on the surviving victim of Jerry Johns, was found near the body. It was estimated that she had been dead between one to four years. A facial reconstruction was made from the skull, but this has not brought forth any clues to her identity. Her name remains unknown.

Then, on 14 April 1985, another body turned up, the fifth in three-and-a-half months. The victim had been dead an estimated three to six weeks before being discovered in Greenville, Tennessee. Death was caused by blunt-force trauma to the head and possibly stabbing. A slight female of around 5'4" tall, weighing 130-140lbs, she had been pregnant around six to eight weeks. She miscarried just before death. She had had dental work done and her fingernails were painted pink. Although the body was in an advanced state of decomposition, it was possible to retrieve fingerprints. These did not help identify her. The woman had light brown, almost blond hair with red highlights.

The body came to be identified in a roundabout way. Another unidentified woman was believed to have been the victim of serial killer Terry Rasmussen. The Lamotte family provided a DNA sample in 2017 in order to compare with the profile of that victim, who was known by the first name of Elizabeth. In November 2018, the UNT Center for Human Identification found a match between the donated sample and that of the body discovered in Greenville. Elizabeth Lamotte was identified 34 years after having gone missing on some date in 1984. Lamotte, from New Hampshire, had been residing in the southern states before her death. She is a suspected victim of the Redhead Murderer.

Estrangement from family and geographical relocation may account for the overdue identification of many of the victims. Moreover, differences in the *M.O.* and inconsistencies of victim type meant that the cases were not linked until much later. Some of the victims were clothed, others had clothing removed; some had been bound, others had not. Evidence of a sexual motive (seminal fluid) was left on at least one of the bodies. And despite the catchy nickname of the Redhead Murderer, only three of the believed victims had red hair; the others had strawberry-blond hair or were dark-haired.

Although investigators will not be drawn to make a connection between the "redhead murders", it is likely that some of this baffling series of killings *were* the work of the same individual, who picked up hitchhikers or sex workers before strangling them to death. His motivation may have been an intense distaste for transient people or those working in a dubious profession. We do not know. Unless there is a break in the case with new forensic evidence the answer may never be known.

The Connecticut River Valley Killer
(active 1978-1979)

THE BOUNDARY BETWEEN THE STATES of Vermont and New Hampshire is illustrated on maps by the gently rolling Connecticut River as it flows in a southerly direction through rich and verdant land. On the west side is Vermont; to the east, New Hampshire. The two states share similar cultures and demography, although the population of Vermont is less than half that of its neighbourly state. They are geographical twins; even a native would be hard pressed to tell the difference between the two. It is generally a quiet and peaceful place to live.

And yet, in the late '70s and early '80s, on a patch of land within the Connecticut River Valley, residents were terrorised by a rapacious knife-wielding killer. New Hampshire bore the brunt of the unknown killer's crimes; this side of the river was his preferred hunting ground. Yet, across the border, Vermont did not escape lightly, for the killer's malignant touch was felt there too. The "Valley Killer", as he came to be known, would claim the lives of at least six women … and possibly more.

Local law enforcement only came to believe that they had a serial murderer on their patch after considering the discovery of three bodies.

The first body found belonged to Ellen Fried. On 20 July 1984, Fried, a 27-year-old senior nurse, stopped at a convenience store in Claremont, New Hampshire and used the payphone there to phone her sister. After talking for almost an hour, Fried became spooked. It was just before midnight and she had noticed a car going back and forth. She remarked upon it to her sister. Perturbed, she briefly stepped away from the phone, turned over her own car's engine to make sure it would start and then returned to the call. After talking a few moments the two sisters ended their chat and bade each other goodbye. That was the last time anyone was to hear from Fried. The next day her abandoned car was found a few miles from the convenience store.

A deer-hunter found skeletal remains on 19 September 1985. It was not until 1 October that the remains were identified as Fried. Finding evidence of some stab wounds, the pathologist failed to determine the cause of death with surety but recorded that she had been stabbed in the neck.

The second body was a recent death that occurred in Westminster, Vermont on 15 April 1986 and the remains were still warm when found. Thirty-six-year-old Lynda Moore was murdered in a confined space in her own home. She had put up a fierce struggle to defend herself for her arms and hands were crisscrossed by deep slash wounds. Her husband, upon his return from work, found the bloodied body just a few hours after the assault. It was a very grisly sight. The victim's hands were clenched into fists, except for one pointing finger, which had failed to tighten into a _post mortem_ fist, probably due to a severed tendon. The pathologist revealed that Moore had died by the stabs of a long knife to her throat and abdomen. The husband's involvement in the death was quickly ruled out. Witnesses reported having seen a youngish, slightly stocky, dark-haired, bespectacled man in the vicinity on the day of the murder. The lead was developed but it ultimately went nowhere and the trail grew cold.

Third to be found was Bernice Courtemanche, just four days after the remains of Lynda Moore were found. The pretty, dark-haired 17-year-old nurse's aide had last been seen at around 15:30 on 30 May 1984 in Claremont, New Hampshire by her boyfriend's mother. She set off to visit her boyfriend eight miles away in Newport, New Hampshire. She had decided to hitch-hike to her destination and she was spotted thumbing for a lift along Route 12. She was not seen alive again.

Courtemanche's remains lay undiscovered for nearly two years until, on 19 April 1986, her skeleton was found by two fishermen off a dirty road near Kelleyville, New Hampshire. The body had been dumped on a narrow forest lane close to where Reid had been discarded. Due to the condition of the remains a *post mortem* examination could not identify with certainty the cause of death; however, it was likely that she had died from stab wounds to the neck. She was identified by her dental records.

Investigators believed that these three deaths were connected; the similarities were felt to be too great to be coincidental. Then they cast their minds back to two New Hampshire cold cases from 1978 and 1981, another two murders which seemed consistent to the *M.O.* of their sadistic serial killer.

Cathy Millican was an attractive 26-year-old employee of a local publishing house and she was probably the killer's first victim. On the afternoon of 24 October 1978, Cathy, a keen birdwatcher, was seen photographing birds at a wetland preserve in New London, New Hampshire. The next day, her body was found near to where she had been last seen. She had been stabbed to death, her body containing at least 29 wounds.

And on 25 July 1981, dark-haired Elizabeth Critchley was hitchhiking near Interstate 91, travelling towards Waterbury, Vermont, where she lived. The body of the 37-year-old university student was found just over two weeks later in a wooded area in Unity, New Hampshire. Due to the decomposed state of the body the medical examiner was unable to determine how she had died. Both women, investigators now considered, were possible victims of a burgeoning serial killer in their midst. The locality of the dump sites (all bodies had been found within a 10-mile patch of forested land), the specific wound patterns, the comparable victim-type – these indicators pointed to all five murders having been committed by common perpetrator. If this was the case, it was likely he would kill again.

Shockingly, the investigators' fears were confirmed sooner than they thought possible.

Just a week later, on 25 April 1986, another body turned up. This would turn out to be factory worker Eva Morse, a 27-year-old single mother, who had been missing since the morning of 10 July 1985 after leaving the factory where she worked. Her intentions had been to hitchhike to visit a friend. She never made it. Loggers found her body around 150 yards from where Elizabeth Critchley's corpse had been discovered. Her skeletonised remains showed evidence of stab wounds. Now investigators knew a serial killer was stalking their bucolic borderlands.

Nine months later, the killer struck again. Barbara Agnew, a 38-year-old nurse, was murdered on or around 10 January 1987. She disappeared whilst travelling home from a skiing trip. Her abandoned car was found, parked in an unlit area near a Vermont rest stop just 10 miles from her home. That evening, a snowplough driver noticed the car door cracked open and blood on the steering wheel. Eleven weeks were to pass before Agnew's body was found across the river in Hartland, Vermont under an apple tree – as the snow began to thaw. Indications were that she, like the others, had been stabbed in the throat and abdomen.

Investigators were perplexed as to the reason why Agnew interrupted her journey home that snowy day. Perhaps the answer lay in her occupation. Agnew was a nurse, the third nurse to die on the slayer's roster of murder. Had she pulled over to help a stranger in need? Agnew's sister would later say that doing so would have been very much in character for the nurse whose caring nature and professionalism were unquestioned.

People reacted as expected: they bought guns for self-defence and attended self-defence classes; they offered rewards for information. And inevitably, they grew suspicious of neighbours and strangers alike.

The _Boston Globe_ described the pall-like dread that blanketed the district:

> _The nurse's death – following four other savage murders in the last three years – fed a fear that licks this valley like wisps of morning fog: Is there a single murderer, a "serial killer," at large along the Vermont-New Hampshire border?_
>
> (_Boston Globe_, Boston, Massachusetts, 1987)

The newspaper also reported the investigators' uncomforting depiction of the serial killer as a decent, outwardly average man, hiding in plain sight under the cloak of propriety:

> *Vermont police ... released some conclusions about the psychological profiles, which portray a murderer who may be living an otherwise normal and respectable life in the nearby area: a family man, perhaps, with a good job and a house in a quiet neighborhood.*
> (*Boston Globe*, Boston, Massachusetts, 1987)

Detective Sergeant Ron DeVincenzi appealed to the public for help:

> *"We're looking for someone who is your next-door neighbor type, but someone who is a little weird, perhaps. Who goes to work, has a family, children – but goes out certain nights and stays out all night."*

A criminal profiler who was tasked to develop an insight into the mindset of the killer visited the sites where the bodies of the victims had been found. John Philpin believed that the killer was a local who pre-selected his sites, choosing them in order to induce fear and panic in his prey before killing them. The residents of the area were not exactly comforted by the details of this description. However, there were no more random killings using the same *M.O.* and, as it seemed as if the killer had ceased his monstrous ministrations, the inhabitants of the valley began to breathe a little easier.

And then detectives got a break – of sorts. At around midnight on 6 August 1988, 22-year-old Jane Boroski, who was seven months pregnant at the time, was returning home from a country fair. She stopped at a closed convenience store in West Swanzey, New Hampshire where she bought a soft drink from a vending machine and then returned to her car. As she sat in the car, downing her drink, Boroski noticed a Jeep parked alongside her.

In her rear-view mirror she noticed the owner of the Jeep walk around the back of her vehicle. He approached the driver's side of her vehicle and spoke to her through the open window, asking her if the payphone was working. Immediately, he grabbed her and pulled her from the vehicle. The man accused Boroski of beating up his girlfriend and asked her if she had Massachusetts plates on her car. Boroski stated her car had New Hampshire plates, but the man was undeterred, proceeding to stab her 27 times with a long-bladed knife before leaving his victim at the edge of death.

Incredibly, Boroski survived. Severely wounded and bloodied, she returned to her car and began to drive herself two miles towards a friend's house for help. However, on the way she was horrified to see a Jeep travelling on the road in front of her and realised it was her attacker. She arrived at the house of her friend and the occupants immediately came to her aid. But the driver of the Jeep appeared to have noticed Boroski's movements; the vehicle lingered a moment, made a U-turn and stopped in front of the house for a while, before suddenly speeding off into the pitch night.

Boroski was treated for her considerable injuries at hospital. Fortunately, her baby survived, but not without suffering complications of her own. Boroski was able to give a description of her would-be slayer and the first three numbers of his license plate. She was able to remember under hypnosis that her attacker had been extremely cold, calm and collected throughout the assault. She also recalled that once she had stopped struggling he lost interest and stopped the attack. Her recollections enabled a police artist in the preparation of a sketch of a thin-faced white male of around 35-40 years of age. Despite this and another composite sketch, no arrests were made. After the attack on Boroski, the Connecticut River Valley killings ceased and the investigation came to a standstill.

Three names have become attached to the case. Delbert Tallman, a convicted child molester, raped and stabbed to death 16-year-old Heidi Martin whilst she jogged in Hartland, Vermont.

Her body was found in swampy ground behind a local school. Tallman confessed to the crime, was arraigned on homicide charges in 1984, tried and convicted. He later recanted his confession and was acquitted. Tallman was never really a serious suspect as the Valley Killer. There was no evidence against him, connections were tenuous, the timeline simply did not fit, and the age given by Boroski of her attacker did not match that of Tallman at the time of that attack. It is believed that Tallman is currently serving a prison sentence for unrelated crimes.

Michael Nicholaou became identified as a suspect although his connection too is uncertain. A veteran of the Vietnamese war, he was once described by company colleagues as a man "with a dark side", who had once left camp with a knife seeking hand-to-hand combat with the enemy. His wife disappeared in 1988, and in 2005 he killed his second wife, his daughter and himself in a murder-suicide. Nicholaou lived in Virginia when at least three of the Connecticut Valley River killings occurred. However, it is thought that he was familiar with the killing ground area and it is known that he owned a Jeep. Jane Boroski stated that there was "some resemblance" between Nicholaou and the man who attacked her, but this was not until 2006, some 18 years after the attack.

In a couple of interesting side-notes, Nicholaou's first wife had been a nurse – just like some of the victims of the Valley Killer – and his mother had worked at a hospital. Furthermore, Nicholaou was a black belt in karate. Jane Boroski had also recalled that her attacker had used martial arts during the attack. To this day, however, Nikolaou has not been conclusively linked to the Connecticut River Valley killings. DNA profiling may yield results at some stage but so far none has been forthcoming.

In a final twist, Gary Westover, a paraplegic from New Hampshire, made a deathbed confession of his involvement in the murder of Barbara Agnew. He recounted to an uncle that on the night of Agnew's murder, three friends had picked the wheelchair-bound man up for what he called "a night of partying".

They loaded him into their van, then drove to Vermont where they abducted and murdered Agnew and then dumped the body.

On his deathbed, Westover gave the name of the three men who had killed Agnew. Westover's uncle recorded the names on a piece of paper and reportedly gave it to police and it is believed that the scrap of paper is still in their possession. It is not known whether police enacted upon the information given to them.

John Philpin, the criminal profiler, believes that Westover's deathbed confession may have some credibility: "Given the point that this guy was at in his life, I can't see why he would be telling anything other than the truth. What does he have to lose? What does he have to gain?" Could Westover have been used as bait to lure Barbara Agnew from her car during a snowstorm? There is speculation that Westover came to know Michael Nicholaou through veteran connections. The supposition is certainly plausible.

The case is still in the hands of the Vermont and New Hampshire Police's cold cases unit. The newspapers refer to it now and then, and Internet sleuths occasionally come up with and deliberate over new theories, but so far no prime suspects have been named and the case remains unsolved.

The Tube Sock Killings
(active 1985)

MINERAL IS A SMALL VILLAGE set in the rural countryside of Lewis County, Washington. As its name suggests, the bucolic town of Mineral originally began life as the residence of miners prospecting for gold in the late 1800s. Instead they found coal and arsenic. But when those mines eventually failed many of the town's residents left to find their fortunes elsewhere. There is not much in Mineral – a small school, a couple of taverns, a municipal centre – but the village does have the honour of being the locale of the smallest post office in the US. With an accompanying creek and a rich, blue-watered lake going by the same name, these days Mineral is primarily a tourist attraction for day-trippers and anglers. In its heyday, the town once boasted 4,000 residents, but now there are fewer than 300.

In 1985 Edward Smith and Kimberley La Vine, aged 26 and 27 respectively, were an engaged couple enjoying their lives together. The good-looking couple had first met at university in Dartmouth, New Hampshire where they fell madly for each other. After their graduation they crossed the States, moving to Kent, Washington on the west coast, working there as accountants in a government agency. They became engaged and planned to tie the knot that summer "back home" in the east.

On Saturday, 9 March 1985, the couple went away for the weekend. They had plans to explore the scenic surroundings and landmarks of Grant County, Washington, three hours journey along the I-90, travelling in La Vine's vehicle. Their actions or movements that Saturday during the trip are not known, but the next day the deceased body of a young white adult male was found by hunters in a gravel pit in Beverly, not far from the Wanapum Dam. His hands had been bound behind his back, his feet were bound, and his throat had been slashed. No car, however, was to be seen in the vicinity. There was no documentation on the body and identification could not be established at that time.

The following Monday, after the couple uncharacteristically failed to arrive for work and could not be contacted by telephone, their employer reported them missing.

Two weeks later, La Vine's car was discovered on a high overlook above the Columbia, abandoned around 10 miles from where the body in the gravel pit had been found. The car and body matched descriptions already known and it was quickly established that the body belonged to Edward Smith. His fiancée could not be found and investigators had little hope of finding her alive. A single fingerprint, not belonging to the couple, was found on the vehicle.

Five months later, on 19 August 1985, the skeletal remains of Kim La Vine were located, purely by chance, in a sage bush, one-and-a-half miles away from where Smith had been murdered. She had also been bound by the hands and feet. The cause of death could not be established due to the state of the remains; however, the pathologist unsurprisingly ruled that she had been murdered. The single fingerprint found on La Vine's car was not to be identified until four years had passed, and not before another four homicides had been committed.

Twenty-seven-year-old Stephen Harkins and his older girl-friend, Ruth Cooper, aged 42, were both employees of a vocational school. After leaving a wedding reception on 10 August 1985, they went on a weekend camping adventure at Lake Tule, near Tacoma, Washington, bringing their dog with them. When they did not return to work the following Monday they were reported missing by their families. Four days after when they were last seen, hikers chancing upon the remote campsite found Harkins dead in his sleeping bag with a fatal shot to the head. It seemed as though he had been shot whilst sleeping. The dog, nearby, had also been shot dead. A skull was found four months later, along a dead-end road near Harts Lake, Washington. The decapitated body was found a short distance away, with a tube sock around the neck. A purse was nearby. Corroborating dental records later identified the skull as belonging to Cooper. Little else is known about the crimes, but the medical examiner recorded that Cooper had died by "homicidal violence" by reason of a gunshot wound to the abdomen. Police suspected that the case was connected to the recent murders of Smith and La Vine.

Four months later the idyllic Washington forests would again turn bloody. On 12 December 1985 Mike Riemer, aged 36, and his 21-year-old girlfriend, Diana Robertson, went for a trip to Nisqually River to search for a Christmas tree, taking with them their two-year-old daughter, Crystal.

That evening Crystal was found wandering the carpark of a K-Mart, 30 miles away in Spanaway, Washington. She had been crying and was distraught but she was otherwise unharmed. Her parents were not to be found in the vicinity and so locals contacted the police.

Two days later, Robertson's mother saw Crystal on the news and came forward to claim kinship of her granddaughter. When asked where her parents were, all Crystal could say was, "Mommy was in the trees."

It was not until 18 February 1986 that a development in the case arose. A motorist who had stopped to walk his dog found a partially decomposed female body in snow on Washington State Route 7, deep in a thickly forested area. A tube sock was fastened tightly around the woman's neck. A red Plymouth pickup truck was nearby. Blood was spattered across the front seats and left inside the car was a note written on an envelope with the words *I love you, Diana*. These developments led investigators to determine that the female body belonged to Diana Robertson. A pathologist reported that she had suffered 17 stab wounds. There was no sign of Mike Riemer.

Riemer became the prime suspect in the death of Robertson and, due to the similarities of the deaths, also of the murders of Stephen Harkins and Ruth Cooper.

Riemer had a history of domestic violence and had been arrested for assaulting her in October 1985. He was known as an outdoorsy man, who supplemented his income by trapping minks, bobcats and other wild animals for their fur, and it was thought that he would have had the expertise to survive in the wild. He remained a strong suspect in the strange "Tube Sock" murders for many years.

Four years later, the cold case was revived with fresh evidence. The single fingerprint found on Kimberley La Vine's car was identified as belonging to Billy Ray Ballard, an inmate in Wyoming State Penitentiary. The former truck driver pled guilty to the double-murder as part of a plea bargain to avoid the death penalty and he now serves a life sentence for the crime. His earliest date of parole in 2021. A local county prosecutor, John Knodell, is not enthusiastic about any imminent release: "We don't ever want to have him see the light of day."

Then, twenty-five years later, came a late development. In March 2011, the partial skull of Riemer turned up, not a mile from the location where the remains of his girlfriend, Diana Robertson, were found. An autopsy was not able to conclude how he died, although lack of damage to the skull ruled out suicide by gunshot to the head. However, investigators have now eliminated him as a suspect in the deaths of his girlfriend and Stephen Harkins and Ruth Cooper. Nevertheless, some believe that Riemer may actually have had some involvement. Could he have dropped his daughter Crystal off at a store 30 miles away, then doubled back, ended Robertson's life and then his own? It's certainly possible. Or did an unknown killer slaughter both Riemer and Robertson and then conceal Robertson's body in order to make it look like a murder-suicide? This would seem a risky strategy given that such an individual would still have had to deal with the couple's two-year-old daughter without arousing suspicion. It may be that the perpetrator of the two unsolved double-murders is already languishing in a prison, serving a sentence for yet another double-murder. Although implausible, without evidence these theories cannot be conclusively discounted. If guilty, Billy Ray Ballard, up for parole in 2021, is unlikely to volunteer a late confession.

It may also be possible that the unknown killer, whose arousal is kindled by disturbing thoughts of tube socks, may still be prowling Washington's deep woods … or further afield.

The Honolulu Strangler
(active 1985-1986)

THE HAWAIIAN ISLANDS, in the Pacific Ocean, is America's newest
state and the only one located outside the North American landmass. A paradisal archipelago, it basks in tropical heat all year
long. Its golden, sun-drenched beaches attract countless tourists
annually, the majority of them flocking to the island of Oahu.
Honolulu is the state's party-loving capital. Its name means
"sheltered harbour" or "calm port". With good reason. Honolulu
is widely accepted as one of the safest US cities to live in. However, for a while in the mid-1980s that perception changed, for
it was during that time that the streets of Honolulu had the misfortune of being the haunting ground of a strangling serial killer.

Vicki Purdy was the very attractive 25-year-old wife of an
army helicopter pilot. Although she was only 5'5" she could be
feisty and was known to stick up for herself. Raised in North
Carolina, Vicky had only been married to husband Gary for five
years. Three-and-a-half years after getting hitched they moved
to Hawaii, where Vicki found a job at a local video rental store.
It was said that life on the island was not quite what Vicki had
expected. She was an outgoing girl who liked to party, but it
seemed that she fell in with the wrong crowd.

On the evening of 28 May 1985 Vicki went out clubbing in
Waikiki, a district of Honolulu. She was known to be a head-
strong socialite who would often go out without her husband.
When she did not return home as expected her husband grew
worried, relentlessly paging her to no avail. The next morning
he set out to look for her and found her car, complete with a
newly minted dent, in a hotel parking garage. Friends reported
that she had phoned at 22:00, arranged to meet them, but did not
show up. She was last seen by a taxi driver who told police that
he had driven her to the hotel garage at about midnight.

Vicki was found on the morning of 29 May 1985. She had
been bound with tape, raped, strangled to death and dumped

unceremoniously at the edge of Keehi Lagoon. She was still wearing the yellow jumpsuit she had donned to go dancing in.

It transpired that the video rental store where Vicki worked had gained a reputation for renting X-rated videos, and that the previous year two female employees of the store had been stabbed to death inside the premises. Given the sexual nature of the crime against Vicki, police speculated that a customer of the pornographic video store may have developed a lethal obsession with her. This tenuous lead, however, drew a dead-end. Vicki's husband told the *Honolulu Star Bulletin* that his spouse had been "streetwise", and "a woman who knew who not to trust, and so tough it would take two people to abduct her". He later left the island promising never to return until her killer was found. Presumably he has never returned.

Regina Sakamoto was a 17-year-old high school senior who had plans to attend university. On 14 January 1986 Regina had the misfortune of missing her early-morning school bus. She phoned her boyfriend from a payphone to tell him she would be arriving late. She did not arrive at all.

Regina's mother (also called Regina) and her adoptive father had separated acrimoniously a couple of years earlier. Mr Sakamoto, a military man, warned Regina's mother that the pretty teenage was a "target" in the dangerous community where her mother had chosen to settle. It was a tragically prescient forewarning. Regina was, indeed, a very pretty girl, having long dark-blond hair and an easy smile. She was known to be very kind and very careful and, although shy, a girl who was still able to make friends. At 4'11" tall and 105lbs, she would have been no match for a sadistic torture-killer intent upon taking her life.

The next day her body, naked from the waist down, was found on the same stretch of embankment where Vicki Purdy's body had been dumped. Her hands had been tied behind her back. She had been raped, and haemorrhaging in the eyes gave testament to a violent death by strangulation.

Although police noticed similarities between this death and that of Purdy over seven months earlier, they made no public

announcement at the time that the killings may have been related.

Another body followed with indecent haste. Three young
fishermen found the decomposing body of a young woman at a
narrow canal. It had been wrapped in taupe and the bundle
seemed to have been rolled down the muddy embankment towards Moanalua Stream, which drains into Keehi Lagoon. The
victim's hands had been tied behind her back, like the two previous murder victims and, similarly, she had also been strangled. The victim was named as Denise Hughes, a 21-year-old
former resident of Seattle, Washington who had only moved to
Hawaii five months previously. At 5'8" tall, a newspaper referred to her as a "hefty" 154lbs. Hughes had worked as a secretary in a telephone company; her military husband served in
the navy. Despite not being long in her job she was a valued
member of staff who had quickly made friends and was apparently much loved by her colleagues. She enjoyed hiking and skiing and had volunteered in a local Christian youth group.

Like Purdy before her, Hughes used the local bus service to
move around. Her mother reportedly felt that the street on which
Hughes had lived was remote and she remarked that her daughter always planned her departures in the morning so that she
would not have to wait long at the bus stop by herself.

By now, because of the emerging *M.O.*, local law enforcement
was convinced that they had a serial killer on their idyllic island
patch. They set up a 27-person taskforce, aided by the FBI and
investigators from the Green River Killer[*] case. Profilers believed the killer to be an opportunist who happened upon lone,
vulnerable women, not one who stalks his victims. He most
likely resided or worked in the area. He was organised in his
killing – he came prepared with binding, leaving little evidence

---

[*] Gary Ridgway, born 1949, was known to have killed in excess of 49 women
in a crime spree spanning 16 years. He was eventually caught in November
2001 and sentenced to 48 life sentences with no possibility of parole.

behind him. Forensics examiners determined that the binding used on all three women was parachute rope. This pointed to the killer having a military background. The three victims had connections to the military. Hawaii was home to a huge military population. It seemed a reasonable conclusion.

Louise Medeiros had planned to catch a bus on the last day she was seen. Twenty-five-year-old Medeiros, originally from the neighbouring island of Kauai, seemed to have fallen upon hard times. An itinerant drifter who spent much of her short life wandering, she was now living in Waipahu on the island of Oahu.

However, on 26 March 1986 Medeiros was back in Kauai, where she had returned to attend the reading of her mother's will. Her family had found the prodigal sister a different person, telling the *Honolulu Star-Bulletin* that she was "centered and motivated, no longer the alienated rebel". Keen to get back to her three sons and boyfriend on Oahu, however, Medeiros caught a night plane, despite the warnings of her sister about waiting at bus stops at night. She disembarked the plane … and then promptly disappeared.

At 5'5" tall and weighing less than 90lbs, Medeiros would have been no match for the psychopathic strangler she encountered upon her return to her adopted island. Her diminutive body, clad only the blouse she had been wearing when boarding her plane, was found on 2 April by roadworkers near Waikele Stream in Honolulu. She had been sexually assaulted and, like the others, her hands had been tied tightly behind her back.

The taskforce now implemented a sting operation, sending undercover female officers to act as decoys at bus stops around Honolulu International Airport and Keehi Lagoon. The ruse proved fruitless. A month later a fifth body turned up.

According to friends, Linda Pesce was a vivacious, carefree spirit – opinionated, self-centred and tough. She had migrated from her home in Marin County, California, hitchhiking across the country alone in search of adventure. Ending up in Honolulu, she worked as a dancer in a nightclub before settling down upon the birth of her daughter. By 1986, 36-year-old Pesce was a sales representative for a telecommunications company on the island of Kauai, and on 29 April she had just been informed that she had been promoted. Things were looking up. She left work at half-six that evening in a great mood.

As Pesce had not returned home as expected, her roommate contacted police the next morning and reported her missing. The description – a very pretty, petite brunette – did not inspire police with much confidence that she would be found unharmed. They set up roadblocks and questioned commuters. Some of those quizzed remembered having seen Pesce's car on the night she disappeared, and a Caucasian or mixed-raced man driving a light-coloured van near her car.

A man, Howard Gay, came forward and told police that a psychic had told him the whereabouts of Pesce. The psychic had apparently told him that the body or bones of Pesce were on Sand Island, a recreational area overlooking Keehi Lagoon. On 3 May he took police to the exact spot he reportedly believed the body to be, only to find nothing. Pesce's body was later found in another area of Sand Island. A group of friends fishing for squid had noticed a strong odour and then turned their vehicle around to check. "I looked and I thought it was a mannequin," one of the finders told the *Star-Bulletin*. "When I really looked at it, it was a human being with [her] hands tied in the back with a cement block on her back." She was naked.

Suspicion immediately fell upon the local informant whose uncannily intuitive psychic-given knowledge led the police eventually to Pesce's remains. The suspect was a 43-year-old mechanic who worked near Lagoon drive. The police followed him and watched from a distance as he scratched the company insignia from his van. They interviewed his ex-wife and girlfriend, who both described him as a smooth talker, obsessed by sex, whose fetishism involved having sex with them with their hands bound behind their backs. Furthermore, the suspect's girlfriend recounted that on the nights of the murders the two had argued, resulting in him storming out of the house and not returning until much later. "He'd go on the prowl," said one investigator who believed he had found the impetus for the killer's murderous rage.

A break came when a witness came forward and picked a receding-haired middle-aged man out of a photo line-up. It was the suspect. He came with police voluntarily to speak with them on 9 May. The suspect failed a polygraph test but, without more incriminating evidence, police were obliged to let him go.

Two months later, another witness came forward with the information that she had seen Pesce with a man on the night of her murder. She successfully picked the suspect out of a line-up. However, she declined to cooperate further, citing the fact that the man had also seen her that night. She said that she had not come forward earlier because she was afraid the suspect would recognise her.

Without any stronger evidence police have not been able to make any further arrests, and prosecutors are reluctant to press for trial without more incriminating evidence. It is an incomplete circle. Police believe they had their man yet had to let him go. They continue to monitor their number one suspect. They clock his movements and activities. If he goes to the mainland, they notify local police in advance. He has not been linked to any other murders in Hawaii or anywhere else. To date, the degenerate Honolulu Strangler continues to cock a snook at investigators by evading justice.

The Frankford Slasher
(active 1985-1990)

FRANKFORD IS A NEIGHBOURHOOD in the northeast quadrant of Philadelphia, Pennsylvania. Like most city districts it has a chequered history and suffered its fair share of ups and downs. Once an elegant, prosperous area, by the 1980s it seemed to be on a downward turn, and many of its respectable former residents had fled for the suburbs. During this time the area's main thoroughfare, Frankford Avenue, and its immediate environs fell into a sort of Jekyll-and-Hyde existence. By day it was host to a contingent of mainly reputable businesses, run by professional businesspeople who were struggling to keep afloat. As darkness fell the streets were left to the offscourings of society, who ran their own trades on less-regulated business models. Petty crime and prostitution were endemic; drug use was common. It was in these bleak surroundings that the first victim of a serial slasher was found … in fearsomely gruesome circumstances.

On the morning of 19 August 1985, two railway workers were arriving for work at the yard of the Frankford Transportation Center, a terminal station for the Frankford elevated train. The sight they saw stopped them dead in their tracks. On an intersection where Penn Street meets Bridge Street lay a corpse. Unmistakably female, the body was naked from the waist down. The legs were splayed widely as if posed for a gynaecological examination and the blouse had been pulled up to expose the breasts. The unfortunate victim had suffered 47 vicious stab wounds to the head and chest, and a slash across the abdomen was so deep that the intestines had spilled out. In addition to the gross indecency she now suffered in death, the woman had been sexually assaulted prior to having her life extinguished. Her name was Helen Patent.

Patent's husband confirmed that the body belonged to his 52-year-old wife and attested to the fact that she had left their home in Parkland, a town in nearby Bucks County, the previous week without saying where she was going. This, apparently, was not unusual, as the pair lived separate lives.

Police could establish no motive for the crime. However, subsequent reporting intimated that Patent, who frequented bars in the Frankford area, was engaged in prostitution, and that she could easily have met a stranger with murder on his mind.

On a cold winter night the killer struck again. This time 68-year-old Anna Carroll was the unhappy victim. She was found just over nine miles away on 3 January 1986 in the South Philadelphia apartment where she lived alone. The door to her apartment lay open and inside Carroll was found sprawled on her bedroom floor, naked from the waist down. She had been stabbed six times in the back with a deep slashing wound from breastbone to groin which police felt may have been an attempt to gut the body. Police were easily able to ascertain the murder weapon – a large kitchen knife – for it was still embedded in the body. Like Patent before her, Carroll was thought of as a Frankford barfly and, likewise, no discernible motive for the murder could be established. Notwithstanding the distance between the two murders, due to the similarities of *M.O.* the police considered a possible linkage between them, although it would take further deaths before they actively made a connection. However, with little evidence to work on the investigation stalled.

It should be noted that police can very often be reluctant to link cases, even when there are strong similarities. This has been seen in previous serial murder cases and it was the case now in Philadelphia. Authorities do not want to cause undue worry or to panic people, especially when they simply do not have the evidence to support their suppositions. It is only when overwhelming similarities in further murders present that investigators feel they have no option but to alert the public that a repeat offender might be walking the streets unapprehended. Then it becomes an absolute necessity to warn the public so that they can pass on any information relevant to the police enquiry, and also be on their guard to minimise the risk of becoming a victim of the unidentified serial killer themselves.

The killer waited nearly a year, striking again on Christmas Day 1986, and for Susan Olszef it would be her last. The killer presented the body in startlingly similar fashion to his last two offerings. The door of the Richmond Street apartment was left open. Inside, the victim herself lay on the floor. She had been stabbed in the back six times. At the age of 64, Olszef, like the other victims, had been an older woman. She had been a familiar sight at the bars of Frankford, in particular one called the Golden Bar (known locally as "Goldie's"), an establishment that Patent and Carroll had also been known to frequent. However, other than her fondness for alcohol, little else is known of Olszef. Nevertheless, despite parallels in the three slayings, local investigators were still unwilling to officially link the cases. But before they could even catch their breaths, the killer struck yet again.

On 8 January 1987 Jeanne Durkin's body was found. She was a much younger victim at 28 years of age. Durkin, who had been homeless and lived mostly in the doorway of an abandoned building near to Goldie's, would have been seen as an easy target for a rapist and murderer. She was found next to a fruit and vegetable stall just a block from where Helen Patent had been killed. Durkin was naked, spread-eagled and bathed in a pool of her own blood. She had been stabbed 74 times in the chest, back and buttocks. During their investigations, detectives discovered that Durkin used to go into Goldie's seeking warmth during the winter. She was a familiar face to the wider community also. "She was quiet and sort of nice," a friend told the *Durkin Pennsylvanian Enquirer*, "but she kept on coming back to the doorway here. I loved her. I really did."

Now, with four bodies in the morgue, law enforcement could no longer deny that they were dealing with a serial killer.[*] But

---

[*] In the mid-1980s, the term – "serial killer" – was relatively new. It had probably been coined in 1981 by FBI agent and profiler Robert Ressler after he had

unfortunately, Philadelphia around this time was already experiencing a wave of serial violence against women. One series of crimes was committed by a man called Gary Heidnik. This sadistic psychopath was discovered when one of the women he was holding hostage managed to escape. She told a tale of unimaginable horror. Heidnik's pleasure was to kidnap women, keeping them hanging in chains from the basement ceiling, playing the radio loudly to drown out the sounds of their screams. He would strip them naked and rape them repeatedly as his own personal sex slaves. When one died from asphyxia, he cut up the body and forced the other women to eat the flesh. He forced one abductee to electrocute another whom he had deemed "uncooperative". He would ram a screwdriver into the ears of his victims until drawing blood. With the help of the escapee, detectives caught Heidnik. He was tried, found guilty and sentenced to death, eventually dying by lethal injection in July 1999.

Around the same time, the people of Philadelphia were to learn about the crimes of Harrison Graham, who had been evicted from his apartment due to the foul odour emanating from it. After the eviction of their unhygienic tenant, the owners made a search of the apartment. However, they soon discovered that the overpowering stench was caused by more than the piles of

---

heard descriptions of some crimes which occurred in series. He said that the description reminded him of the classic "serial adventures" shown on television, which ended with a cliff-hanger, the audience wanting more. He said it was the inconclusive nature of the series that struck a chord for him in his thinking about this apparently new type of killer. The word "serial" seemed apt when referring to these sequential murders, for they are committed by people who remain agitated and dissatisfied, always lured back by the thrill of the crime to repeat and repeat and repeat it with no desire to get caught. However, despite its newness, the term "serial killer" caught on. It did aptly describe this breed of killer who was becoming more widely known in both fiction and real life, to the horror and fascination of the public – and the public needed to be warned about them.

rubbish and rotting faeces they found inside and contacted the police. Behind a locked door, concerned investigators found the bodies of seven women, in various stages of decay. Under questioning, the former tenant eventually admitted to having killed the women during sex whilst he was under the influence of drugs. He was sentenced to life in prison for the crimes.

And so it was under these sensational circumstances that Philadelphian newspapers began to awaken to the fact that a serial killer was working the city streets of Frankford ... and began to put pressure upon the police to do something about it. It was around this time also that journalists began to use the nickname "The Frankford Slasher" to identify this particular slaughterer.

And then another killing. Catherine Jones, a 29-year-old waitress, was found half-naked, frozen and covered in snow on a sidewalk in Frankford's Northern Liberties area. She had been bludgeoned to death, her skull shattered and jaw completely destroyed. Whilst she was also a patron of Goldie's bar, there remained some doubt as to whether she was a victim of the Frankford Slasher's madness.

Police, meanwhile, canvassed the patrons and staff of Goldie's. Those who had interacted with the killer's first two victims, Patent and Carroll, reported that the women had been streetwise and savvy and would not easily have let their attacker take advantage of them. This led police to conjecture that the killer had known his victims.

For a while it seemed as if the killer had vanished. No more similar deaths occurred for several months. Then, on 11 November 1988, two students found the viciously slashed body of Margaret Vaughan in the inner vestibule of their apartment building. Vaughan, aged 66, had recently been evicted from her home for failure to pay rent and it was there that she had seemingly sought refuge from the weather. She did not escape her killer's ministrations. Her body had suffered 29 stab wounds to the head, neck and torso. She had not been sexually assaulted and the $200 she carried remained in her possession. This was another apparently motiveless crime.

Police returned to Goldie's to interview staff and patrons. A barmaid was able to provide a missing link by recalling that Vaughan had been in the bar in the company of a round-faced Caucasian who wore spectacles and walked with a limp. The first composite sketch was produced and distributed around the neighbourhood, but no new witnesses came forward to offer any new leads.

Two months later, 19 January 1988, produced the next victim. Thirty-year-old Theresa Sciortino's remains were found by her landlord in her third-floor apartment unit not far from the former residence of Margaret Vaughan. Naked but for a pair of white socks, Sciortino had been stabbed 25 times on the face, arms and chest. Her body lay in a large puddle of blood and there were the signs of a prolonged struggle in the apartment which had moved from room to room. The killer had discarded his murder implement, a large bloodstained knife, in the kitchen sink. Also in the kitchen was a three-foot-long piece of wood, which had been used to sexually violate the victim.

Sciortino was also known to have frequented Goldie's. However, on the evening she died she had been trying to pick up a man at another bar, the Jolly Post Tavern. According to the barman there she had been unsuccessful in her mission and left alone. "She used to walk in, stand there, and just stare at you," a patron of the Jolly Post told the *Philadelphia Daily News*. "It was a scary look. A weird look. I'd say she had some kind of problem." Indeed she had. Sciortino had been in and out of psychiatric hospital many times and had the marks of needle use on her arms indicating a regular drug habit. She had been trying to get her derailed life back on track again but she could never hold onto a job. As she kept getting the orders wrong in her waitressing job she had been fired from three neighbourhood restaurants in the three months before her death. Newspaper reports hinted that by now Sciortino was earning a living as a sex worker. One of her neighbours noted wryly, "She had a lot of company." Although police were not yet prepared to speculate about the possibility of a serial killer's involvement, unofficially a detective told the _Philadelphia Daily News_, "There's a kook running around up there. All these jobs look like they were done by the same man."

For a second time the killer lay low. It seemed as if he were toying with the police. However, his urges eventually got the better of him and, on 29 April 1990, 46-year-old Carol Dowd became his eighth victim. Her body was found by a patrol officer behind a seafood store on Frankford Avenue. The condition of the remains was horrific. Thirty-six stab wounds covered her face, neck, chest and back. She had defence-wounds on her hands. Her left nipple had been cut off and her abdomen was sliced open to expose her intestines.

A witness recalled having seen Dowd in the company of a white male on the evening of her murder. However, police instead focused their attention upon a black man who was employed at the fish market near where the body had been found. There had been a lot of break-ins around that time and during the course of investigations the man told them that he had known one of the earlier victims, Margaret Vaughan. This, police now believed, was the man they sought – the Frankford Slasher. His name was Leonard Christopher.

Christopher's acquaintance with the area and the victims put him under suspicion. Police asked him where he had been the previous evening. He told them he had been with his girlfriend, but she did not vouch for that alibi, saying that she had spent the night alone. A search of his apartment uncovered clothing with blood on it. A work colleague, however, told a newspaper that their employer had told Christopher to clean up some blood in the alley and that this could have accounted for the blood. Others who knew Christopher assured police of his good character. His landlord stated that the only problem was that he made too much noise.

Christopher was arrested, arraigned and charged for robbery, murder, abuse of a corpse and possession of an instrument of crime, and he was ordered to stand trial in December 1990.

Now the neighbourhood could return to normal. Or so they

thought …

Whilst Christopher was remanded in prison another murder occurred. Michelle Dehner, aged 30, was killed on 29 April 1990 and it held all the hallmarks of the same killer. The victim was a hard-drinking female, described as "unconventional" and "a paranoid loner". She frequented the same Frankford Avenue bars that the other murder victims had frequented. On the day before she died she had left the bar with a white man. Could this man, knowing that another man was in custody, have killed one last time? Might he have been trying to let the police know they had the wrong man? Possibly. Certainly, some people began to feel that the police *had* arrested the wrong man and called for Leonard Christopher to be released.

Meanwhile the citizens of Frankford continued to provide information. One woman reported that she had dated a white man who looked like the police composite sketch. A couple of psychics got together to pray for a vision of the man police should be looking for[*]. Angry girlfriends called to inform on their boyfriends. But no one came forward to report seeing anyone covered in blood on the nights of the killings.

Nevertheless, the prosecution of Leonard Christopher persevered. Dowd's murder was the only case that went to trial. The jurors were persuaded by evidence that Christopher's behaviour had been "strange" and that he had lied to the police. He was found guilty – of the murder of Carol Dowd – despite there being no physical evidence linking him to the scene, there being no injuries on him, there being no murder weapon recovered and there being no reason to view him as a murderer. He was sentenced to life imprisonment where he died from cancer still asserting his innocence.

One woman from the Frankford Slasher's roll received a dubious sort of justice. The others received none. The perpetrator

---

[*] The measure of their success has not been recorded.

of those crimes, if he still alive and at large, walks free. He has literally got away with murder.

The Colonial Parkway Killer
(active 1986-1989)

THE COLONIAL PARKWAY is the narrowest national park in the United States. Linking three key points of Virginia – from Yorktown, through Williamsburg to Jamestown – the 23-mile road was designed to be a pleasantly scenic and unbroken journey through historic, bucolic landscape. Bridges are plentiful – there are 35 of them – and an abundance of splendored woods line the route, shielding the traveller from the constructions of modern development. It is not a journey *to* anyway; it is a trip through time. Toll-free, free from trucks and with speed limits between 35-45 miles per hour, it is little wonder that the Parkway is a magnet for tourists and day-trippers seeking to unwind and enjoy the area's charming and unique attractions.

Alongside the majestic York River there are many turnouts and overlooks, where visitors can park up and sit for a while to enjoy the views of the mighty blue waters passing by. In time, as so often happens, these parking spots became the haunts of courting couples, attracted by the quietude and privacy the idyllic locations afforded them.

In the mid-1980s, the Colonial Parkway also became the haunt of a violent serial killer whose prey was couples in their car. He was not the first to target such victims. The Phantom Killer of Texarkana and Zodiac also found these individuals satisfied their needs … at least for a while. However, for whatever reason, these two serial killers allowed some of their quarries to live – and, because of this, the victims were able to describe their assailants' appearances to some extent. The hooded mask of the Texarkana Phantom protected his identity and he has never been brought to justice. Zodiac, who also wore a sinister mask on at least one occasion, made a game of his crime spree. He blundered too, having been seen on at least three occasions and a physical description of the killer exists.

But the Colonial Parkway Murderer made no such mistake.

To suggest that the killer made *no* mistakes is inaccurate; he made his fair share of slip-ups. But leaving his victims still alive was not one of them. There are no witnesses. The killer remains formless, featureless. He left no workable clues. He does not even have a "catchy" moniker by which to catch the public imagination. He simply arrived, executed his heinous deeds with clinic fastidiousness, and then left the scene as covertly as he entered. In fact, the apparent *ease* with which this murderer committed his acts may be the only clue about him ...

It started on the night of 9 October 1986 when two women decided to take a drive together. Cathleen Thomas was an attractive 27-year-old redhead coming from an Irish family. A graduate of the naval academy at Annapolis, Maryland, she had dedicated five years to the Navy before probes into her private life eventually pushed her to leave the service – for Cathy was a lesbian at a time when homosexuality was still considered a security risk. Undaunted, the driven and intelligent woman began a civilian career in a brokerage firm and became very successful in it. On 9 October Cathy drove herself over to William & Mary College in Williamsburg, Virginia to pick up her friend Becky.

Rebecca Dowski, aged 21, was a senior student at the college, majoring in business management. The pretty, dark-haired young woman was also known to be driven and enthusiastic. She was a keen athlete and summer camp counsellor. According to a newspaper report she was "serious but not sombre".

Becky was helping a friend with a computer project when Cathy arrived to meet her. The pair of women had been introduced by Cathy's ex-girlfriend and it is thought that they were in an early-blossoming relationship. They decided to go for something to eat and to spend some time together. Becky's car was packed with belongings – presumably she had been planning to drive home to Poughkeepsie, New York for Columbus weekend – and so they chose to take Cathy's white Honda Civic.

On 12 October a jogger spotted a white car down an embankment. Thinking this was the scene of an accident, he clambered down the bank and smashed the back window of the car in order to rescue the occupants. The sight that greeted him quickly alerted the would-be rescuer to the fact that this was no accident. Neither of the occupants was in the driver's seat. One of the women – Cathy – was stashed at the rear of the vehicle, under the hatchback. She was bound and gagged and had had throat cut so deeply she was almost decapitated. The second woman – Becky – was in the back seat. She had suffered similar ministrations.

Both victims, autopsies would later confirm, had been strangled with a thin cord. There was evidence of rope burns on both their wrists. Both victims were fully dressed. There had been no sexual molestation. Money was left visible at the site. This had been an execution, pure and simple.

The bodies lay on federal land and so it became a case for the FBI. Investigators found a piece of cord wrapped once around Cathy's neck, a cord which had also been cut – not once, but twice. It seemed a curious way in which to strangle someone. Could it have been an attempt to render the woman insensible, only to revive her and repeat the action? Or could it have been the botched work of someone whose intention was to kill? If this were the case, why the need to slash the necks of the victims? This was overkill – twice – by a slayer who had come well prepared to kill.

Furthermore, found between Cathy's fingers was foreign hair. She had evidently put up some fight before being overcome – her thumb had a defence knife-wound. Becky had fought also. How could the killer have overpowered two strong women fighting for their lives? This would have been difficult. Could he have incapacitated one of them whilst he attended to the other? Plausible, certainly. Could there have been more than one perpetrator? Some investigators seemed to think so. The attack appeared to have been prolonged and involved. How could this have occurred without the killer (or killers) being seen by any travellers in passing cars? Had the abduction occurred somewhere else and was the Parkway used merely as a dumping ground? There were more questions than answers.

On and inside the car, crime scene specialists found over 150 partial latent prints, as well as some full prints. A careless mistake perhaps, but they did not match anyone's prints already on the FBI database.

There was a strong smell of diesel in the car and on the bodies. Someone had doused them with the fire accelerant and tried to destroy the evidence. The higher ignition temperature of diesel denied them that. It seemed that the car had then been driven to the embankment and pushed over the edge in the hope that it would roll into the York River and be swept into Chesapeake Bay and then out to sea. This failed too, for the car came to a rest nose-down almost at the river's edge.

There seemed to be no motive. It is possible that the killer had deliberately targeted two women he had seen parking in a lovers' lane and attacked them in raging moralistic fervour. It is possible that he mistook the two women for a heterosexual couple and the moral aspect of the motive is negate. What is certain, however, is that few leads were generated and eventually the trail grew cold.

The killer lay silent for a year. On 23 September 1987 a jogger was running along the across the tundra-like terrain of a nature reserve on the south shore of James River. The area is bleak and eerily open, buffeted by strong winds coming in off the sound. It is not the sort of place someone would expect to run – almost literally – into a dead body, but that is what happened. A partially clothed young female lay dead on the ground, her life ended by a shot in the back of the head, execution-style. The jogger took in the body, about-turned, and ran back to the parking lot. Arriving at a gas station-convenience store he announced that he had found a woman's body on the beach and the police were alerted.

Whilst law enforcement officers were at the site where the female had been found, a man came along the beach. He was searching for his young adult son. It was he who found the second body, that of his deceased son, who was near to a copse of trees away from the shore, also partially clothed.

The bodies belonged to 20-year-old David Knobling and his 14-year-old girlfriend Robin Edwards. They had been missing since 19 September, a rainy night. When David's abandoned pickup truck was noticed in the parking lot of the Ragged Island Wildlife Refuge, the keys were in the ignition, the radio was playing, the driver-side window was down, the wipers were on and Knobling's wallet was on the dashboard. Two pairs of underwear – both male and female – were found in the vehicle. Nobody was nearby the car to explain the way it had been left.

The female victim had had recent sex, an autopsy showed. It is not difficult to imagine the sequence of events that happened three days before the bodies of David and Robin were found. A young couple, late at night in a petting spot. A car pulls up and the driver gets up. The couple, caught *in flagrante*, hastily attempt to arrange their clothing. The newcomer approaches the couple's car and shines a flashlight into their vehicle. Thinking this is a cop, the young driver winds down his window. Suddenly a gun is thrust through the window, and the "cop" orders the couple out. He instructs them to walk, and he marches them over a mile towards the beach where he shoots the girl in the head. As the young man runs to escape, the "cop" shoots him, hitting him in the shoulder, before approaching and shooting him also in the head. It is a plausible scenario.

There are questions. Why did the killer not commit his crime at the carpark? Why did he feel a need to march the couple for mile away before shooting them dead? Perhaps he needed to feed off their fear. He was taking an enormous risk that his own car would be found. Perhaps an evil toady aided the killer by waiting in the car or driving it away to avoid eliciting suspicion. Was it possible that the killer, before fleeing the scene, arranged the victims' pickup truck – door open, radio playing, wipers on – in order to attract attention to it? It would not have been the first time a killer sought to draw attention to his own wrongdoings. All the same, there were plenty of questions … but precious few answers.

The wildlife preserve was on State-controlled property and the investigation was undertaken by Virginia State Police. However, they could not garner any leads. There were no witnesses and not even a set of footprints remained at the scene; the rainy downpour had washed them all away. The case eventually stalled and grew cold.

On 10 April 1988 a young couple mysteriously disappeared. Their car was found on a turning spot over a mile from where the bodies of Cathleen Thomas and Rebecca Dowski were found.

Cassandra Hailey and Keith Call, aged 18 and 20 respectively, simply disappeared. The two colleges students had gone out on a first date, Keith first collecting Sandra in his red Toyota Celica for a party in Newport News, Virginia. They attended the party and left sometime later. They were never seen again, alive or dead. Keith's car was spotted the next morning at a turning spot along the Colonial Parkway. Keith's father, who was commuting to work, noticed the car parked in the turnout at seven o'clock. He drove on, knowing that his son had had a date the night before but assuming that he and his date had gone for a romantic walk along the shore.

A ranger, investigating the same car at about 09:00, had more cause for concern. He looked in the car and noticed a wallet containing a small amount of money and some clothes. The keys had been tossed on the front seat. The owner of the car was nowhere to be seen. Owing to the clothes in the car, the ranger considered that the occupants could have gone skinny-dipping. Possibly they had drowned. However, this was unlikely. In April the water would have been very cold and the beach difficult to access from the point where the car had been abandoned. Nevertheless, the car was towed and investigators awaited two bodies to surface. None did. An extensive search of the local area turned up nothing. In considering the young couple's disappearance the FBI now presumed that they had been murdered. The finding of their clothes indicated that they had been taken by surprise in a petting spot. There was no sign of a struggle, as if the couple had been compliant with their abductor.

It appeared as though their car had been driven from some other place and abandoned quickly in the turnout. There was no clue as to where it had been driven from. Did the killer have an accomplice who followed in a separate car? The bodies of Sandra and Keith, if they *were* dead, had obviously been cleverly hidden. Why? Had their disappearance been staged as the accidental drowning of two skinny-dipping youngsters? Or had the killer merely been planting false clues? There were no answers to these questions, but one horrific theory was beginning to emerge from the scattered clues …

The task-force connected this murder to the other two cases and now became concerned that they were the work of a serial killer. Corporal Bob Hayes, a spokesman for the joint task-force said that police had already come to one horrific conclusion: "The killer may have dressed as an authority figure, such as a police officer, to win the victims' cooperation and lure them to their deaths."

The killing "cop" bided his time. It would be a year-and-a-half before the next attack.

David Lauer, aged 21, was in the process of moving house. He and his brother's girlfriend, Annamaria Phelps, aged 18, left late at night to make the four-hour journey from Amelia County, Virginia to Virginia Beach, Virginia, driving eastward along the I-64. David's beloved tan-coloured Chevy Nova was loaded with his possessions, household items and some food that Annamaria's mother had prepared. It was 5 September 1988, just after the Labor Day weekend.

A couple of hours into their journey, they stopped at a rest area. They were still a couple of hours short of their destination. The reason they stopped is not known. It might have been for a bathroom break, or something may have spooked them. Nobody knows, but it was not due to a mechanical failure of the car. But whatever happened, the young couple vanished.

The next day Daniel's car was found in the rest area on the westbound side of the road – the wrong side of the road – parked in a bay area designated for large-rigged vehicles. It had been left at an odd angle – half on the road, half on the shoulder – and the driver's window was half-down. The key was still in the ignition. It was almost an invitation to a would-be car thief. But there was one other odd thing. Beside the key, dangling from the front window was Annamarie's peacock-feather roach clip. This was usually attached to a rear window. It was as if the killer had moved it to arrogantly taunt the police.

A search was initiated. The New Kent County Sheriff's Department and the State Police covered the area by helicopter, but dense woods covering vast acres made it well-nigh impossible to spot anyone on the ground. Eventually the search ended. The families never gave up hope that their young relatives would be found alive. Sightings in Williamsburg and other places proved to be false leads. The press made a quick link between this disappearance and the other Colonial Parkway murders, but police downplayed the link, even though they could see it too. They did not wish to cause panic.

Six weeks later, on 19 October 1989, two skeletonised bodies were found by turkey hunters. They were 30-miles away, near to the I-64, which passes by the Colonial Parkway. The dumping site was a little distance off a secluded logging trail, deep in the woods. The bodies were covered by Annamarie's electric blanket, which had been removed from David's car.

The remains were identified as David Lauer and Annamarie Phelps by their dental and medical records. The cause of death could not be determined by autopsy but neither puncture wound or strangulation could be definitively ruled out. Annamarie's remains had the mark of a sharp weapon on one of its fingers. She had obviously fought her attacker at some stage. Her locket was found on the pathway. The authorities could only guess as to its purpose. Had she dropped it there in the hope that someone would find it and come to investigate? Had it fallen off during a struggle? Or had the killer placed it there to point searchers in the right direction?

As before, the killer left no evidence other than suppositions that can be drawn from the locations of the crimes. He would have had to have some prior knowledge of the rest stop. There was no mud on the tyres of David's car. Evidently the killer had transported his abductees in his own vehicle. That meant a degree of knowledge about that particular area in the woods, with its narrow logging road, otherwise he risked his own vehicle becoming stuck, and the peril of discovery that that would have entailed.

Like the previous murders there is no motive other than the homicidal compulsion of a madman. Like the previous murders the killer did not want the bodies to be found quickly. Like the previous two cases the victims appeared to have gone at least some of the way without struggling with their killer, suggesting they thought they were dealing with a figure of authority ... or someone posing as such a figure.

> *Each of the four couples, investigators said, appears to have been commandeered by someone in authority.*
>
> *"There was no sign of any struggle. These people were placed under control early on, and they became compliant," said Irvin B. Wells, special agent in charge of the Norfolk FBI Office.*
>
> (*The News-Press*, Fort Myers, Florida, 1990)

Unlike the others, though, Lauer and Phelps were not dating, nor were they resting in a known petting site. Could the killer have made an error of judgement, or had he simply seen a couple in a car and seized the opportunity?

The killer seemed to have staged the victims' cars in the latter three cases. The first case, that of Thomas and Dowski, seems to have been rushed and hence botched. Could this have been the work of a criminal just learning?

Officially, the deaths of Lauer and Phelps would be the last linked to the Colonial Parkway Murderer case but were there others?

Julianne "Julie" Williams, aged 24, and Laura "Lollie" Winams, aged 26, were a dating couple who had decided to take their dog, a golden Labrador called Taj, and go camping and hiking in Shenandoah National Park, Virginia on 19 May 1999. When they failed to return home as expected on 27 May friends became worried. Their bodies were found by a park ranger on 1 June near the spot where they had been camping. Both had been bound and gagged. Both had had their throats cut so severely that their heads had been almost decapitated. Julie was discovered naked in her sleeping bag, Lollie still inside the tent. She had been stripped of her clothes. Taj the dog was waiting not far off, unharmed.

The horrific attack bore some striking resemblances to the murders of Catherine Thomas and Rebecca Dowski: (i) both were lesbian couples, (ii) sexual assault was not a motive, (iii) a knife was the murder weapon, and (iv) it had been used in an equally brutal way in all four murders. Law enforcement officers found a late suspect who was charged on the basis of circumstantial evidence five years after the deaths of Williams and Winams. However, the case against this suspect scuppered due to a lack of physical evidence.

Heidi Childs, aged 18, and David Metzler, aged 19, two students at Virginia Tech went for a walk on 26 August 2009 at some time between 20:00 and 22:00. They were found dead the next morning by a man walking his dog in a camping area in Jefferson National Park, Virginia. They had both been shot multiple times. David had been shot in the chest through the open window of the driver's side of the car. Heidi was shot as she tried to escape. Police remain tight-lipped as to whether sexual molestation occurred.

Some items of value were stolen from the scene, including a credit card that was never used. At the time of the murders, the suspect of the killings of Williams and Winams was in prison serving time for an unrelated crime. The crime scene lies some 250 miles east of the Colonial Parkway, and there is no concrete evidence to link these two murders to the Parkway killings, yet there are some similarities. As with those double murders, no discernible motive can be attached to the crime. It, like the

Parkway murders, appears to be an entirely random slaying.

In 2009 a former Gloucester, Virginia deputy called Fred Atwell requested a meeting with a TV news journalist. Atwell seemed to have taken a great interest in the Colonial Parkway Murders, starting his own private investigation and remaining in touch with the families of the victims. Atwell told the reporter that he had heard that the owner of a security company had been using images from the Colonial Parkway murder crime scenes for teaching purposes. He said that he had tried to get the FBI to investigate this lead but they had not done so. Instead, the FBI later considered Atwell a suspect. The former deputy denied any involvement. He was later jailed for other crimes and passed away in prison on 16 December 2016. The cold case had briefly warmed before cooling again. It has little current traction and, unless there is a late breakthrough, the Colonial Parkway Killer – or Killers – will be unlikely to be brought to justice.

The New Bedford Highway Killer
(active 1988-1989)

THESE WERE THE WOMEN. The prostitutes. The drug addicts. The spurned women who scratched a living on the streets after sundown. Who wantonly put themselves into risky situations. Low profile women with lower expectations. Women to whom no one paid attention. In whom the media took little interest. These were the women the killer chose, and he chose them well. For they were the women that no one realised were being killed ... until they turned up dead.

Yet they were somebody's daughter, somebody's sister. Between them they were mothers to 15 children. They were the 11 victims of the New Bedford Highway Killer.

The latter months of 1988 was a terrifying time for the women of New Bedford, Massachusetts. An unknown prowler was stalking the streets of their small city, picking off victims with an apparent ease and ruthlessness, and it was only as the year progressed, and the bodies began to mount up, that people began to realise that dreadful fact.

Six women would disappear before the first grim discovery was made. On the afternoon of 2 July 1988 a woman driving along Interstate 140 took an urgent need to answer the call of nature. She pulled her car over the side of the road and clambered down the bushy embankment seeking a private place in which to urinate. Instead she found a sight that would stay with her a long time.

The body was a skeleton by this stage, having been rotting away for several months. The smell – that unmistakeable stench of death – hung heavily in the air. It appeared that the deceased person had died whilst lying backwards, for the legs and arms were spread outwards. A bunched-up pair of panties were by the side, and a bra was still twisted around the neck, the only indications that the decedent was a woman. She turned out to be 30-year-old Debra Medeiros, a drug user and occasional sex worker who had last been seen by her boyfriend in New Bedford just over a month earlier. It would take eight further months before the pretty, dark-haired woman was positively identified.

However, before the month was done, and whilst Jane Doe no. 1 remained unidentified, a second body turned up. On 30 July, two motorcyclists found a body on Route 195 near New Bedford, placed amidst brush at the side of the road. The "weathered" body had been left to the elements and by now little more than a skeleton remained. It had been hastily but well hidden – around 15-feet along a narrow rural path, the sort of path formed by someone making a shortcut. Investigators would later wonder if the path had been formed by someone returning to the scene to "visit" the body. They also began to cast their thoughts back to the body which had been found under similar circumstances earlier in the month.

Jane Doe no. 2 was identified as 36-year-old Nancy Paiva. She had been missing for over two weeks. Her sister made the identification in December that year after viewing a few pieces of clothing and jewellery laid out on a table. Nancy, a secretarial school dropout, was later to become a heroin addict who had had a few dealings with law enforcement over drugs. She was also the very supportive mother of two girls, and a grandmother too. Her family asserted that she was not a prostitute and there are no police records of her having been arrested for soliciting sex. On the evening of her disappearance, Nancy's boyfriend had had just had an argument with her and ordered her out of The Whispers Bar. She was last seen walking home through the rain, tears unmistakably in her eyes.

Just over three months later, a road crew clearing brush found the third body near a road in Dartmouth, Massachusetts, concealed within a copse of trees. Clothes had been strewn about the nearby foliage. Identification was made two days after Christmas 1988. This was 35-year-old Deborah DeMello, the mother of three children. She had walked away from a prison work-release programme in Rhode Island on 18 June 1988 whilst in the midst of serving a sentence for prostitution violation. Strangely, some of the clothes – and some jewellery – found nearby turned out to have belonged to victim no. 2, Nancy Paiva. The discovery only gave more questions. Had De-Mello gained access to Paiva's apartment, and her possessions? Or had the killer returned to Paiva's body, retrieved her clothes and jewellery, and the left them with DeMello's body? Whatever the answer, it strongly pointed to a connection between the two, and investigators now believed a serial killer was roaming New Bedford's highways.

A search dog found the next body on 29 November 1988 near the I-195. The remains were identified two days later as Dawn Mendes, aged 25, a known drug-user and prostitute, but also the devoted mother of a young son. She had been due to attend a family christening on 4 September but did not show up.

There was little respite. Two days later, on 1 December, a fifth body was discovered. Police with search dogs were out in force scouring the area. They were rewarded with the discovery of a fully-clothed skeleton in a wooded place just off Route 140 in Freetown, Massachusetts. Inexplicably, a sack of clothes lay nearby. It was not until March 1989 that the remains were identified as 25-year-old Debroh McConnell. She had been reported missing since May the previous year when her family became worried after she failed to phone on her 10-year-old daughter's birthday.

Nine days later, on 10 December, the police had a sixth murder victim on their hands. This body had lain undiscovered for over seven months before being chanced upon by hunters in a disused gravel quarry off the I-196. The remains belonged to 28-year-old Rochelle Clifford Dopierala, a drug user who had been due to give evidence against a man who had been accused of rape. She never got to make her statement.

Two bodies were found in a single week in March 1989. Robin "Bobby Lyn" Rhodes, aged 28, was found by a search dog alongside Route 140. She was the first to go missing but the seventh to be found. Whilst the mother-of-one was addicted to heroin and cocaine and was not known to have been involved in prostitution she did frequent the same saloons as Paiva, Mendes and Clifford. She was also known to have been a friend of the second skeleton found that week, Mary Santos, aged 26-years, a mother-of-two who was found alongside Route 88.

On 24 April 1989 the final body, that of Sandra Botelho, aged 24, was found beside the I-195. She had gone missing in August 1988 after leaving her apartment to go for a stroll. Like many of the other victims, Botelho had been a drug addict and prostitute.

In addition to the nine bodies found, two women who fit the victim-profiles of the killer disappeared. Christine Monteiro, a 19-year-old sex worker with addiction problems, went missing in May 1988. Marilyn Roberts, 34, Monteiro's next-door neighbour, vanished in June 1988. She had her own struggles with addiction. Both women are presumed to have been slain at the hands of the highway killer. Both had connections to the police: Monteiro's mother was engaged to a policeman; Roberts was the daughter of a retired police officer. Were these coincidental connections?

The New Bedford murderer's wicked spree began sometime in March 1988 and ended seven months later in September. In July 1988 a woman needing to relieve her bladder inadvertently launched one of the largest criminal investigations in Massachusetts with her accidental discovery of a body on a patch of hardscrabble at the side the I-140. Some of the women had been strangled; others were so decomposed it was not possible to determine the manner of their deaths. The victims seem connected by complications that came into their troubled lives – domestic abuse, drug addiction, prostitution. They might have been thought of as "throwaway people", but their lives were important to some. It took a street-savvy detective to realise that several prostitutes were going missing and failing to return, and it was only when the bodies began to pile up that the reason for this became clear.

Local and state investigators threw everything they had at the case. The trouble was, there was so very little to go on. All the witnesses were dead. The murderer left little by way of evidence behind. The bodies themselves had been wiped clean by time and nature. Tips dried up, but the fear and suspicion remained.

A few names have been tossed into the suspect pile.

Anthony DeGrazia was alleged to have been a frequent violent abuser of prostitutes in the area. Witnesses to those crimes identified him by his distinctive flattened nose. One witness, a prostitute, reported that during an attack he had tried to snap her neck and told her that he "was going to do to me like he did to the other bitches". DeGrazia was charged with six attacks on sex workers and released on bail. Whilst out he fixed his nose, started a business and attacked another prostitute. After initially evading arrest he turned himself in and was arraigned on the latter charge. However, the charge was dropped after he ended his own life in his sister's house under a picnic table. His secrets, if he had any, he took to the grave.

Kenneth Ponte, a New Bedford attorney, also had connections to sex workers and drug use. In particular, he had a connection with Rochelle Clifford Dopierala, the prostitute who had been due to give evidence against him on drug charges but for the fact that instead she turned up dead, one of the 11 known victims of the Highway Killer. Indeed, Ponte's name _kept_ popping up in the investigation. He had represented Mary Santos, and Nancy Paiva. Dawn Mendes had once been seen knocking at the door to his residence, a place in which Rochelle Dopierala had been known to have also stayed. Furthermore, according to her sister, Robbin Rhodes had dated a lawyer, who turned out to be Ponte. A heavy drug-user himself, his habit seemed to have caused paranoia and weakened his inhibitions. He was known to occasionally lock a working girl in his house and bolt the door behind them both. Rumours circulated that he had watched snuff movies, with one woman claiming he had watched a video depicting a death by strangulation.

Ponte was arraigned on a single charge of murder – a decision some investigators were queasy about – but this was dropped due to a lack of evidence. His behaviour became increasingly erratic, and he would frequently call the media to rant that the authorities had ruined his career and life. No positive evidence that tied Ponte to the murders was ever uncovered. In 2010, his bloated dead body was found lying on two stacked mattresses in his squalid New Bedford home.

David Tavares Jr., a "skinny little runt", whilst in prison for the knifing to death of his mother, indirectly claimed to have been responsible for the Highway Killings. He is currently sentenced for two unrelated murders.

Around March 1989 information came to light that an anonymous letter had been sent to the office of the Bristol County District Attorney. The letter purportedly stated that if a body were found near Route 88 in Westport, the author of the letter would come forward to the D.A. and provide further information. It was around this time that the body of Mary Santos was found – near Route 88. It was reported that someone *did* come forward, but the D.A. would neither answer questions about the letter nor its author. Questions arose as to whether the letter actually exists and whether a person did come forward.

As is always the case, theories also remain as to why the killings suddenly stopped. The usual postulations that come of the fore are that the perpetrator is in prison, is incapacitated, is dead or has moved on to "fresh pastures". Or he could still be free, living and working alongside the people of that New England city, having literally got away with murder. Meanwhile, there are no answers and no closure for the families of those left behind. The case remains frustratingly unsolved.

The Smiley Face Murder Theory
[active 1990s–2000s]

ACCORDING TO FBI STATISTICS, at any one time the US has around 50 active serial killers. Generally, these killers are split into two groups – the ones who get caught and the ones who don't. But there's a third kind – more silent but just as deadly – and they are the ones who are so elusive that they are not even recognised as serial killers. The only trace they leave might be a trail of disappeared people – a vague, unfathomable suspicion that something is awry. The Smiley Face Killer could be just that sort of killer. In this case, sound evidence of his existence is somewhat lacking to say the least. A statistical anomaly. Some graffitied "autographs". Scant evidence indeed. However, some authorities, after examining patterns of "accidental" deaths, have concluded that a serial murderer of young men *does* exist. His preferred victim-type is the young, popular, athletic male. His *M.O.* is to take them whilst they are inebriated and to stage their deaths like unintentional drownings. Others dismiss this hypothesis, stating that it really isn't so out-of-the-ordinary for college-aged students, whilst under the influence of alcohol, to accidentally fall into a body of water and not come out again alive.

The theory was developed in 2008 by two retired New York detectives, Kevin Gannon and Anthony Duarte, together with a criminal justice professor, Dr Lee Gilbertson. They believe that over 40 cases (the number could be around 100) of apparent drowning across the mid-west and north-east of America are linked. They are convinced that these deaths, from the late 1990s onwards, are the hideous business of a serial killer – or a net-works of killers, working together – who travel the country hunting young college men. They allege that these victims did not, as law enforcement agencies concluded, accidentally drown, and they believe they have the evidence to back up their theory.

These are the facts. Between 1997 and 2008, in more than 25 cities across northern North American states, the dead bodies of more than 40 young white males were pulled out of lakes and rivers. They mostly fit the description of being popular and athletic. Most had been last seen leaving bars or parties whilst inebriated.

Police, quite reasonably, supposed that the men had become drunk, wandered off, got too close to water, slipped in and, trapped or incapacitated by their inebriation, had simply drowned. However, Gannon and Duarte, who were at the time investigating the case of an accounting student of Fordham University, Patrick McNeill, drew an eerier conclusion.

Twenty-one-year-old McNeill disappeared on 16 February 1997. Standing at 6-feet tall and weighing in at 195lbs, he was a clean-cut all-American boy who was well liked by both his male and female associates. That night he had been out with friends at the Dapper Dog, an uptown Manhattan watering hole popular with Fordham students due to its *laissez-faire* serving policies and frat-like atmosphere of free-flowing booze and loud music. McNeill, it is fair to say, had been enjoying the hospitalities of the establishment and ended up drunk. After he threw up in the bathroom of the Dapper Dog he left, waiting outside for one of his friends. When she failed to appear McNeill took off himself. In the early hours of that morning bystanders observed him stumbling southeast along Second Avenue, sometimes falling down and then getting up again. They also noticed a double-parked van apparently shadowing him. When McNeill stopped so did the van. When McNeill turned left onto East 90th Street so also did the van. Then McNeill disappeared.

There was no obvious conclusion to be drawn about the disappearance. McNeill had been a popular student with many friends, a good-looking "ladies' man". He was doing well in class; he was motivated, having ambitions to join the FBI. There was no evidence that he was depressed or feeling suicidal. He had no cause to leave without telling anyone.

McNeill's family, understandably distraught, canvassed the

area for over a month, enlisting volunteers in coordinated searches and the distribution of fliers. The search for McNeill proved fruitless.

Then the unthinkable. On 7 April 1997 a body was seen floating next to the 65th Street Pier in the East River. The badly decomposed remains, dressed only in jeans and socks, were recovered and identified as the missing student. The medical examiner could not determine a cause of death. His blood-alcohol level was 0.16. This was "more than a little, less than a lot", the New York City's chief Medical Examiner ruled, a level at which a disoriented imbiber has reduced control of motor skills and experiences perceptual impairment and poor judgement. Not unreasonably, the New York Police Department who were investigating the case believed that McNeill had drunkenly staggered towards the river and fallen in.

Gannon did not concur with this conclusion. He believed that McNeill had been "stalked, abducted, held for an extended period of time, murdered and disposed". And the evidence, a rational person might conclude, does suggest some oddities could be attached to the notion of accidental drowning. The East River would not have been an easy destination to reach. To get there one would have to cross the FDR Drive, a fenced, limited-access expressway. One does not simply stroll across it. Access to the river itself would not have been easy. It has barriers designed, indeed, to prevent accidental falling. Despite his probable poor judgement, it is highly unlikely that the young man would have decided to go for an early morning swim. The temperature in New York that winter's night was at freezing point. Disturbingly, the autopsy of McNeill's body suggested that he had been bound and burned before ending up in the river. In addition, fly larvae were found in the groin area of the body, and flies do not lay eggs in the cold temperatures that were happening outdoors when McNeill purportedly drowned. The larvae were of an indoor fly, "so we have a body that was already dead before it was placed in the water," said Dr Cyril Wecht. Also, further evidence from the autopsy – discrepancies of lack of skin "slippage" – suggested that the body had not been dead for the full period during which McNeill had gone missing. The body was found *upstream* from the part of Manhattan in which McNeill had last been seen. It was found floating face-up, not face-down, contraindicating blood lividity observations, and it did not possess the typical semi-foetal posture that is the norm for drown victims. Lastly, McNeill's body was found in the same location as that of another handsome young college student, Larry Andrews, who had disappeared under similar circumstances a year before. McNeill had not, Gannon was certain, flung off his clothes to go for a midnight swim in February in the uninviting waters of New York's East River. And he was not the first college-age male to have died under suspicious circumstances.

Gannon and Duarte then began to collate and examine the evidence surrounding other suspicious deaths of young men, similar to that of Victim Zero, Patrick McNeill. Eventually they came to hypothesise that many of the victims had been murdered, either by a single deranged individual or by a coordinated group of killers. The "Smiley Face" designate that has become attached to the theory comes from the discovery of graffiti in the vicinity of where the bodies were found in at least a dozen of the cases. This is perhaps unfortunate. Sceptics point to the fact that this graffiti image – a simple, easily-drawn design – is ubiquitous; its discovery next to the dump sites is nothing more than coincidental, a misleading motif. A close inspection of the graffiti supposedly planted at the sites shows different versions of the smiley face – some very simply drawn, others more complex. This suggests that different individuals have made their mark there at different times, who would in all probability have had no connection whatsoever to the accidental drownings. It does not, however, conclusively rule out that many different individuals, of diverse artistic ability, may have "signed off" their crimes with their own style of graffiti. It is also possible that the smiley face *does* have some significance and is not merely coincidental. The bodies may have moved between being disposed of and being found (many were found in flowing water), in which case the location of any smiley face graffiti would not be immediately identifiable.

The fact of the matter is this: in that north-and-north-eastern region of the US there is a higher rate of drowning deaths amongst the demographic of college-age males, a rate that is statistically significant. Of course, the raised alcohol intake more likely to be prevalent amongst that population may have skewered the data, but even taking that into account there is still an anomaly.

The FBI National Press Office issued a statement in 2008 on their current position on the theory:

> *The FBI has reviewed the information about the victims provided by two retired police detectives, who have dubbed these incidents the "Smiley Face Murders," and interviewed an individual who provided information to the detectives. To date, we have not developed any evidence to support links between these tragic deaths or any evidence substantiating the theory that these deaths are the work of a serial killer or killers. The vast majority of these instances appear to be alcohol-related drownings. The FBI will continue to work with the local police in the affected areas to provide support as requested.*

Some disagree. The debate is hotly contested. The coinage of the Smiley Face moniker seems to be an unfortunate distraction, and the fact is that many of the deaths have been ruled as accidental or undetermined drownings, exacerbated by excessive alcohol consumption. Nevertheless, the theory of malfeasance persists. Gannon and Gilbertson continue to argue the case that these men did not drown. Instead they were targeted, abducted and murdered by a network of coordinated criminals who remain at large. Their *motive* may be jealousy – the target being the privileged white male, society's "*crème de la crème*", the perpetrator being an unpopular, unemployed loser.[*]

Another motive may be that the young men were killed as some sick kind of gang initiation rite. The victims were drunk and alone on the streets at night, and so the *means* and *opportunity* can be easily explained. Horrifyingly, as the theory becomes more widely known and develops traction, the idea of copy-cat killings cannot be discounted.

Another conjecture is that the killings have occurred in locations that can be pinpointed on a map – that is to say, the killers are creating a frightful dot-to-dot puzzle, with the United States being the gigantic canvas upon which the puzzle is drawn, and if one were to connect the dots the image of a smiley face emerges. The idea is astounding in its audacity.

A disappearance that fits the circumstances associated with the Smiley Face Killings occurred around Halloween 2002 in Minneapolis, Minnesota. Chris Jenkins, a 21-year-old Minnesota student, was out socialising with friends at the Lone Tree Bar and Grill. At some stage during the night he spilt drink on his trousers. Security assumed he had urinated himself and ejected him from the bar. Unfortunately, Jenkins' fancy dress costume of a Native American did not have pockets and so he did not have his wallet, keys or cell phone upon him that bitterly cold night. Unable to get back into the bar, and with no means to arrange a lift home, Jenkins began to head home. He was last seen walking northeast along Hennepin Avenue … towards the Mississippi River.

On 27 February 2003, Jenkins' body, still clad in the Halloween costume, was found floating in the Mississippi River beneath a bridge near Upper St Anthony's Dam. Since he still wore the costume it was assumed that he had drowned that same Halloween night. However, a few discrepancies arose. Private

---

[*] Gannon, Kevin and Gilbertson, D. Lee (2014) *Case Studies in Drowning Forensics*. CRC Press: Boca Raton, Florida

investigators hired by Jenkins' family could not trace the drowned man's steps to the river. Security cameras footage showed no sign of him. He had not completed his solitary walk home. The PIs hired K-9 units, which followed a scent to an underground carpark. There the investigators found blood droplets and some cloth, string and feather fragments that could well have come from a costume.

In Jenkins' blood, the pathologist found traces of GHB, a so-called "date-rape drug" which is used to render people insensible. Jenkins' blood-alcohol level was .12 percent, which indicates significant a concentration of alcohol intake but not enough to cause intoxication. The body was inconsistent with that of a drowning victim. Jenkins was found with his trousers tucked in and his slip-on moccasins still on; his arms were crossed in front of him. There were no bruises on his body. Jenkins' family thought this unusual. As a lacrosse player he often had bruises on his body. His family believed that he may have been kept alive long enough for any bruising to heal. Finally, it was supposed that a body could not have remained in the river at that point without being spotted by a passer-by. It was beginning to look as if the body of Chris Jenkins was placed into the river at some stage after his death.

The evidence was reviewed and the case reopened and upgraded from accidental death to homicide. The case certainly fits a grim pattern. However, no smiley face has been found in the area where the body was found and no one has been charged for this or any of the other supposed Smiley Face Killings. In many circles the theory has aroused much incredulity and ridicule, with law enforcement agencies pouring scorn on conspiracy theorists whose objective it is to find connections and patterns that are simply not there. And yet inconsistencies highlighted by forensics and evidence *do* exist. The victims themselves are consistently "of a type". The frequency of their deaths is statistically significant. The bodies often do not correlate with those of true drowning victims. There may be some staging involved in the placement of the bodies.

There are many theories and possibilities and they all continue to stimulate debate and fuel speculation: One, there is one serial killer who has been extremely prolific and expert in evading law enforcement. Two, a group of serial killers have been working in collusion under the umbrella of some nefarious motive. Three, a homicidal cult or sect has been slaying young men as a form of unnatural sacrifice. Four, the killings are part of a fearsome gang that demands death as an initiation rite. Five, the deaths are intentional but unconnected, the dreadful doings of vengeful or motiveless individuals, or copycat killers. Six, the deaths *really are* the results of either unforeseen, tragic, accidental drownings of young college-age men who have drunk too much, or of these men's deliberate, equally tragic suicides. Until convincing evidence arises to point a finger at one or more of these potential theories, the jury is very much out.

The I-70 Killer
(active 1992–1994?)

INTERSTATE 70 is a major highway that spans 2,500 east-west miles of American soil, through 10 different states from Maryland to Utah. As the chosen killing ground of many a serial killer, the I-70 has also been dubbed "America's Sewer Pipe". In fact, so many serial killers have haunted this infamous stretch of freeway that two of them share the same appellation, the "I-70 Killer". One of these killers, who is also referred to as the I-70 Strangler, is believed to have been Herb Baumeister, a successful businessman, a husband and the father of three children. Strong evidence suggests that he killed around at least a dozen young men in the early 1990s. When the investigative heat became too strong Baumeister fled to Canada where he ended his own life by a bullet to the forehead on 3 July 1996. His suicide note stated the reason for his action had been his failing marriage and business difficulties. Dead bodies were not mentioned. It was only after his death that the remains of 11 men were found on his farm near Carmel, Indianapolis.

But there is *another* I-70 Killer, one who remains unidentified and unapprehended. He killed in Indiana, Missouri and Kansas, and is suspected also to have killed in Texas.

The spree began in spring 1992 and six shop workers were to have their lives cut short after four short weeks had passed. The killer struck at small "speciality" stores which were located a few miles off the I-70. His victims would have been similar in many respects, apart from in two cases, in which the killer is thought to have made tactical errors.

Robin Fuldauer, aged 26, was the first to die. On 8 April 1992, the kind and caring young woman was working at a discount shoe store in Indianapolis, Indiana. That day her co-worker had called in sick and so Robin was manning the store by herself, a task she had been called upon to do before. It is not known exactly what happened that afternoon, but police believe that at some time around 14:00 a man entered the store, forced Robin into a storage room and shot her in the head with a .22 calibre gun. Taking what small amount of cash there was in the register, the killer then left the store via the back exit and walked off in broad daylight.

Customers arriving at the store would come in only to find the store unmanned. With no surveillance cameras to thwart them, some of them would grab some free shoes and leave. It was some while before Robin's body was discovered in the storeroom. The police were shocked. The dispatching of a defenceless store assistant was nothing less than a cold-blooded execution.

A witness reported that he had seen a man in a green jacket arrive on foot and scout the shoe store for around half-an-hour before entering. "I'm telling you," the witness said, "he was either on drugs or had mental problems," apparently basing his diagnosis on the fact that the man "looked like a guy who had been sleeping in his clothes" and that he had been talking and giggling to himself. The witness reported that the man disappeared for a short while. The witness then caught a glimpse of the man as he calmly hitched a northbound lift on the highway.

Three days later, on 11 April 1992, and nearly 700 miles away, a man appeared at a bride and groom clothing business in Wichita, Kansas. The owner, Patricia Magers, aged 32, and her assistant, Patricia Smith, aged 23, had already closed up shop for the evening. They had, however, prearranged to admit a man who wished to collect a cummerbund after-hours.

When the customer arrived at the store as agreed, a slight, red-haired man with a semi-automatic gun was already on the premises and he tried to get the customer to enter the store and go into the back. After a brief dialogue the customer managed to make his excuses and surprisingly the red-haired man allowed him to leave unharmed. The customer immediately put in a call to police.

By the time they arrived Magers was already dead and Smith lay dying. They had both been shot execution-style with a .22

calibre pistol and the gun-toting assassin was gone. Nevertheless, the witness who had called the police was able to give a detailed description of the man in the shop and a composite sketch was compiled by a police artist. Some money was missing from the till but it is believed that robbery was not the motive for the crime. Police also assumed that the killer had chosen the bridal shop in the belief that only a single clerk worked there and that he had been surprised to discover two on duty.

On 27 April 1997 Michael McCown, aged 40, was working at a ceramics store in Terre Haute, Indiana, 600-miles eastward. The shop belonged to his mother. Its name was Sylvia's Ceramics and Michael wore his long hair in a ponytail. It is possible that these two facts were the unwitting downfall of the only male to be killed by the I-70 Killer, who may have shot a man believing him to be a woman called Sylvia. Michael was shot in the back of the head as he knelt on the floor reaching for a small white ceramic house. The weapon was a .22 calibre gun. Michael's wallet was stolen, but the money in his pocket and what cash there was in the tills was untouched. No one saw anyone enter the shop and the killer left no traces. It quickly became a cold case of no leads.

On Sunday, 3 May 1992, nearly 200-miles west of Sylvia's Ceramics, the first and last customer of the day entered a footwear shop in St Charles, Missouri. Nancy Kitzmiller, aged 24, opened up the store at noon and admitted the man who would coldly shoot her in the head. Like the murder of Michael McCown no one heard any shot, but one shopper was able to describe seeing a man of medium height with dull red hair in the vicinity. This individual was more than likely the I-70 Killer and he had just ended the life of the fun-loving cowgirl with a single bullet from a .22 calibre semi-automatic. Nancy was his fifth victim and robbery did not seem to be the motive for the attack.

Just four days later, over 200-miles west along the I-70, the killer's last confirmed attack occurred. On 7 May 1992, in Raytown, Missouri Sarah Blessing was working in her gift shop. It was half-past-six, nearing the end of Sarah's shift, when an unidentified man entered her shop. A witness heard a loud *pop* sound and then saw the man exit. Another witness saw the man scramble up an embankment towards the I-70. Upon investigation, Sarah lay lifeless, her legs half-out of a backroom, in a pool of her own blood. She had been shot at point-blank range with a .22 calibre bullet. Witness accounts of a "nondescript" sandy-haired man with lazy eyes hanging around the mall correlated with the witness statements taken after the bridal shop murder of Magers and Smith and the mumbling man who had been seen lurking outside Robin Fuldauer's shoe shop.

It was only after a St Charles detective suspected a connection that the cases were linked due to the *M.O.* and victim-type of the crimes. The pattern seemed to be dark-haired women working alone, all shot in the back of the head. There was no sexual motive to the crimes, and although all were robbed, this did not seem to be a motive either. Bullet analysis would prove the connection. However, investigators were stymied. "We don't even know what the hell we're looking for," the frustrated police chief in Terre Haute admitted.

Some believe that the I-70 killer killed again in Texas in September and November 1993, and made an attempted killing in January 1994. Again all victims had been shot in the back of the head with a .22 calibre gun. However, ballistics tests showed that it was not the same weapon in the earlier killings and other than some similarities there were no reasons to suspect that the cases were linked.

A break in the case seemed to emerge briefly in June 1992. Thirty-seven-year-old Donnie Waterhouse was arrested for the murder of his mother and stepfather in Dyersburg, Tennessee using a .22 calibre gun. Waterhouse had a passing resemblance to the description of the I-70 Killer but other than that there is no evidence to link him to the case. The slim lead, however, went nowhere and Waterhouse is currently in prison awaiting parole in 2021.

Another theory exists. Some consider it possible that the I-70 Killer may actually have been the supposed I-70 Strangler, Herb

Baumeister. He certainly did fit the description given by witnesses – a thin, red-haired man with drooping eyes. He might seem a strange suspect given that he was a sexually-motivated serial killer who targeted gay men. It is telling that the I-70 Killer's victims were mostly women and that they were not sexually molested. The question of motive arises. Perhaps he did it merely because he could – for the thrill of it. Notwithstanding, there were no I-70 killings after Baumeister's death in 1996, so the theory may have some merit.

It is unlikely that the case of the I-70 Killer will ever be solved. The ghostly monster simply came, killed and went, leaving no trace, and only fear in his wake. There are no clues as to _why_ he killed. If robbery actually was the motive then the pittance he got away with was pitifully little for the grief and bewilderment he left for the families of the bereaved.

The Long Island Serial Killer
(active 1996–2010)

"IS THIS MELISSA'S LITTLE SISTER?" The strange call came through on 16 July 2009 using Melissa's own mobile phone.

Sixteen-year-old Amanda replied, "Yes."

"Do you know what your sister is doing? She's a whore."

The calls would only come in the evening, and the caller would only talk to Amanda. If anyone else picked up the phone he would hang up. In each of the six calls, a low, calm voice would taunt the sister of Melissa Barthelemy, revealing that she was a prostitute. The caller kept his conversation – if that were the right word – short. The man continued to make increasingly disturbing "vulgar, mocking and insulting" calls to Amanda over the next five weeks, asking her if she was "a whore like her sister", eventually culminating with him telling her that Melissa was dead and that he was "going to watch her rot". Amanda's mother kept a log of the calls, and police were able to trace them to Times Square and Madison Square Garden, New York and a town called Massapequa at the southeast end of Long Island, New York. However, as the caller never stayed on the line more than three minutes, and the calls were made from crowded locations, the police were never able to catch him. They were beginning to think that the man could be involved in law enforcement, for he did not make mistakes, and he seemed to always be one step ahead of his pursuers.

Melissa Barthelemy was last seen on 12 July 2009 outside her Bronx, New York apartment. A surveillance camera at her bank recorded her depositing $1,000 cash, and she was then observed withdrawing $100 from an ATM before heading out the door.

The information imparted by the caller to Melissa's sister was partially correct. Although her family had not been aware of the fact, Melissa, in fact, *had* been working as an escort, and that evening she had another "date" lined up somewhere on Long Island. Her working name was "Chloe", and "Chloe" was a very attractive 24-year-old blond woman. In his first unsolicited call to Amanda, the strange man had initially alluded that her sister was alive. At that stage she was very probably *not* alive. The exact details of what happened to Melissa that night are not known but they can easily be surmised, for her decomposed remains were discovered near Gilgo Beach on Long Island on 11 December 2010.

The body of 25-year-old Maureen Brainard-Barnes was found on an unspecified date in December 2010, a few days after the body of Melissa Barthelemy was discovered. She had gone missing on 9 July 2007, having last been seen in her hotel room in midtown Manhattan. Shortly after her disappearance, a friend received a call from an unknown man who stated that Maureen was alive and staying at "a whorehouse in Queens". The man refused to identify himself but stated that he would call the friend back with details of the address where Maureen was staying. He never did phone back.

On 1 May 2010 Shannan Gilbert, a 23-year-old escort, was working at a client's house in Oak Beach on Long Island. The client's name was Joseph Brewer, and waiting outside the house was her driver for the night, a man called Michael.

At 04:51 Shannan made a panicked 23-minute call to 911 dispatchers saying that "they" were after her and "they" were trying to kill her. After screaming and banging on the door of an Oak Beach resident's home she ran off into the night, screaming for help. Shannan subsequently disappeared without trace.

Her mother received a phone call two days later. The caller, who announced himself as Dr Peter Hackett, claimed that he "ran a home for wayward girls" and that he was taking care of Shannan. Three days after this, Dr Hackett spoke to Shannan's mother again (by phoning Shannon's mobile) and during the call he denied that he had seen Shannan. Two calls *were* made from Hackett's own mobile phone for they were confirmed by phone records.

These unsolicited telephone calls, which could have been interpreted as malicious pranks, would soon come to be viewed as attempts as diversion, as if someone were trying to place the three missing women somewhere else, somewhere other than on Long Island. By now, however, Shannan's mother had filed a missing person report, and it was the impetus provoked by this that ultimately created a chain of events that led to the uncovering of a series of killings on Long Island. Meanwhile, the list of victims seemed to grow and grow with no answer as to who was responsible.

On 20 April 1996 two female legs were found in a plastic bag on Fire Island. It would be another 15 years before the skull of "Fire Island Jane Doe" was found on Tobay Beach.

On 28 June 1997 another Jane Doe was found, this time a young African-American female. She had been dismembered and her torso was dumped in a plastic bag by the side of the road. Arms, legs and head had been removed and have not been yet found. Investigators called this body "Peaches" on account of a tattoo of a peach on the woman's breast.

On 19 November 2000 hikers near Manorville on Long Island found the naked, headless body of a woman in her 30s cut into pieces and stuffed into plastic bags. She would be referred to by investigators as Jane Doe No. 6. Her body, head, hands and right foot would be found 11 years later, in a plastic bag around 20 miles away, across the bay on Fire Island, enabling investigators to identify her as Valerie Mack, a 24-year-old escort who had last been seen in the spring or summer of 2000. Nobody had reported her missing.

On 23 November 2000 hunters found the body of man dressed only in boxer shorts in woods in Manorville. He was either white or Hispanic and had black hair. His crushed larynx suggested that he had been strangled to death.

A headless and limbless body was found on a pile of scrap wood on 26 July 2003. These remains were identified as Jessica Taylor, aged 20. A tattoo of a red heart and angel wing on the body had been mutilated with a sharp implement. In similar circumstances to Valerie Mack, the rest of Taylor's remains would be found across the Great South Bay on Gilgo Beach eight years later.

It was speculated that another body found in Manorville on 10 November 2003 could have been dumped at the same time as Jessica Taylor. The white victim, aged 35-50, had died around four months earlier and she remains unidentified.

"Cherries", a dark-skinned unidentified female was found on 3 March 2007. Her torso washed onto a Mamaroneck, New York beach in a suitcase. Both her legs washed up on Long Island later that month. "Cherries" had a tattoo of two cherries on her breast. Because she had been dismembered in similar fashion to "Peaches" and Valerie Mack, "Cherries" is linked to the Long Island Serial Killer's official victims.

Mother-of-three, Tanya Rush, aged 39, was found on 27 June 2008. Like many of the other victims, Rush was a sex worker. Her dismembered remains had been crammed into a suitcase and dumped in grass on the side of the road on Long Island. Her killer had made little attempt to hide his handiwork.

Mid-December 2010 was a busy time for the Suffolk County Police. On 11 December they begin looking for the body of Shannan Gilbert at the behest of her mother who, after receiving the two strange phone calls from Dr Peter Hackett, became convinced that something untoward had happened to her daughter. Police with dogs instead found the remains of Melissa Barthelemy, whose sister had also received a series of unusual phone calls from an unidentified man. Melissa's full skeleton was found wrapped in hessian fabric on Long Island's Gilgo Beach.

Nearby, police found the remains of Maureen Brainhard-Barnes, whose friend had also received the unsolicited call from a mysterious man who claimed that she was staying "in a whore-house in Queens".

The remains of Megan Waterman were also found close by. Twenty-two-year-old Megan had last been seen on 6 June that year, heading towards a convenience store in Hauppauge on Long Island. Megan was an escort who advertised her services on Craigslist.

Amber Costello's skeletal remains were also found at the

Gilgo Beach site. The 27-year-old sex worker who had battled against addiction was last seen getting into a client's car just a few months earlier in September. In late January 2011 Suffolk County District Attorney announced that the so-called "Gilgo Four" victims were escorts who had advertised in Craigslist.

Skeletal remains were found between Oak Beach and Gilgo Beach on 4 April 2011. These were revealed to belong to an Asian male who had been bludgeoned to death. He was missing four teeth. It was assumed that the man, who was aged between 17 and 23, had been working as an escort; he had been dressed in female clothes at the time of his death. His identity remains unknown.

Also found at the same site and on the same day were the remains of a 16-32-month-old girl. DNA analysis showed that Baby Doe was the daughter of "Peaches", the female body found in 1996.

Eventually, to the obvious distress of her long-searching mother, on 13 December 2011, the remains of Shannan Gilbert were discovered on Oak Beach. The next day, a 48-year-old businessman, James Bissett, ended his own life in a carpark in Mattituck on Long Island.

Two further discoveries would be made in 2013. A woman walking her dog in January found intentionally buried remains near Lattington, New York. These were believed to belong to an Asian woman of around 20-30-years of age. An autopsy indicated that her bones showed signs of trauma. And the remains of a woman, later identified as 31-year-old Natasha Jugo, were discovered in June after washing up on the Gilgo Beach. Her family reported that she had a history of paranoia. Neither of these findings has been officially linked to the Long Island Serial Killer case.

And there was an older case that had bewildered law enforcers at the time and was still unsolved. On 1 February 1982, Tina Foglia, aged 19, went missing from a rock music venue in West Islip on Long Island. Her dismembered remains were found two days later in three separate plastic bags along the side of the road.

There has been a lot of speculation about the profile of the killer, and much of the conjecture seems to conform to common sense. He was most likely to be a white male aged between 20 and 40 who had intimate knowledge of the South Shore of Long Island as this is not an area which one just stumbles upon. He was probably married, or had a girlfriend. He had a job and was financially secure, and will have had access to a car or van. He is organised. As part of his job or interests, he also had access to hessian fabric. Four of the victims had been wrapped in this particular material, which is not that commonly available. Could the killer have been a landscaper or building contractor?

As the killer was able to meet women some distance from their own homes at night, he will have been rational and persuasive, able to demonstrate social skills; he may even have been charismatic. He was your "Average Joe". The people who lived and worked with him will have had no inkling of his deeper psychopathic tendencies.

Some have speculated that the killer may have had knowledge of law enforcement procedures or telecommunications. The fact that untraceable calls were made to the families of three of the victims suggests at least some knowledge.

The summertime disappearances offered another clue. The killer may have been a holidaymaker, or he may only have visited his relatives during the summer months. It is possible that his wife and family or his own parents departed from Long Island for the summer, hence giving him the opportunity to indulge in his homicidal recreations whilst alone there. Or the summer months may have had some sort of ritualistic or fantasy meaning for him.

The killer targeted sex workers, subjecting them to psychosexual sadism. He enjoys pain, and he gets a kick out of taunting others. He was able to lure his victims to an address many miles from his home in order to kill them. This was not impulsive or disorganised behaviour. The killer was able to demonstrate a degree of care and carefulness to have done this without being caught, and he is therefore likely to be an intelligent, educated and methodical individual. The fact that he left little in the way of viable clues (as far as is known) suggests that he may have knowledge of forensic techniques. Could the killer be a serving or former cop?

There are suspects.

James Bissett, the businessman who ran a nursery, which was known to have been a supplier of sacks made from hessian. He killed himself in December 2011, the day after the remains of Shannan Gilbert were found. The motivation for his unexpectedly suicide caused rumours to swirl locally. Perhaps the heat had become too strong after the discovery of Gilbert's body. Certainly, the victim's mother had been very vocal in her determination to get justice for her daughter. It is possible that living under the cloud of suspicion had become too much for Bissett.

Suffolk County resident John Bittrolff was a hunter who reportedly enjoyed killing animals. He was a suspect in at least one of the Long Island murders. In 2014 he was arrested on the basis of familial DNA profiling for the murder of two prostitutes in 1993 and 1994. He is currently serving two consecutive life sentences for each crime. There are similarities between the known murders of Bittrolff and those of the Long Island Serial Killer. Authorities say that he is suspected of a third murder but not in the Long Island cases. They have declined to reveal the exculpatory evidence.

Oak Beach resident Joseph Brewer was the john who hired Shannan Gilbert on the night she disappeared. He reported that some hours after her arrival Shannan suddenly became irrational and fled from his house into the night. He claimed that she had become paranoid after taking a large quantity of drugs. During the 911 call she was heard screaming and crying that "they're trying to kill me". Police investigated but, finding no evidence of wrongdoing, cleared Brewer as a suspect.

Also of interest is James Burke, former Suffolk County Police Chief, who was sentenced to 46 months in prison in November 2016. His crime had been to attack a man who had stolen a bag from his car. The bag contained sex toys and pornography. Allegations have been made that Burke paid for sex and treated prostitutes roughly, pulling them by the hair and enjoying causing them pain.

Dr Peter Hackett was confirmed by telecommunications records that he had made phone calls to the mother of Shannan Gilbert shortly after her disappearance in 2010. He claimed to have given the panicked Shannan medication to help her calm down, and that he had tried to get in contact with her family to come and help her. Shannan's remains were found a year-and-a-half after this in marshy ground next to Hackett's Oak Beach house. He was later ruled out as a suspect by police.

Two separate "sex kidnapping" incidents occurred on Long Island in October 2018, according to the *New York Times*, which reported that the women had gone to meet a man, 54-year-old Andrew Frey, who had agreed to pay them for sex. Instead he forced them violently into his car and drove off. The women escaped by throwing themselves from the moving car, injuring themselves in the process. On one of the occasions, the sinister man later returned with a weapon to hunt the woman down. Fortunately for the woman she was able to escape a second time. Police searching his house found ropes, zip-ties and manuals on how to tie knots. It is not clear what the man's intentions had been but they do not seem well-meaning.

The Long Island Serial Killer could actually have been more than one individual, a team working together, hunting prostitutes for sport, or indulging themselves in a series of dreadful sex games which ultimately resulted in the women's deaths.

Alternatively, there might have been more than one series of killings. Each individual killer might separately but coincidentally have chosen Long Island for its convenience as a desolate dumping ground. For preferential reasons the individuals may have independently chosen different areas of the island that suited their own disposal needs.

Investigators, it seems, are no closer to uncovering the answers. There have been recent breakthroughs in identification of some of the bodies, but others remain whose identities are still a mystery. For their friends and families, it is hoped that someday resolution will eventually come. However, the investigators' best chance may have already come and gone. The series of taunting phone calls to the sister of Melissa Barthelemy was a rare lucky break – but by the time New York detectives had triangulated the signal and arrived at Times Square, the killer was already gone. He had slipped like a phantom into the crowd and was never to be seen. And after that single call to the friend of Maureen Brainard-Barnes he was not to be heard from again either. For now, the face of the Long Island Serial Killer remains unseen, his identity undetected.

The Edgecombe County Serial Killer
(active 2000s)

SEVEN BRIDGES ROAD in Rocky Mount, North Carolina already had a somewhat spooky reputation. It is said that a motorist driving eastwards from Rocky Mount to the tiny village of Leggett would count seven bridges. Travelling on the return journey the motorist would count only six. One of the bridges has disappeared.

It is an optical illusion, of course, but some locals point to a darker reason. The more superstitious residents believe that this stretch of road is haunted and that it can mess with people's heads. There are stories of a weird individual seen in car rear-view mirrors, and certainly, there have been plenty of freak accidents on this 10-mile stretch of asphalt over the years. But a proportion of the deaths were not merely misfortune, and at least 10 women are thought to have died at the hands of a depraved miscreant.

Edgecombe County does not often make the news; the small-town city Rocky Mount even less so. The city has a population of just over 50,000, nearly two-thirds of whom are African-American. Mid-century integration gave rise to the movement of some of the less-embracing white people from the district. In a once prosperous area of cotton fields, textile mills and tobacco warehouses, as the jobs disappeared so the town itself became impoverished; but the surrounding the city is rich with lush, green countryside containing plenty of acres of deep woods and open and bountiful fields. A perfect place, as one person clearly felt, to dispose of a dead body … or more.

The first of those disposed bodies was to be found towards the end of May 2005. A farmer near the Seven Bridges Road was taking down an electric fence when he was drawn towards a foreign odour. After a search he stumbled upon what he initially mistook for the rotting carcass of a deer. With horror, the farmer quickly realised that this was nearly-skeletonised human remains, lying face-down, beetles and maggots crawling over the remnants of the flesh. This would prove to be the body of Melody Wiggins, a black 29-year-old lady. She had been killed by blunt force trauma to the head and had also suffered stab wounds.

Christine Boone and Joyce Durham, in 2006 and 2007 respectively, appeared to simply vanish from the face of the earth. Christine's bones were found four years later in a wooded area 45 miles away. Her sister said in an interview after the remains were found, "My sister was a very loving and caring person who got caught up with the wrong crowd." Christine had been 43 when she died. Joyce Durham, who was aged 46 when she went disappeared, remains unaccounted for.

Ernestine Battle, aged 50, was last seen getting into a vehicle with an unidentified black man on 1 February 2008. Her remains were found in a wooded area off Seven Bridges Road in March, in the same remote field where the body of Melody Wiggins had been dumped. The same field was also to produce the remains of two other women, Nikki Thorpe, aged 35, and Jarneice "Sunshine" Hargrove, aged 31.

Nikki Thorpe, who was known locally as "Miss Jackie", had had dreams of being a fashion model and had taken pains to look after her appearance. In school she had written poetry and been a cheerleader. After school she held down a respectable job with a cable company. Then things seemed to slide and before long she made a move into the sex business. Nikki had a highly regarded talent for doing hair. For braiding the hair of local crack dealers she would sometimes accept a rock of crack from their wares as payment. Like Melody's, Nikki's rotting body was found along the Seven Bridges Road. There was not enough left of her to determine the cause of death. "Miss Jackie" had had her head and an arm cut off.

Jarneice Hargrove was discovered on 29 June 2009 by a Mexican labourer who had gone to relieve himself behind a bush. There was not enough left of Jarneice to determine the cause of her death. The examining doctor, however, was able to determine that six of her teeth had been beaten from her skull. Her family were able to recall a woman of some self-possession who, despite a diagnosis of bipolar disorder and an addiction to crack, enjoyed writing and performing her own rap at a local club. She was the seventh black woman from Edgecombe County to have been killed in similar circumstances.

It seemed with this seventh death that authorities were now able to connect the cases and bring in State and federal investigators. Politicians became involved. The media were alerted, billboards were erected and an invitation was made by a TV news channel to the mother of one of the murdered women to talk on air about her daughter.

Unfortunately another news story broke, and the victim this time was a missing white woman – a "beautiful Florida newly-wed". The media turned their eyes instead towards the Sunshine State and the mother of the slain Edgecombe County woman was duly dropped from the TV news schedule.

Then, in Edgecombe County, two further sets of remains were found. One set would be identified over a year later as belonging to Roberta Williams, aged 40. She had a history of drug use and prostitution. After her disappearance she had not officially reported missing, the unfortunate fate of too many a sex worker.

The second body wore only a black bra and white socks. A tattoo – "Tara" – on the arm of this corpse aided the identification of 28-year-old Tahara Nicholson. She had been strangled, her neck fractured, and multiple abrasions covered her body.

Tara had been trying to get off drugs and get off the streets but her boyfriend would not let her. Every time she made progress he would rattle a vial of crack before her and the cycle would begin again. Shortly before her disappearance, Tara's mother gave her a warning: "There's someone out there killing these girls." And Tara would reply, "I don't jump into cars with people I don't know."

Maybe Tara *did* know her killer. In finding a sample of foreign DNA on her remains, the authorities were able to put a name to her killer, and on 1 September 2009 they made their arrest. Antwan Pittman, aged 31, was already languishing in prison at the time for failing to register his latest address as a registered sex offender. Six months later he was indicted for the murder of Tahara Nicholson.

Numerous mugshots show a black man with blank eyes. A high school dropout having a mild learning disability, Pittman had worked a series of low-grade jobs in or around Rocky Mount. On the surface there was little about the man to inspire the interest of neighbours, but already on his record was the fact that whilst still a teenage he had attempted to rape a two-year-old child. His arrest record was already chequered: underage possession of alcohol, assault, taking indecent liberties with a child, resisting arrest, driving whilst under the influence, the solicitation of prostitutes. Authorities believed that they had their man, and even as the prosecution prepared its case the bodies continued to turn up.

Missing since 2009, Yolanda "Snap" Lancaster, aged 37, would eventually be found by a hunter in January 2011 in a wooded area outside Rocky Mount. That same month another body was found. A prison clean-up crew came across the unclothed skeleton in the woods. Eight months later the remains would be identified as Elizabeth Smallwood, aged 33, who had a record of prostitution and drug charges. Today the numbers hold at 10 dead and one is missing. Antwan Pittman is in prison and the killings have stopped.

Pittman admitted to having had sex with Tahara Nicholson on 1 March 2009, giving her $20 and taking her to the Carolina Inn for consensual sex. Two former prostitutes testified to similar, independent sexual encounters with the defendant, and that after each encounter he had driven his "date" to a secluded location where he had strangled her.

Pittman was convicted of the murder of Tahara Nicholson. As the verdict was read out in court he yelled out, "You all are sending an innocent man to prison for life. I did not kill that woman." His mother, predictably, would later say, "I don't believe he did it. I don't care what evidence they have, I can't believe my son would do that."

The circumstantial evidence against Pittman is strong. As a teenager he had lived with this grandparents a few miles from Seven Bridges Road. He had worked on farmland near where some of the bodies were found. He had also lived near to where the body of a male crossdresser[*] was found. Christine Boone's body was found 45 miles away from the other victims, but only a few hundred feet from an old trailer Pittman had used to live in. In April 2009 he was found in his car at the side of the road. The Highway Patrol trooper who found him slumped in the front seat noticed that his boots were muddy and his flies undone. Two months later, just 200 yards away from the site, the body of Jarneice Hargrove would be found by the Mexican labourer. Pittman is known himself to have used prostitutes and taken drugs, and hence it is possible he had had some acquaintance with the victims. All of the victims were African-American, like Pittman himself.

Pittman continues to deny responsibility for any of the other Edgecombe County murders. Authorities continue to question his involvement. It is not known whether the case is still open and actively being investigated.

---

[*] The crossdresser was believed to have had a similar background to the female victims, but unlike the majority of them he had been dismembered.

The Chicago Strangler
(active 2001–2018)

THE MURDER ACCOUNTABILITY PROJECT (MAP), a non-profit organisation, is the brainchild of Thomas Hargrove, a retired journalist. The idea is simple but surprisingly effective. It is based upon the fact that each year, in the US, around 5,000 people kill other people and do not get caught. Undoubtedly, some of these people have killed more than once. The aim of MAP is to use a computer algorithm to mine a collected archive of homicides in order to find statistical anomalies. MAP searches the archive to find murders that are related by geographic location, date and time, method of killing, and by the victim's gender. The goal is to find and disseminate information about unsolved killings and possible serial murderers in the US.

Between 2001 and 2018 at least 75 women have been strangled, smothered or otherwise asphyxiated to death in Chicago, Illinois. Only one-third of the cases have led to arrests, with 13 assailants being arrested and charged. The killers in the remaining 51 cases have not been found. Many of the women struggled with addiction; many were sex workers. Some had no discernible troubles. None of them deserved the fate dealt to them by the hands of another. And the killings are still happening …

The ages of the women range between 18 and 58. The majority of the women had histories of prostitution, and some of those held down other jobs too as they tried to conquer their addictions and move on with their lives. Many were mothers. One was a grandmother to 20, a great-grandmother to two. One was an expectant mother, eight months pregnant. Most of the victims were black.

Nearly all the victims were dumped in empty places – in abandoned buildings, down alleyways, in deserted parks. Some were disposed under snowdrifts, others in garbage bins. Over two days in November 2007, two women were killed, their bodies discarded with the rubbish and set alight.

Casual violence seems to be an unwritten clause in the job description of the street prostitute, and many of the 75 murdered women had recent injuries and bruises. One of them had a broken nose; others had received blows to the head. Being choked during sex also seems to be an occupational hazard in the sex-for-sale business. *Don't let a john near your neck* would be an important piece of advice, one that a canny prostitute should heed. With good reason. Seventy-five corpses that passed through Chicago's mortuaries would attest to that. If they could …

Why strangulation? For a very good reason. It is up close and personal. The instrument of dispatch – rope, cable, wire, bra or bare hands – forces a new type of relationship between predator and prey. For during those shared moments the void between torturer and torture-victim is both intimately narrow and colossally wide. The greater the victim's panic and pain, the greater the killer's sense of control. It is a moment he enjoys, savours, longs for. It is truly addictive. Ironically, for the killer, it is during these moments when he takes a life, by demonstrating his complete lack of humanity, that he himself feels at his most alive and human.

Why prostitutes? For another good reason. They are accessible. They are desperate. Their desperation pushes them to do things and take risks that another person in the same position would baulk at. They are also seen as marginalised people – transient, unwanted, unloved. They are more likely to be looked upon by law enforcement as the victims of an unsatisfied john or an abusive pimp, and if they were to go missing or die then no one is going to care. That is how the psychopathic killer sees it.

The statistics speak for themselves. Fifty-one unsolved murders since 2001. All of which follow a grim pattern – black women involved in drugs or prostitution or both, all of them strangled and dumped in empty places.

Before 2018 the killings were thought to be the work of many different perpetrators. MAP's algorithm took in the data and signalled red immediately. The killings were concentrated in three specific areas – Washington Park, Garfield Park and the far south of the city. The "Chicago Strangler" killed between 2001 and 2014 but then suddenly stopped. There were no murders of similar *M.O.* between 2014 and 2017. Serial murderers do not easily give up their habits. He must surely have been in prison, away or otherwise incapacitated during this hiatus. Then, in 2017, the killings restarted, further confirming that this murder spree was the work of a serial killer. Or more than one serial killer.

So far, police, if they have any leads in the case, remain mute. But the truth of the matter is that they have no concrete evidence upon which to base an arrest and make charges. If they had it they would use it. The shockingly inhumane killings continue. The many victims and families of the Chicago Strangler have yet to receive justice.

The West Mesa Bone Collector
(active 2003–2009)

A MORE DESOLATE PLACE would be difficult to imagine. West of the Rio Grande, southwest of Albuquerque, New Mexico, the West Mesa is an elevated landmass characterised by wide open plains of low-lying stubbly grass, tumbleweed and sandy gravel. It is a large span of desert, stretching over a dozen sun-baked miles. Over the years, Albuquerque's city sprawl has encroached outwards onto the flat and barren land of West Mesa, laying down large areas of housing and business development. By the mid-2000s, wide plots of land had been earmarked for the construction of residential buildings. However, as developers soon discovered to their horror, their invasion of a nondescript patch of land was to have consequences that would disturb the ground of a mass burial site and release its wretched secrets from beneath.

The housing bubble collapse of 2008 temporarily put a halt to the building work on the nondescript patch of land. However, before this happened, the filling in of an arroyo (a dry creek) caused flooding. Residents who had already moved into the area complained about this, and so the developer built a retaining wall that channelled storm rainwater into a retention pool, directly on top of the patch of nondescript land.

On 2 February 2009 Christine Ross and her husband, recently moved-in residents, took their dog for a walk through an area designated for development. Due to the recent housing market collapse work had stalled, and the only indication that plans had been afoot was some recently overturned soil.

The dog, a curious three-year-old Shar Pei-Labrador mix called Ruca, was eagerly sniffing the ground, as dogs are inclined to do. Running ahead, an object jutting out of the ground caught Ruca's attention. As Christine and her husband came closer for a better look they became concerned, for what Ruca had found appeared to be a human bone. Christine took a snap of the bone on her mobile phone, sent the image to her sister, a nurse, who in due course replied that the bone did seem to be human in origin. Christine contacted the police to alert them of her suspicion, and shortly afterwards officers arrived at the scene. If there was one bone, they reasoned, there were likely to be others, and they determined that the site was likely to be a crime scene. Unbeknownst to them, as investigators gathered and began to dig, they were about to unearth Albuquerque's biggest ever unsolved crime.

There was more than one set of remains. In fact, the amount of bones recovered surprised investigators. One challenge for the investigators was the previous disturbance of the soil in the region, caused unwittingly by the developers who had moved and levelled large tracts of land. Scavenging animals more than likely contributed to the displacement. Many of the bones were discovered in shallow graves; others as deep as 15-feet underground. Some bones could not be recovered at all. It all amounted to a colossal, macabre jigsaw puzzle for the medical experts tasked to assemble the bones into complete skeletons.

What became clear soon, though, was that several bodies had been buried in the same area, a rectangle of 10-by-30 metres, an occurrence unlikely to have been mere coincidence. Satellite imagery of the site from the early 2000s showed tyre marks and patches of disturbed soil, giving good indication of where remains might lay. Moreover, the bones had been recently interred. This was not the ancient burial site of a long-gone indigenous community.

Two of the sets of remains were identified fairly quickly.

Victoria Chavez had disappeared in 2004. The 26-year-old mother-of-two had been in and out of prison numerous times on prostitution charges. She was a known drug user and had had repeated run-ins with the law. After having not been seen for about a year, Victoria's family reported her missing. She was not to be found (by Ruca the dog) until four years had passed when, on 2 February 2009, her skeletal remains were pulled from beneath 18-inches of dusty West Mesa ground. She had been buried naked and without any personal effects and could only be identified by her dental records. The medical examiner was not able to determine the cause of Victoria's death due to the advanced degree of decomposition, and only a vague estimation – around 2004-2005 – could be offered on the date of her death.

Before the month had passed four further sets of remains were discovered, two of them a mother and her tiny foetus.

Gina Valdez – also known as Michelle, her middle name – was the 22-year-old mother of a daughter and a son and she had reportedly tried hard to give them stable lives, despite the chaos that had infiltrated and taken over her own existence. During her teenage years, Michelle, a fun-loving girl with a bubbly personality, fell in with the wrong crowd. Drugs played a major part in the unravelling of her life, and she would repeat the pattern of disappearing for weeks on end only to reappear to family or friends. Usually with a request for money. Then people noticed that she did not reappear and a month passed without any contact from her.

Michelle's father filed a missing person report. Unfortunately, she was not to be found alive. A body was pulled from the West Mesa ground, along with that of a foetus. The victim, whether she had known it or not, had been an expectant mother. She was the second identified victim.

During a press conference, Albuquerque Police Chief Ray Schultz was to shy away from stating that a serial murderer was responsible for the women's deaths:

> *"We have linked two of the victims with similar life-styles now. That gives detectives a good place to start. This is where the real work begins. At some point in time, their lives crossed paths, whether it was each other or some other individual who was involved in their deaths."*

A few days later, Chief Schultz was still keen to downplay the notion that a serial killer was stalking Albuquerque's streets:

> *"The remains are all old; they've been there a number of years. Had we been finding fresh bodies, I'd be much more concerned. Everybody can be reassured that there's not an active serial killer in Albuquerque actively killing and preying on people."*

His words did little to assuage local concerns, especially amongst the community of prostitutes and young women.

In time, investigators would discover and identify a total of 12 remains from West Mesa – nine women, two 15-year-old girls and the bones of a four-month-old foetus. All had disappeared between 2001 and 2005. All were Hispanic, apart from one woman who was African-American. Most of them had been involved with drug use and prostitution.

Thirty-two-year-old Cinnamon Elks had had dreams and aspirations as much as anyone, but drugs took over her and her problems escalated. Her charge sheet for prostitution offences was long but, in order to feed the habit she could not give up, such activities were regrettably necessary. When Cinnamon failed to phone her mother to wish her a happy birthday suspicions were aroused. After her daughter was pulled from the ground in February 2009, Cinnamon's mother was able to tell investigators that Cinnamon had known the first two identified victims, Victoria Chavez and Michelle Valdez. She would also be able to add to that list the name of the next victim to be found.

Juliean "Julie" Nieto had always been a very petite girl. Her mother had constantly to alter clothing just so that it would not hang on her daughter's slim frame. Julie first dabbled in drugs at age 19, but quickly spiralled into dependency and prostitution. She disappeared around August 2004, aged 24, leaving behind a son upon whom she had doted very much.

Four victims who had all moved within the same social circle. It was becoming likely that the same killer was responsible for having dispatched them all. Police were, however, reluctant to use the phrase "serial killer", not least because of the panic that the words would inflame. Nevertheless, Chief Schultz would continue to point to commonalities within the lifestyles of the women – Hispanic women involved in narcotics and prostitution. An unkind inference might have been taken that they were nothing but drug-addled hookers.

It was around this time that Cinnamon Elks' mother began to claim that she had received numerous phone calls in the previous five years warning her that her daughter had been decapitated and buried in West Mesa. She also stated that Cinnamon herself had heard similar rumblings, and had believed that a "dirty cop" had been killing women and burying their decapitated bodies in the desert. These rumours had also been heard by the mother of Michelle Valdez, who, like Cinnamon Elks' mother, had passed the report to police at the time. No one had paid any attention at the time. Well, the bereaved mothers must have thought, they were starting to show a little interest now.

The fifth victim to be publicly identified was 28-year-old Veronica Romero. Too little of her body remained for forensic investigators to learn much about her death. Whilst growing up, Veronica had been an only child. It is possible that this influenced her decision to have five children of her own. She was last seen getting into a white truck in the east of Albuquerque in February 2004.

Single-parent Monica Candelaria, aged 21, was last seen in southwest Albuquerque in May 2003. Not much is known about her, but it is thought that she had ties to local gangs and that she was involved in drugs and prostitution. Just after she disappeared[*], rumours surfaced that Monica had been killed and was buried in West Mesa. Indeed, it is believed that her family went searching in the area where her remains were later to be found.

Compared to the other victims, Doreen Marquez seemed to

---

[*] Candelaria disappeared some six years before Ruca the dog found a bone.

have had a stable life. She appeared to have no issues growing up as a teenager. She kept a nice home in a good area and was able to provide a good life for her two daughters. She looked after her appearance, getting her hair and nails done regularly, buying fashionable clothes. Friends and family would remember her as a bubbly, lively individual. Things took a downward turn in Doreen's late 20s when her boyfriend was sent to prison and she turned to heroin as an ill-advised replacement and it was not long before she was in the throes of a fully-formed addiction.

It is not known exactly when she disappeared, for Doreen would often go missing for long periods before returning to her daughter. Police believed that during her vanishings she was somehow involved in the sex industry. She went missing for good sometime between 2003 and 2004, only to turn up dead in April 2009. She would be identified from dental records created during her single incarceration on a drugs charge.

Meanwhile, investigators were still declining to call this the work of a serial killer, preferring to suggest that they were "related" and speculating about a "single offender". Rumours abounded. Perhaps the crimes were related to drug use, or prostitution, with possibly gang or cartel involvement. The case was featured on *America's Most Wanted*, but this only seemed to inspire insights from psychics. Tips came in – mainly from people attracted by the lure of a sizeable reward – but no concrete leads were generated and nothing useful was learned. The police had finished their shifting of the West Mesa soil in the belief that they had recovered 90 percent of the expected bones and that no others remained. The FBI were now involved, but months would pass before the next identification was made.

One of the victims appeared to be a black teenager who had broken her nose at some point not related to her murder. Her name was Syllania Edwards from Harris County, Texas and she had been living with foster parents in Lawton, Oklahoma, some 500 miles east of Albuquerque. She was 15. Details of her movement were sketchy, but police speculated that she may have been part of a travelling group of sex workers, colloquially termed "circuit girls" by authorities, moving along Interstate 40 under the aliases "Chocolate" and "Mimi". Syllania's true identity had been difficult to uncover. Her description did not match any names on the list of missing Albuquerque women, she was of a different ethnic group, younger than the others, and she was not known to have had ties to any of the other victims. It was only after police requested dental records from out-of-state that a match was made.

Virginia Cloven, aged 24, was described by family, friends and teachers as a feisty yet personable youngster, affecting many with her bright personality. Yet life was not perfect. Shortly after her brother was shot and killed she left home and shacked up with her boyfriend in Albuquerque. Disaster struck again: her boyfriend was hit by a car and became comatose. Now broke and living on the streets, Virginia found herself slipping into drug addiction and prostitution. After being released from a spell in prison she contacted her family to tell them she was soon to marry her new boyfriend. Her family were never to hear from her again. They reported her missing, but it would be five years before they learned of her fate.

Evelyn Salazar's history is similar to many of the others. Although the caring mother of two daughters, she had somehow slipped into a life of drug use and prostitution. On 25 March 2004 Evelyn and her 15-year-old cousin, Jamie Barela, left a family gathering and were going towards a local park near the Albuquerque International Airport. It is not known if the two cousins made it to their destination but they were never seen alive again. Relatives did not believe that Jamie had been involved in any of Evelyn's illicit doings, and there had been no reason for her to run away. The unexpected and totally uncharacteristic disappearance of both cousins confounded police; the two had simply vanished into thin air. Then, in 2009, came the news that the family had been dreading, when both bodies were disinterred from West Mesa. Jamie – the last of the victims to be identified – would also turn out to be the youngest.

After six months of investigation, police announced that they had narrowed their list of suspects to five names. "But we're still waiting for that one person to come forward with that last little bit of information we need to seal it," said Chief Schultz, who was a great believer that the reward of $50,000 would "motivate" a potential tipster.

And tips *did* come in. Hundreds of them. There were tips from disgruntled wives and girlfriends, tips from citizens concerned about a "strange man" in their locality, offers from prison inmates who wanted the reward upfront before they could release their information, and the usual array of predictions from psychics. One lead thought to have legs concerned a man with a shrine in his apartment, complete with photos of the West Mesa victims and Post-Its bearing information about the women.

> *Detectives got excited after receiving several tips about a man who had a makeshift shrine, complete with photographs of the West Mesa murder victims and sticky notes bearing other information about the women in his apartment.*
>
> *But like a number of once-promising leads in the biggest murder mystery in Albuquerque history, the guy with the shrine fizzled.*
>
> (*Albuquerque Journal*, Albuquerque, New Mexico, 2009)

Detectives got a search warrant and entered the man's apartment. They thought they had struck gold, but after questioning the owner they realised their lead had no legs and crossed the man off their list of suspects.

Nevertheless, detectives continue their investigation still, determined to find their man. They realise they have their work cut out.

> *"But this will be a good, extensive court case when it does come together," [said Commander Mike Geier].*

"There's not a rock we haven't turned over. It would be just our luck that the guy on the corner with the cardboard sign has the tip that breaks the case and we don't check it out. So we're checking everything out. We spent two or three weeks on the guy with the shrine."

Years later, and the although the case remains active the trail has gone cold. Police are candid – they have still not got the one piece of concrete evidence they need to break the case.

It is likely that the victims were all buried by the same person, and as far as is known that is the assumption that the police are currently working on. No official suspects have been named, although some have attracted police attention.

Fred Reynolds was a person-of-interest for several months after his death by natural causes in January 2009. An alcoholic and drug addict, Reynolds had worked as a pimp in Albuquerque. He is believed to have had a connection with several of the victims, owning nude photographs of some of them, and showing an above-and-beyond interest in their disappearances and wellbeing. Police no longer believe that he is responsible for the crimes.

Lorenzo Montoya lived three miles from the burial site and it was reported that trails led from his trailer to the site. Montoya died in December 2006 after being shot in revenge by the boyfriend of a teenage girl he had strangled. It may be coincidental, but the Bone Collector killings ended with Montoya's death.

Several properties of an unnamed photographer and businessman were searched by police in August 2010. They confiscated "tens of thousands" of photographs. The man had reportedly visited Albuquerque to visit the New Mexico state fair. Investigators believe the West Mesa murders may be linked to a larger trafficking ring operating at regularly scheduled events such as this fair. Little else is known of this person's activities or how the photographs are considered significant.

In December 2010 convicted Colorado serial killer Scott Kimball was investigated for the killings, of which he denied involvement. He is not currently considered a suspect.

A finger has been pointed at a local rapist, Joseph Blea, who is currently serving a 90-year sentence for four violent sexual assaults unrelated to the West Mesa case. It is known that he frequented Albuquerque prostitutes, acted creepily and spoke disparagingly of the West Mesa victims, calling them "trashy". Circumstantial evidence against him (admittedly weak) is the discovery of a plant tag found in the grave of one of the buried victims. Detectives were able to trace the tag to a Californian nursery that transported plants to Albuquerque. Business records belonging to Blea showed that he had bought plants from the Californian nursery.

Other than identifying the victims' remains, breaks in the West Mesa Bone Collector case are scant. And, but for the complaint of West Mesa residents about a flooded retention pool, and the chance finding of an inquisitive dog, in hindsight even those were very lucky breaks. To all intents and purposes, the trail has gone cold and, unless there are other lucky breaks, the elusive serial killer is unlikely to be found.

Sleuths speculate about motives. The victims were mostly sex workers and drug addicts. Perhaps the perpetrator targeted these victim profiles simply because they were unlikely to be missed. It is possible he used religious fervour or the social stigma associated with this victim-type to justify their murder. Or maybe the use of violence was the only thing that stimulated him and he was disinclined to resist his appetite for death. It is almost certain that there was a sexual motive to the crimes; all the women were young, good-looking and were naked at the time they were buried. Revenge cannot be ruled out. Had the killer been treated badly by women, or had he acquired a sexually transmitted disease? Had he sought to punish them for some other spurious reason? Without the culprit the answer is unlikely to become more than mere speculation.

Meanwhile the prostitutes of Albuquerque remain fearful, mindful that the West Mesa Bone Collector is still at large. They mitigate danger as best as they can: they spend more time talking to johns before agreeing to go with them; they remain alert to nervous tics or shaky hands; they make sure car doors have working inside door handles and functioning windows; they ask johns to stop the car, and if he does not comply they jump out or yank the central brake. The working girls also talk about "bad dates" and regularly send investigators a list of men who have attacked or raped them. The killer could be still out there, merely biding his time before he begins his murderous onslaught again.

Jeff Davis 8
(active 2005-2009)

JUST OVER 10,000 INHABITANTS make up the population of Jennings, the parish seat of Jefferson Davis County, Louisiana. Founded as a stop-off point for trains midway of the larger cities of Lafayette and Lake Charles when the pace of life was slower, now the town offers fewer reasons to stop. Spotting alligators, hunting wild boar and angling for crawfish seem to be the main attractions for out-of-town visitors. A convenient rest-stop for journeypersons along Interstate 10, Jennings, however, latterly became a hotbed for drug traffickers, who kindled and encouraged a thriving trade in crack. The history of Jennings, it is not unfair to say, was entirely unremarkable. Unremarkable, that is, until 2005, when local women began to die of unnatural causes at a shocking and terrifying rate. And it was at this point law that enforcement agencies turned up – alongside the national media – and scraped at the veneer of small-town Cajun-country Jennings to expose its fetid, sordid underbelly.

It began on 20 May 2005 when a body was fished from a canal on the outskirts of Jennings. A fisherman on a bridge spanning the Grand Marais Canal had been casting his line into the murky waters below. At first, he thought the outline of a human body floating beneath the surface was a mannequin. He had recently heard a story on the news about mannequins having been stolen so the idea was not entirely irrational. But as he peered closer he came to realise that this figure was no plastic model.

No one knew it at the time but it was a discovery that marked the beginning a four-year period of suspicious deaths and unsolved murders in the network of swamps and canals ringing Jennings. Eight bodies would be pulled from the water in total. Collectively, the eight women would come to be known as the Jeff Davis 8, and Loretta Lewis was to have the dubious distinction of being the first victim found.

Loretta, aged 28, had last been seen three days before. A wife and the mother of two boys, her marriage was crumbling and life was on a downward trajectory. In a deep thrall to the crack to which she was addicted, Loretta traded sex for drugs. Caught in a "high risk" lifestyle she partied hard with the roughest and toughest street players of Jeff Davison. On 20 May 2005 Loretta's partially clothed body, without shoes, was found in a rural but public area. It appeared that after death she had been tipped over the low railing of a Highway 1126 bridge into the canal waters below.

Officially, Loretta is the victim of homicide. No cause of death could be determined, but the medical examiner found that high levels of cocaine and alcohol were in her system when she died. There was "no evidence of significant injury", reported the coroner. There was also early speculation that Loretta had been killed in reprisal for her robbery of a group of migrant Mexican workers in town. A witness informed a documentary filmmaker that Loretta had died accidentally as a result of a drugs overdose. Her associates, not wanting the inconvenience that accompanied an unexpectedly dead body, simply disposed of it in the most expedient manner they could think of. The unidentified witness purportedly had "a lot more to tell" about the incident.

Much had gone wrong in Loretta's life, and even after her death the pattern was to continue. Despite her body being found on 20 May, the date of her passing is marked on her gravestone as 27 May.

Ernestine Patterson had been a lifelong resident of Jennings. An African-American, Ernestine came from a large family of three brothers and six sisters and had four children herself. She had worked at a local fast-food establishment, Wendy's, but at the time of her death at the age of 30 she was employed by Louisiana State University. Her partially clothed body was found by froggers in a draining ditch a few miles outside Jennings on 18 June, two days after she had last been seen. The cause of death was ostensibly easy to rule: her throat had been slit. A newspaper reported that she had been stabbed in the mouth. Like Loretta Lewis, there were high levels of drugs and alcohol found in Ernestine's system. Also like Lewis, there was speculation that she had been killed by Mexican workers for allegedly robbing them. Mindful of rumours that she had been stabbed in the mouth in addition to having had her throat slashed, whisperers would evoke the phrase "snitches get stitches", suggesting that a motive for the murder may have been to silence her.

Twenty-one-year-old Kirsten Lopez's completely naked body was found by a fisherman in the Petitjean Canal on 18 March 2007. The site, in a rural spot around 20 miles southwest of Jennings, must have been chosen by someone familiar with the area. She appeared to have been involved in a high-risk lifestyle of drugs and prostitution and it was not unusual for her to disappear for long periods on end. She was not reported missing before 10 days had passed after her last sighting. Friends and family remember an "outgoing and well-liked" young woman who had made some poor choices in life.

In the days before her death Kirsten had reportedly become "withdrawn" and would constantly look over her shoulder. Whether or not such paranoia was caused by drugs-induced psychosis is in the realms of speculation. Certainly, toxicology results revealed elevated levels of drugs as well as alcohol in her system. The cause of her death was indeterminable.

The fourth body to be found belonged to Whitnei Dubois. Whitnei had had a difficult start in life: she and her two siblings were abandoned by their mother. After many years of being shuffled back-and-forth Whitnei and a brother were legally adopted by the Dubois family. At the age of 26 Whitnei herself was the mother of a five-year-old daughter who was believed to have been in the care of extended family.

Whitnei was a known police informant. Her disappearance was reported by someone also known to be a police informant. On 12 May 2007 a couple found a naked body lying on a dirt roadway in an area mostly used by farmers and local residents. Whitnei's police charge sheet for drug possession and forgery would prove useful to authorities: fingerprints on file allowed for the identification of her body.

Whitnei's was the first body not dumped in water and it was not as decomposed as the others. It was hoped that this would provide valuable evidence in identifying her killer. It did not. The cause of death was not released, and reports conflict as to whether there were marks on her body: some reported that there were no visible signs of attacks; others stated that she had been badly beaten. Like the other victims, however, there were high levels of alcohol and drugs in her system. Investigators wondered if the victims were being deliberately staged to appear as if they had died from accidental drug overdose.

Local sheriff Ricky Edwards now publicly connected this death to the previous three, commenting that he had a "serial dumper" on his hands. He speculated that Whitnei had died at another location and disposed of where she was found.

Born and bred in Jennings, 23-year-old LaConia "Muggy" Brown spent her last days living in fear, as if knowing something bad were about to happen to her. She ran in the same circles as the previous four victims and on 29 May 2008 her premonitions came to dreadful fruition. Her clothed, shoeless body was found within city limits on Racca Road, next to a police firing range, and so it was that a police officer found her, just six hours after she had been dumped on the road. She had been missing two days.

LaConia's throat had been slit. The blood-drenched body was doused in bleach, an effort, it seemed, by her assailant to rid evidence from the scene. There was some speculation that she had witnessed one of the other murders in the series and had to be silenced for that reason.

LaConia was the second African-American to be killed by the mysterious murderer. Her killer made a three-year-old boy motherless. Her survivors also included her mother, a brother, two sisters and her grandmother.

The case threw up many interconnections between the murder victims. LaConia, it transpired, had been interrogated by the investigative taskforce about the murder of victim no. 2, Ernestine Patterson. There were also suggestions that LaConia had been the discoverer of victim no. 1, Loretta Lewis. Furthermore, allegations have come to light that LaConia had been helping the police with their enquiries in the murder cases and that she had predicted her own death, telling a family member that "three police officers were going to kill her".

Crystal Zeno enjoyed music – singing and listening to it – and fishing. The 24-year-old was employed at a fast-food drive-in, Sonic. As a people person she reportedly enjoyed the job and relished spending time with her friends and family, above all her young daughter. Uncharacteristically, Crystal went missing on 29 August 2008.

A hunting trip on 11 September 2008 led to the discovery of Crystal's remains a couple of miles southeast of Jennings. Found by hunters on a levee (raised embankment) in a wooded area, the badly decomposed body could only be identified by DNA. Authorities would release neither the results of toxicology nor cause of death, suggesting that by now they had begun to feel these details would become significant following any subsequent apprehension of a suspect. They allowed, however, that Crystal had been the victim of homicide.

Shortly after Crystal's remains were found, a man from Lafayette, Louisiana called the parish district attorney's office to report that he had seen three African-American men leaving the same woods where Crystal's body had been found. The witness's name was Russell Carrier. On 10 October 2010, in the early hours of the morning, Carrier was struck and killed by a train in Jennings. He had simply lain down on the tracks and was run over … apparently.

On 2 November 2008 Brittney Gary left her home to go to a local convenience store to buy prepaid minutes for her mobile phone. She made it to the store and then exited alone. Surveillance cameras recorded nothing untoward about the visit to the store. Seventeen-year-old Brittney enjoyed swimming, listening to music and hanging out with friends. Family and friends could think of no discernible reason for her disappearance. In light of the recent serial killings they began to fear the worst. Thirteen agonising days passed before these fears were realised. Brittney's remains were located around five miles west of Jennings in a wooded area. Toxicology reports and the cause of death were not released, although leaks have indicated that asphyxia ended the teenager's life.

Brittney's family, although acknowledging that she had a history of drug use, stated that she had been clean of drugs and denied that she had been involved in prostitution. There was no denying, though, that she or her family knew or had some involvement with each of the previous six victims to some degree. Brittney and victim no. 3, Kirsten Lopez, were cousins. She and victim no. 6, Crystal Zeno, had shared accommodation. Prior to her death, Brittney had disclosed that she was scared and did not know who she could trust anymore.

The last of the Jeff Davis 8 was a feisty prostitute, Necole Guillory. Aged 26, Necole was known to be streetwise and savvy. In addition to her four children, her enjoyments were music and being outdoors. She was also a crack addict who had spent time in prison for possession and her lengthy rap sheet included theft, burglary, assault, resisting arrest and criminal damage. For some unknown reason, all these charges were formally and mysteriously dropped, with the district attorney's office citing unwillingness to proceed with the charges against her.

Before her death there had been rumblings from a local prostitute that Necole "might be the next victim", and as it approached her 27th birthday Necole began to believe it herself. In her final days she was reportedly "scared of someone", but would not say who, and made arrangements for her four children to be placed with relatives. Later, reports emerged that she had confided to a relative: "It's the police killing those girls." The story was eerily similar to the forebodings of other victims.

On 16 August Necole disappeared. Her mother contacted the authorities on 19 August, but before the ink was even dry on the missing person report her daughter's remains were found, discarded like trash alongside the I-20, around 10 miles east of

Jennings. She was nude from the waist down. Cause of death was ruled as asphyxiation. After this, the killings ended.

Charges of second-degree murder for the murder of Ernestine Patterson, victim no. 2, were levelled at Byron Jones and Lawrence Nixon. Several witnesses had implicated them. However, again, shoddy forensics work caused the cases to collapse and the two men were released, the charges dismissed.

For a while local strip club owner and suspected drug dealer, Frankie Richard, was a suspect in the murder of victim no. 3, Kristen Lopez. He admitted to having "shared something" with the murdered women, alluding to the relationships being mutually supportive ones. ("I was their friend no matter how fuckin' low their life was," he told author Ethan Brown.[*]) Issues with conflicting witness statements and a botched piece of physical evidence scuppered the case against him and he was released after the charges were dropped. Nevertheless, Richard, according to Brown, continues to assert his innocent, stating that *he also* now has a hit on his head. In conversation with Brown, Richard was keen to point out that the dumping sites were all within a three-mile radius of the residence of Jennings' former sheriff, Deputy Danny Barry, and that since his passing the murders have stopped.

Allegations against the investigative authorities abound. The murdered women, all thought to be police informants about the local drug trade, were believed to have provided information about other Jeff Davis 8 victims prior to their own deaths. The shooting of a drug dealer by a police officer in a botched raid was alleged to have been impetus to the killing of many of the Jeff Davis 8 murders. Witnesses believed that the murders occurred only to bring about the victims' silence. Many of the Jeff Davis 8 had been present during the drugs raid. Also, the

---

[*] Ethan Brown's book, *Murder in the Bayou: Who Killed the Women Known as the Jeff Davis 8?*, is the authoritative account of the mishandling of the investigation.

brother-in-law of victim no. 1, Loretta Lewis, reportedly told the brother of victim no. 4, Whitnei Dubois, that "I'm close to finding out who killed your sister". He was later discovered stabbed to death in his apartment. His murder is unsolved.

There are further allegations of witness statements being deliberately "disappeared" and the disposal of evidence. A sergeant who took statements was reportedly edged out of his job. The investigation as a whole did seem to be steeped in misconduct and corruption:

> *My investigation raises a number of very real questions about the prevailing serial-killer theory of these murders, [Ethan Brown concluded], and it also indicates that local law enforcement is a hindrance, not a help, to a resolution being reached. Whatever the truth, these eight women, and their surviving families, deserve a fresh inquiry by an outside investigative body.*

"We are still looking into different information and tips as they come in," CID Commander Chris Ivey blandly told the *Jennings Daily News* in 2014. Whilst Sheriff Ivy Woods added without preamble, "We can't go on the belief that the person or people responsible is from this area." It is clear that progress on the case has stalled if not stopped completely.

Whatever the truth of the matter – a single serial killer, a network of corrupt cops covering their tracks or merely the coverup of a run of accidental overdoses – the crimes linked to the Jeff Davis 8 remain unsolved.

The Eastbound Strangler
(active 2006)

SOME SERIAL KILLERS enjoy their own predilections – a signature
so unusual that there is nothing for it but that the media must lap
it up and tag the fiend accordingly. With surgical precision
Charles Albright (born 1933) removed the eyeballs of his three
victims and took them away with him. He became known as
"The Eyeball Killer". It was his fondness for ladies' shoes that
earned Jerry Brudos (1939-2006) his nickname. In his teenage
years he would knock women unconscious and steal their shoes.
Later in life he graduated to killing and posing the bodies pro-
vocatively in different undergarments and footwear. He even cut
the foot off one victim so that he could use it to model his col-
lection of high-heel shoes whilst himself dressing up in heels
and masturbating. He is known as "The Shoe Fetish Slayer".
Lawrence Bittaker (1940-2019) and Roy Norris (1948-2020)
became known as "The Tool Box Killers" due to the instruments
of torture they submitted their unfortunate victims to – an ice
pick, pliers and a sledgehammer.

So alluring can a catchy nickname be that some notoriety-
seeking serial killers choose their own. Dennis Rader (born
1945) requested authorities call him "BTK" after his preferred
M.O. His pleasure was to bind, torture and finally kill his victims. "Zodiac", the elusive North Californian killer, also chose
his own epithet, although for the reason its significance is not
yet known, and may never be discovered.

An Atlantic City, New Jersey killer had his own penchant for
disposing of bodies which gave him a strange appellation. After
garrotting them to death, he placed them in a drainage ditch,
face-down in a row, all pointing east. He came to be known as
"The Eastbound Strangler".

Atlantic City, the seaside resort, has a nickname of its own –
"America's Playground". Within 25 years, after the legalisation
of gambling, the city was transformed from a worn-out resort to

a trendy destination for slot players. Each year, it attracts around thirty-five million tourists, with billions of disposable dollars in their pockets. As with any business, its _raison d'être_ is to remove those dollars from its customers' pockets – a task it performs very well. Casinos reap enormous profits. As for the customers, there are winners and losers. A few winners go away happy; most of the rest less so. And a few of that unhappy bunch can find themselves sucked into a life a drug use and prostitution where the price of a sexual encounter with a charmless john can be as little as $10, or the cost of a rock of crack.

On the streets of Atlantic City drugs and sex are sold openly. Prostitutes stroll the pathways around the clock, congregating around the legendary entertainment centre, the Boardwalk. These are the women who were once seduced by the bright casino lights, but who are now tied by their desperation to the commodity of vice. They came to escape something but instead became enslaved by something more binding and dangerous than what they had fled. They are ubiquitous; yet they are anonymous. And for four of them the age-old tale of suffering had the unhappiest of endings.

In 2002 Kimberly Raffo made a fateful decision to break free from her stagnant suburban life in Pembroke Pines in Miami, Florida where she had once been a PTA mom: she enrolled in a local cookery course. There she had an affair with a fellow student and began to smoke crack cocaine, and so began the addiction that was to define her decision-making and life. Refusing to relinquish either her lover or the crack, Kim moved to Atlantic City where she became a waitress before turning her hand – and other body parts – to prostitution in order to support an addiction to drugs.

On 19 November 2006 Kim had her breakfast at half-past-two in the morning in a local diner and left to work the street. She got into a black Nissan Micra and was not seen alive again by anyone other than her killer.

The next day two women who were walking behind the Golden Key Motel, a cheap flophouse on the Black Horse Pike in West Atlantic City, discovered Kim's body lying in a ditch filled with faecal matter and chemical waste. Not far, around 60-feet away, another body was found … and another … and yet another … All of the women had been placed face-down, facing east. It is believed that they had all been strangled.

Molly Dilts, aged 20, is suspected to have been the first woman killed. Whilst she never earned a record for prostitution it is assumed that that was how she supported herself and her drug habit, for the round-faced woman could often be seen flaunting her body in the seedier parts of town. She did, however, have a record for assault, public intoxication and possession of drug paraphernalia.

Molly had past troubles which continued to haunt her. Her mother had died of cancer and her brother from a fatal shooting the previous year, and it appeared that geographical relocation from Black Lick, Pennsylvania was to do little to ease her heartache. A plump young woman, she had been making herself sick to lose weight … and to attract men. It seemed that she had attracted the wrong sort of man.

Molly was last heard from on 7 October 2006, making a call from a payphone. When found, her body was so badly putrefied she could only be identified by dental records and the cause of her death could not be determined. The dank water in which she was found facilitated decomposition. She left behind a 14-month-old son.

Barbara Breidor, aged 42, was the oldest victim. Growing up in an affluent suburb of Philadelphia, Pennsylvania, Barbara had had ambitions to work in law. She had arrived in America's Playground four years before and she worked as a cocktail waitress and helped to manage her mother's clothing shop. When her mother sold the business, Barbara got work as a waitress. Soon after she became hooked on prescription medications before graduating to the less-therapeutic drugs of heroin and cocaine, a habit which cost her $300 a day. Effectively homeless, she drifted between friends' houses and bedded down in flophouses when she could afford to. She often talked of finding a nice place to lay her head. By this stage Barbara's lifestyle had taken its toll on her body; she was emaciated and her formerly attractive face was ravaged by drug use. She cared little for any possessions … apart from the cherished glass crack pipe which she kept wrapped in a napkin.

By mid-October 2006, Barbara's behaviour had become so erratic that when she left for an errand and did not return friends did not immediately report her missing, waiting several weeks to do so. She was found in the same ditch, on the same day, as Kimberly Raffo and Molly Dilts. The autopsy yielded no cause of death.

Tracy Roberts, a 23-year-old high school dropout from Bear, Delaware, began to use cocaine after breaking up from her boyfriend. She moved between Philadelphia and Atlantic City, and stayed briefly in Georgia before escaping an abusive relationship and ending up in Atlantic City in August 2006, where she intended to earn a living as an exotic dancer. Drug use, however, had left her body unsuitable for the stage and so she turned to the streets. She found abuse here too, and was punched in the throat so hard by a man wanting to be her pimp that she coughed up blood and was hospitalised. She was not the same again, said another prostitute friend.

On 8 November 2006, wanting to leave this life behind, Tracy called her mother to pick her up. However, for some reason she changed her mind and remained in Atlantic City. This was the last she would be heard from. She would soon be dead, presumably asphyxiated as the other victims were thought to have been.

Detectives surmised that the four women had been killed elsewhere and dumped in this fetid ditch behind the motel. Other than the bodies themselves there were no clues left behind; the water hastened decomposition, putting paid to that. The bodies were clothed when found, but their shoes and means of identification were removed from the scene – perhaps to become trophies for a killer, or maybe in order to thwart any investigation. None of the bodies had defence wounds. Either they were attacked when incapacitated (by drugs or by another means) or decomposition had eradicated the evidence of it. Foreign DNA was found under the fingernails of Kimberly Raffo. It did not match that of anyone in the federal databases.

Unbelievably, the investigation was structured so that four separate teams worked a case each, duplicating work and communicating ineffectively with each other. This decision was taken, it was said, because of Atlantic City's reliance on tourist money; it seemed that the prosecutor's office made the decision not to label the killings the work of a serial killer for political and economic reasons. It was probably a costly mistake.

The authorities have yet to report any substantial leads or release the names of any viable suspects they may have. Suspicion fell briefly on a workman, Terry Oleson, who had been allowed to stay at the Golden Key Motel in exchange for repair work around the time the murders took place. His girlfriend at the time implicated him. Investigators making a search of his room found a hidden camera set up with images of his girlfriend's teenage daughter undressing. Oleson has not been connected to any of the murders.

Eldred Burchell allegedly confessed to a prostitute that he had killed people and called himself "The River Man"[*]. However, he also has not been connected to any of the murders.

Internet sleuths point to connections between the Eastbound Strangler and the unidentified Long Island Killer, who worked about 150 miles away, east of New York City. Investigators, although they have ruled this theory out, seem nonetheless no closer to solving the mystery of who *did* kill these four women.

Other prostitutes have died violently deaths – before and after – and most likely will continue to do so. There have been reports of other streetwalkers not seen in weeks. Detectives are uncertain whether the killer has claimed more victims. It is possible

---

[*] Possibly in homage to Gary Ridgway, the Green River Killer, who had been sentenced for his crimes in 2003.

that another dumping site for dead prostitutes exists but has yet to be found.

In the early days after the discovery of the bodies, local officials stated that they did not expect any decrease in visitors seeking the excitement of Atlantic City. Unfortunately, they were to be proved wrong. Since then, five casinos have become closed to business, leaving seven still in operation. It would be difficult to show a link between the killings and the economic downturn – if indeed there is one. The drug-dealing and street-walking still goes on, however, although not so ostensibly. There are fewer on the streets, thanks to the ease with which these unfettered service-providers can conduct their business on social media and via apps. And some might say this is a good thing.

Afterword

SERIAL KILLERS ARE NOT EXPERT in the act of murder from the start. Although they will undoubtedly have fantasised about killing for a long time, like all neophytes they will, by definition, have had no experience before their first kill. They only gain the confidence to kill again after they have successfully committed murder, and in their eyes success is measured by the fact that they have not been caught and remain free to repeat the action. The idea of a serial killer who is so tormented by his clandestine acts of murderous lust or rage that he secretly desires to get caught is nonsense. The serial killer loves to kill and he will not stop unless he absolutely has no choice in the matter.

Part of the serial killer's pleasure is the hunt. It is the targeting, approaching, controlling, killing and sometimes disposal of the body that stimulates this unique type of killer. It all requires meticulous planning and the learning curve is mightily steep. But for the killer, who strives so hard to complete murder and not get caught so that he may kill and kill again, the rewards are immense. It is addictive.

On their journeys towards becoming accomplished in their nefarious careers, serial killers gain experience from their success and they quickly become more emboldened, more confident and empowered. They learn how to avoid making critical mistakes whilst beginning to take more risks. This will enhance their excitement and make the thrill of the actual kill all the more stimulating. It is this circular addiction to the drugs of excitement and risk-taking that eventually becomes the undoing of many serial killers. They come to believe that they will not – indeed, *cannot* – get caught and this leads to the minimisation of problems, sloppy workmanship and the taking of unnecessary risks. In short, most serial killers are undone by themselves. If left to their own devices serial murderers will kill and kill and kill again until they are stopped or die themselves.

And the statistics show this demonstrably. Gary Ridgway, the

Green River Killer, kept on murdering women and girls until he was eventually caught by DNA profiling. If he had not been stopped he undoubtedly would still be slaughtering prostitutes and dumping their bodies in the Green River, Washington. Jeffrey Dahmer, the Milwaukee Cannibal, was only interrupted in his series of murders when one of his intended victims escaped from his lair, by which time Dahmer had already killed, dismembered and sometimes eaten at least 17 young men and boys. Ted Bundy was literally stopped in his tracks after being arrested – twice! – for traffic violations. If this had not happened he would surely have added to his total of 27 murdered women. Likewise, Randy Kraft, the Scorecard Killer, was stopped by police performing an illegal lane change. If not apprehended for this misdemeanour he would have added the names of many more men to his diabolical scorecard.

However, some serial killers *do not* get caught. Some simply decide to call it a day and cease and desist their murdering altogether. It is not that they *want* to stop, it is that for a variety of reasons they *need* to stop. Perhaps the heat is becoming too much. Perhaps they made just one mistake too many and stopping killing is the expedient way to prevent being caught.

But some killers do not stop and are never caught. Perhaps luck is simply on their side. Perhaps they are so slippery and talented and they leave so few usable clues that investigators are unable to catch them. Unquestionably, some killers are also so secretive that the wider world is unaware that a series of killings is actually occurring. All that is known is that people disappear without reason and never return.

Statistics indicate that serial killing is on the decline. In the US in 1974 there were 104 active serial killers. There were 147 in 1984 and 151 in 1994. Now there are only 30 active serial killers.

Only!

The reasons for this decline are surely technological. Advances in forensics, DNA databases and profiling, telecommunications, the wider use of the Internet and social media, instant media news, the ubiquity of 24-hour CCTV surveillance cameras – all these go to thwart the ambitions of even the most determined serial killer. The fear of being caught because of a stray splash of seminal fluid would be enough to prevent a killer giving in to his murderous desires in the first place.

Nevertheless, some serial killers *are* active and are killing with impunity right now. So who are these serial killers? The obvious answer is this: *the authorities do not know, otherwise they would arrest them.* The less palatable answer is that the serial killer could be anyone. Serial killers are a divergent group unlike any other. They are ethnically diverse. Women are included in the group. They do not necessarily live separate, odd existences. They often do not twitch or make themselves known by other stereotypical means. The evidence tells us that it could be your next-door neighbour. It could be a family member. And we only find out if and when they get caught.

Printed in Great Britain
by Amazon